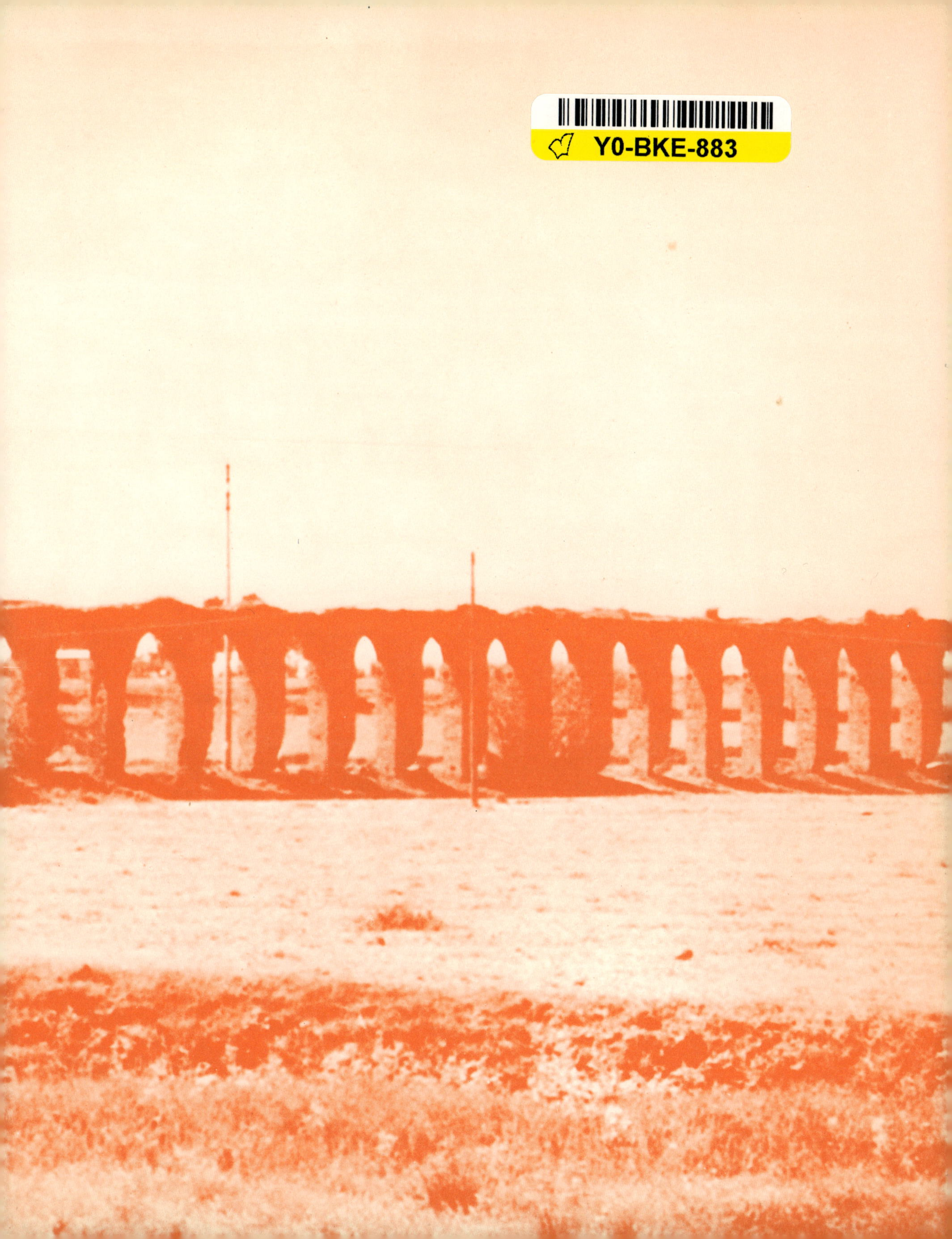

The World of the Romans

The World of the Romans

Text by
Victor Duruy

Translated by Gwenn Lansdell

Minerva

Contents

1. The City 5
2. Way of Life 15
3. The Family 67
4. Arts and Sciences 93
5. Beliefs and movement pattern of ideas 105
Conclusion 146
Outline of Roman History 151
Index 156

End papers: The aqueduct of Claudius spanning the Roman countryside.
Frontispiece: Bases of Columns at the temple of Castor (Forum, Rome).

© *Editions Minerva S.A., Genève, 1972.*

1 - The City

All the virtues have been attributed to the ancient Romans in accordance with the time-honoured custom of eulogising the past. They did indeed possess virtues which made them good citizens.

Equally they had their vices, being enamoured not only of work but of plundering, usury and law-suits. Creditor was harsh to debtor, father to son, master to slave, conqueror to conquered. Was their domestic life more enlightened than it will eventually be? Evil is more apparent in societies which reach the lime-light, while history finds it difficult to reveal obscure ones.

The Romans were honest and kept their word. It was said later on:— "If you entrust your valuables to a Greek, make sure you obtain ten pledges, ten signatures, and ten witnesses, for he will rob you." In Rome the magistrate holds all public money, and his oath is sufficient to ensure that none of it is misappropriated.

It is a puzzle to know in whose hands within the state the law lay,—a problem which threatened the last century of the Roman Republic. Earlier on, an original solution had been found. The consul himself did not pass judgement. He would quote the rule of the law applicable to the particular case, whereupon the judges whom he had nominated would then make the decision. So the law-suit became a dual process— "in jure" before the praetor and "in judicio" before the judges.

The Romans, surrounded by enemy peoples for three quarters of a century, were especially versed in the art of warfare. Not only was the Roman soldier the bravest and best disciplined in the whole of Italy, but he was also the swiftest and the strongest. On route marches, he had to cover 24 miles in five hours, carrying with him weapons,

Characters from Etruscan art. The Etruscans are ancestors of the Romans.

victuals for five days, and stakes to pitch camp, which amounted to sixty Roman pounds all told. Even between campaigns he had to exercise on the parade ground. Javelins were hurled, arrows were shot, swords were brandished in combat and the soldier ran and leapt fully armed or swam across the Tiber. His exercise weapons were twice as heavy as the ordinary ones. Leading citizens took part in these games, and consuls and conquerors would challenge the professional soldier with strength, skill and agility, showing that the generals too possessed the qualities of the legionary.

All forces fought with the mercenaries. Rome alone had a national army which excluded the foreigner, the freed slave and the proletarian. At one time, every well-to-do pleasure-loving citizen had to undergo this rigorous school of training in discipline, dedication, and abnegation. Polybius said:

"No one can be elected to public office unless he has taken part in ten campaigns." This law added tremendous dignity and strength to the army.

Terms of office within the state were temporary or for one year, and more rigidly so in the cities.

Under the empire, concessions made to the ordinary people by those who wanted to become magistrates created the assumption that candidates needed their support. Such mentions in the records are numerous. The assembly consisted of tribes and papal courts (curia), one of which was selected by the drawing of lots to include foreign residents (incolae), who came under Roman city law, or "ius Latii". It conducted elections, voted on motions put forward by the magistrates, and ratified decrees prepared by the decurions. If it were necessary to renew the city's administrative system, the elder of the two magistrates extraordinary would preside. He would hear the statements made by the candidates, and then would ask each one of them the following

The reverse side of a very old silver coin, showing someone casting his vote. Right: soldier and prisoner (Bas-relief from Constantine's arch in Rome).

questions, seemingly taken from the statute laws of Julius Caesar: "Are you born of free parents—"ingenuus"? Have you incurred punishment by law, or followed the livelihood of an incapacitated person? Have you been resident in the city for five years and are you at least twenty five? What offices have you held, and how long ago?"

The president would further assure himself that the candidate was the right sort of person for the senate and of sufficient means to carry out the functions of office properly.

In Malaga the duumvirs and quaestors had to produce securities and underwrite their contract with landed property. The Osuna Bronzes stipulate that the property should be either in the town or its environs within a mile distant so that its revenues could easily be gathered and alienation prevented.

If candidates are fewer than the positions of authority available, the president proposes ex-officio appointments, but those citizens who are let in for such a costly honour are allowed to designate others who can fulfil the required conditions. Names of such appointees are displayed in a place for all to see. Caesar's code also demanded three years" service in the cavalry or six in the infantry. This had to be rescinded when the army became permanent, but all other directives have been preserved and no new provisions have been made.

Once a candidature has been announced, the candidate must control his behaviour carefully. He is not allowed to organise public festivities or to have them arranged during the year before the election, or even to invite more than nine people to his house at a time, and that only the day before. Penalty for non-compliance is five thousand sesterces. It is not desirable that the people should be suspected of selling votes or the candidates of buying them. During her period of austerity, Rome was not more scrupulous in preserving the unblemished integrity of her comitia or in making people believe in it by her laws against bribery. On election day the president asks citizens to vote. Each curia arranges its own voting centre, and voters place their voting tablet or "tabella" in a receptacle held by three citizens from another curia. These men are under oath to receive and count the votes faithfully. First they vote for the nomination of the duumvirs, then the ediles or municipal councillors and finally the quaestors,—after which the president announces the names of those who have obtained the majority vote. Five days later, elected members take the oath of civil obedience and service in all the interests of the city.

An honour such as this was not without considerable expense; the newly elected had to pay honorary dues to the treasury. These were often double the normal amount if great achievements were hoped for. The moneys, which were also paid by priests, pontiffs and augurs were of no mean significance; sums were sometimes known to be as much as thirty, forty or even fifty thousand sesterces, not to mention the games, improvements and embellishments to the town which were carried out at the expense of the new dignatories. A woman from Calamia in Numidia, who was elected priestess for life, presented four hundred thousand sesterces for a theatre to be built, and Dion Chrysostomus recalls that his grandfather, father and he himself compromised their entire fortune because of the offices they held. But what pomp and respect were showered upon them! And how proudly the duumvirs and ediles walked about the town wearing the toga praetexta as if they had administered an ancient magistracy in Rome!

Fasces would be carried before them by two lictors, followed by numerous public officials, ushers, scribes, couriers and heralds, who would take up their position in court on the curule chair to make decisions in the name of the law and pass judgements in the name of justice. From a distance, they could be mistaken for two Roman consuls, and the cities swelled with pride to see their municipal functions performed in the style of the supreme authority within the empire. After the duumvirs there followed the officials who police the streets, public buildings and markets, supervise weights and measures, public baths and games:—in short all concerned with preserving law and order in the city. They also had responsability for supervision of the year's produce (annona), for drawing up edicts which concerned matters of local importance, for cases of default or fraud in business, breaches of the law, for the repair or alteration of public buildings, and the like. After referring each case to the duumvirs, they acted as magistrates in imposing fines on offenders, and saw that all edicts were carried out.

One significant custom was that citizens were divided into two categories; I am not referring to free-men and slaves any more, but rather to the "honestiores" and "humiliores" who were the equivalent of the nobleman and villein of the Middle Ages. So beatings with crossed sticks, lashings to stakes, and casting the unfortunate to wild animals occurred, for such was the common lot of the poor creature who had not escaped his humble birth, were he condemned.

At the one extreme, one can certainly include decurions and magistrates, for they had received honours from the city, and indeed constituted the senate; at the other, with the return of justice, there were settlers, who were the ancestors of the serfs of the Middle Ages, artisans, labourers, and small merchants whom Cicero was already describing as the scum of the cities, and anyone whose job was regarded as rather squalid. Such people were known as plebeians (plebeii), or lower class (tenuiores). There is justification to include the "possessores" or land-owners in the first category, for some of them will be called upon later to take decisions side by side with the decurions, and, in addition veterans, teachers, and doctors.

There were vast numbers of "tenuiores". Many were employed by the state, alongside freed men and slaves, to maintain the temples, serve the magistrates or carry out public works. Their common poverty ironed out any differences of condition or sentiment in a situation where freed men struggled with slaves for the mastery over a most inferior kind of existence. They increased the shops in the streets and squares in great number. They sprang up in houses to supply domestic needs, and outside as a place to hire their labour, advice or products of their industry. They started many industries, of the kind that the rich used to inflict upon their slaves, in any wretched hovel they could find. Rome has always had artisans, but there were many more when the bright tunic of the slave put the often shabby toga of the citizen to shame. The more unworthy his occupation seemed to be to him the more he had to tread the boards like an actor, enter the arena like a gladiator, provide feasts and revelries or else live on charities which were often undeserved and were reserved for the parasite and the client.

To sum up, leaving aside political history,

Magistrates in a chariot. Right: scenes from commerce.

which often does no more than reveal the surface of things, once you probe into life as it really was in Roman times, you discover a society more heavily class ridden than any other. At the bottom of the ladder there was the slave and the commoner (humilior), above him the landowner (possessor), and then a double aristocracy consisting of those on whom honours were bestowed, and those who had money.

Every important occasion celebrated in a rich household was marked by a gift:—a feast or games—to the people. Pliny said, "It is customary to celebrate on a number of occasions:—when a male dons the robe of manhood, at a marriage, or on taking up a new responsibility—and to invite all the senate and even a large number of the lower classes, each of whom receive a small gift of money."

Maximus loses his wife who came from Verona, and he gives a gladiatorial combat to the city in her memory. Combats such as this followed the pattern of a popular old religious custom. First there was blood to appease the ghosts and then blood to amuse the crowds. A dead man had chanced to be making his way along the streets of Pollentia to his tomb further on. The crowd rioted and would only allow the cortege to proceed when the inheritor promised them a present of gladiators, which is no doubt what they normally received when a celebrity died. At Minturnes the following legend appears at the foot of a statue:— "Within four days he presented eleven pairs of gladiators who did not cease to fight until half of them, all Campania's bravest men, had fallen in the arena; he also gave ten wild bears." The inscription proudly goes on:—"Be sure you remember this, noble citizens!"

Anything was acceptable;—contests between one-time athletes, second-rate gladiatorial displays, the killing of wild boars and even hares. Pleasure to the eye was followed by pleasure for the stomach; it might be some small provisions or in the case of richer people a feast. Once, religion exalted these happenings and each event resembled an act of devotion like the early Christian feasts.

Some houses had enormous halls which offered open table on certain days (triclinia popularia). Trimalcion wanted a likeness of himself on his tombstone in the act of emptying a sack of money before the crowd. "You see", he said to the architect, "I gave a public feast at which each guest received two gold coins. Show the triclinia with everyone indulging themselves to their hearts' content."

The feastings became so frequent that they were known as publicae cenea. But the emperors came to distrust them thinking that they would supply a ready source of men for the nobles, "bravi" in fact, that Italian nobles kept in their hire for so long. Nero forbade them, permitting only individual distribution of small gift baskets (sportula). A simplification of this custom led to the gift basket being replaced by a donation of sesterces, more welcome, as they could satisfy other needs than those of hunger. Eventually the donations became suspect in their turn and Domitian suppressed them in favour of the gift baskets.

Gifts of this kind were made in exceptional circumstances, whilst every day others occurred to the benefit of the dependants. Since a dependant would support the election of his patron in the comitia, give his blood for him on the battle field, and show loyalty to him always, patronage became a notable institution inherent in one form or another in all aristocratic societies. During the second century of the Empire, it deteriorated into little more than organised begging or an institution for decadence. If you were poor, or merely disgruntled and lazy, you could join a group of dependants. It was an easy thing to do because it was one of the boasts of the rich to appear in public accompanied by a train of citizens wearing the toga, turba togata. Thus our ancestral lords never appeared at court without a vast number of

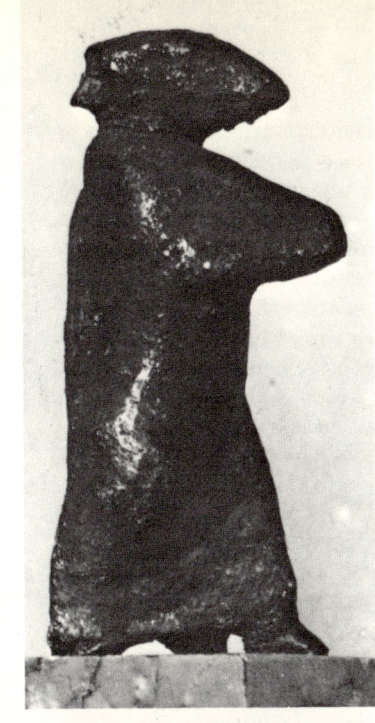

Sculptures representing masks at the theatre of Ostia. An actor wearing a rat's head. The Roman theatre at Fiesole. Bas-relief of a player in his dressing-room.

attendant followers. Costs incurred being commensurate with the number of dependants, patrons would complain bitterly. Juvenal records, "What dense smoke! The food baskets are being given out. One hundred guests rushed forward, each with his cooking things."

Doubtless they would circulate in crowds like this, inspiring secret revolts against "the king and lord", who would appear to be scornful or stingy on some occasions. "You have invited me as your guest, Sextus, and whilst you dine sumptuously, I merely receive one hundred coins (quadrans). Did you invite me to dine or to envy you?"

The clever ones acquired several patrons and if they had mettle they could fulfil their additional obligations. As long as you were not too proud you could make it a way of life. Whole towns adopted one or more rich influential patrons. Canusium had thirty nine, thirty one of whom were Roman senators and eight Roman knights. The southerner was a lover of games, public entertainment, and noisy spectacles, and knew at all times how to exploit the extravagant, those who courted popularity, and the conceited, who could be relied upon to say of him as he was seen to go into the Forum or enter the theatre, "There goes our patron from the great city!"

Patronage offered protection to the towns from the rigours of the governor who had to control the more distant corners of the province through intimidation by formidable prosecutors who could be made to turn against him by an angry mob in the senate in Rome. No secret was made of such self interest; the contract which officially bound people and patron together was often worded like this;—"We are conferring upon you the city's highest honour, in order that you may keep us safe and defend us." If the contracts were relaxed or broken, new ones were formed... renovavit hospitium.

There had been a meeting of the senate to select the patron, and a decree having been prepared by the decurions, it was presented to the public assembly and passed as a lawful bill. Thus a contract was made, linking the posterity of the protector with that of the protected. Bologna came under the patronage of the Antonius', Lacedemonia of the Claudius', and Sicily of the Marcellus' to give some examples. Women and children were also known to be city patrons. Agreements of patronage were engraved on tablets of bronze or marble (tabula hospitalis) which were kept in one of the temples, and a copy of each was ceremonially placed in the patron's house. From that moment on, the patron became the official defender of the city against the government and of the citizens against the law courts. He exhausted his credit and his fortune on his dependants; he rebuilt their crumbling monuments or constructed new ones, organised athletic games, gladiators, festivals and public feasts, and distributed sums of money, a habit described by Pliny as a forerunner of the provident or charitable organisation. Furthermore he would take his place ahead of the magistrates in the town and occupied the seat of honour in the temple, at the theatre or the festivals. He was given presents which he returned a thousandfold, and even during his lifetime inscriptions of honour, busts and statues would be accorded to him. At his death there would be written on his tomb;— "This monument was raised thanks to the financial support of the community by decree of the decurions in recognition for services rendered to the republic by...". The protection of the patron was considered to be more effective than that of Jupiter, and one paid for it as one would atone the gods, with a burst of smoke, pomp and acclamations. So everyone was happy, beginning with the one who faced semi ruination in order to appear a person of some stature.

The Roman town consisted of a number of miniature cities as it were; the units were corporations (collegia, universitates) of all those who found interest or pleasure in getting

Upper part of Titus' Arch (Rome).

together. The right to form an association was exercised without hindrance for many years, and trade groups have been in existence since the oldest period of Roman history. People got together for revelry-making or to celebrate a feast by giving scenic displays, or for practising singing, music or athletics etc... Associations were formed especially for making funeral arrangements, because it was then everyone's major preoccupation to make sure of a tomb for oneself. The rich planned theirs on their own estates whilst the poor would buy collectively a small corner of land, having none of their own to receive the sepulchral urn. Here they would be protected by the other members of he brotherhood better than the knight in his splendid tomb, against abusive scrawls and slogans or sometimes against invasion, when inheritors would try to cut down expenses by placing their dead in an old vault. Nerva had encouraged this kind of institution by providing funds to assist the poor to meet burial expenses, and as societies of this kind were by far the most numerous, having been authorised by a committee of the senate, others adopted similar methods to the funeral college to obtain legal status for groups of a different type.

We are in possession of the rules of a college like this at Lanuvium. The entrance fee was one hundred sesterces plus the gift of a twenty six litre jar of good wine and to retain membership a monthly payment of six small coins (as) was made to the communal exchequer. This ensured a pyre and tomb costing the association three hundred sesterces, that is including payment of fifty sesterces to the members who acted as followers at the funeral. If a member died less than twenty miles from Lanuvium, three brothers would immediately be chosen to go to the funeral and they would be given twenty sesterces to cover the cost of the journey. If a death occurred further away, the customary funeraticum was paid to those responsible for performing the rites. If a master were malicious enough to refuse the body of one of his slaves who had died, the association would nevertheless go through a form of funeral ceremony for him. Suicides were completely unrecognised whilst our repentants from the South, both black and white, provide a lasting memory of the funeral colleges.

A slave member of the college on gaining his freedom had to make a gift of an amphora of wine as a tribute to his joyous accession to liberty. The wine was put into store and members would hold a dinner six times a year. The menu was simple and included two as worth of bread, four sardines and a bottle of the good wine that had been laid in stock. What forethought on the part of a funeral society! But indeed those present were not preoccupied with gloomy thoughts on those occasions. They liked to laugh and even to drink, not to be distracted before reaching the very last drop of the hundred litres (4 amphoras) on the table. The rules say:— "If anyone wishes to lodge a complaint or put forward a suggestion, go to the college meeting. On feast days we want to eat, drink and be merry." As within the city, breaches of the rules were punishable by fines; four sesterces for having taken someone else's place at a feast, twelve for having created a disturbance, and twenty for insulting the president. The fines doubtless served to boost the menu. Those who commissioned the festivities had to provide cushions for the beds and bowls of hot water that they enjoyed adding to the wines which were heavy and sometimes laced with honey.

The fraternity had its patron too. He was earnestly asked to accept the onerous position and requested humbly to allow the incident of his nomination and eulogies in praise of his merit and generosity .to be engraved above his door. Some wealthy merchant was always ready to accept the honour. If not this, some other!

The city became complete with its teaching and public assistance. It provided teachers for the schools and public doctors for the sick. Medical practice which had once been performed by sorcerers or religious quacks had been secularised early on. Hippocrates made a science of it and a lucrative one at that, so that it invited widespread dedication. Doctors were everywhere and medical attention became a municipal service. Every Greek town had at least one public practitioner who visited the sick in the city and its suburbs. They each had a large dispensary (iatrium) where the doctor was available for consultation, assisted by his pupils and public slaves. He also performed operations and distributed medicaments. Beds even were provided sometimes, probably for those patients who had had an operation and were in no condition for transport, or those suffering from serious illnesses. The rich received medical attention at home.

Barristers concerned with the doctors tell us about findings from their estates. There is reference to eye salves and plasters, surgical instruments and apparatus for making medicaments. There is evidence of the terrible responsiblity they had. If a patient died from one of their medicines, the doctor faced exile or death. It was obligatory therefore for a doctor to sign his prescriptions.

Street intersection, Pompeii.

2 - **Way of life.**

The domestic life of the ancient Romans was simple and austere, allowing no luxury and no ease. The master would plough at his servant's side, the mistress would spin in the company of her ladies, and neither the royal nor the rich escaped from work. Bertha, Tarquin's queen Tanaquil and Lucretia as experts in spinning, set an example to Roman matrons. Cato said, "When our forefathers wished to praise a man of substance, they would describe him as a good ploughman and farmer. This was the highest form of praise they knew. "At that time people lived on their own land in rural tribes and were the most highly respected. People only came to Rome for the meetings or the market. The villa, just a primitive sort of construction made of compressed mud blocks, timber and beams, was always a hive of industry. If the weather prevented going into the fields, there was work to be done on the farm, stables

Left, a peasant. Right, the Via Appia Antica.

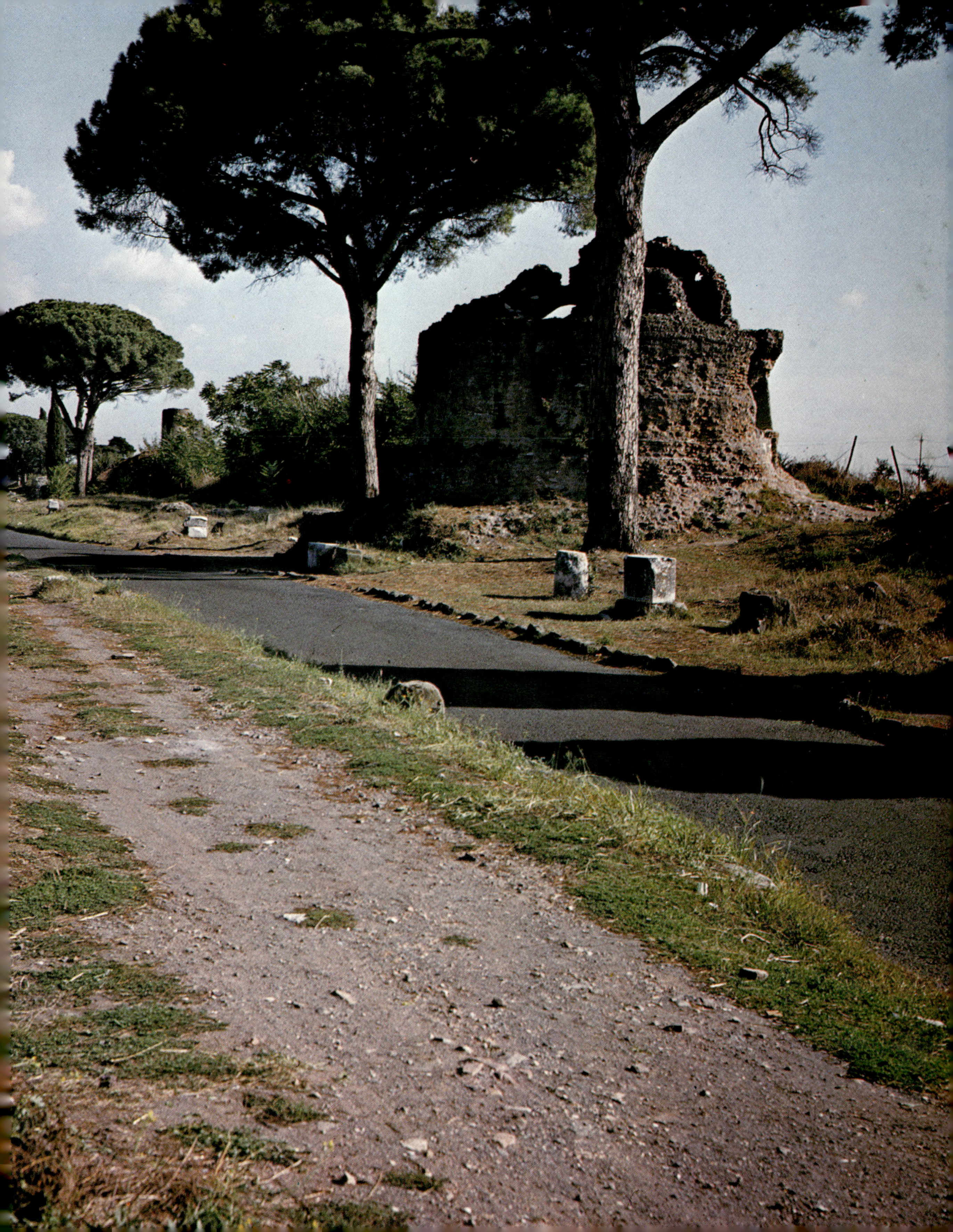

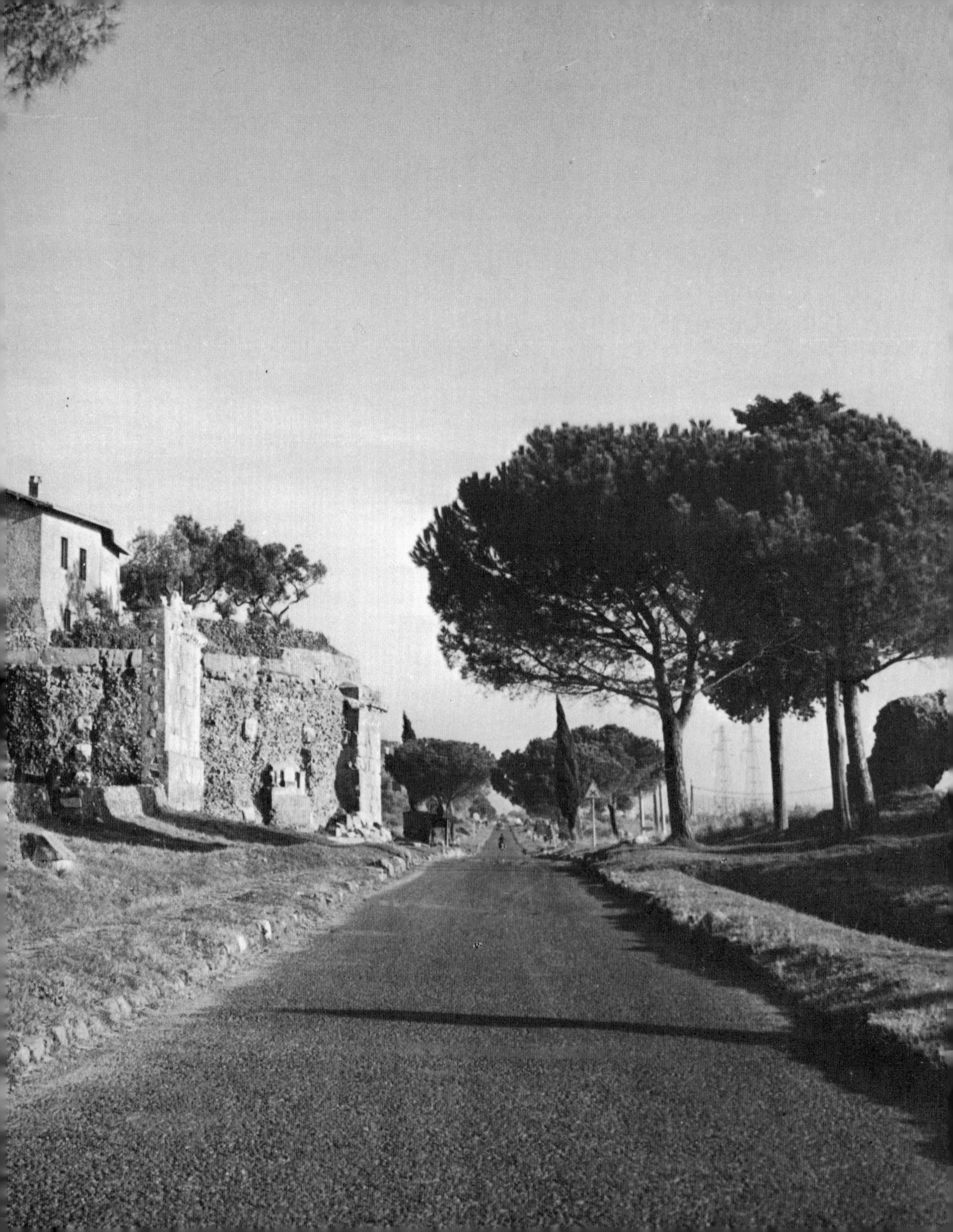

Via Appia aspect. Right, an ancient Roman in the fields.

and farm yard to be cleaned, and worn ropes and clothing to be mended. Even on feast days there were bushes to be cut, hedges to be trimmed, sheep to be dipped, and oil and fruit to be sold in town." In order to put these country tasks in sequence they devised the calendars which we recognise now as the forerunners of our almanacs.

Horace could not have given a more enticing description of ancient custom in the town. "In Rome for many a long year they knew no other pleasure nor festival than to open the city gates at dawn, to read the letter of the law to dependants, and invest money wisely against good securities. They enquired of the older generation and taught the young the art of increasing thrift and avoiding wasteful frivolities." Truly the austerity of the ancient Romans emanated from their poverty rather than their conscience. It took two or three generations before it became a pleasure centre. Till then it knew only frugal banquets and rustic festivals. Now there is eating, drinking and debauchery. Listen to what the eye witness Polybius has to say! "Most Romans live in a strange state of profligacy in which young people go to the most shameful excesses. They abandon themselves to all forms of entertainment, feasts and luxuries and every kind of dissipation, obviously following the example of the Greeks during the war against Perseus." One reads in Cato, "Look at this worthy citizen! He steps out of his chariot, completes a few pirouettes, tells some jokes and makes puns and a play on words. Then he sings or recites Greek poetry and performs some more pirouettes." It became one of the facets of the education of a young nobleman to emulate degenerate Greece. Scipio Aemilianus says, "When I entered one of the schools the nobles send their sons to, there were five hundred young girls and boys receiving instruction in the lyre, singing, and posture, surrounded by actors and people of dubious character. I also saw a child of twelve, the son of a candidate, performing a dance worthy of the most immodest slave."

Another wound created perhaps more harm because it aggravated the first. Titus Livy said, "The legions of Manlius introduced the luxury and indulgence of Asia, bringing beds decorated with bronze, rich carpets, fine cloths and textiles. It was after this period that singers, buffoons and harp players appeared at feasts, and that more research went into the preparation of meals, making an ordinary craft turn into an art." At this time a beautiful young slave could be seen to fetch more money than a fertile field, and a handful of fish more than a team of oxen. Rome had a fascination for the mind which changed man and his surroundings out of all proportion; Titus Livy and Corneille have often overpraised ancient heroes, whilst we make the same mistake in reverse as we rate the Romans of the empire too low.

Life in ancient Rome had to follow a regime of poverty and it was because of inevitable transformation that the new ways of empire were founded on wealth and ease. Setting aside one or two blatant exceptions which always occur, the standard of luxury was no more extravagant than ours nor were their fortunes greater than ours, given that they attract titles and decorations to their fortunate owners.

When the followers of Romulus triumphantly entered the heart of the Palatine palace bearing the sheaves gathered on enemy soil, their houses boasted no marble columns, nor their wives shimmering fabrics, nor their provisions variety to appease their hunger. Their homes were huts made of mud and tree branches and they lived off the land and animal rearing, buying tools with the small

Dining-room of a house, Pompeii. Roman beds, and someone having a meal: a servant offers him a drink.

amount of money they could scrape together from the sales of the vineyard and the cornfield. The women-folk wove the tunic and the toga. Were they of greater worth than their descendants? Certainly they were from a civil and military point of view, for they were both soldiers and citizens, whilst the Romans of the Empire were neither. Speaking of them as private individuals who can be sure that in their modest conditions their standards of morality could be compared with others?

Critics thought that the ancient way of life was indispensible to the Republic. This would have been so if Rome had remained a country town and had not become the world capital city. They were against indulgences at table, the finery of the women, the golden decorations, and even certain dishes involving the fattening of chickens and table birds which appeared to them to be a public hazard. When Tiberius was in power moreover, the town councillors wanted to revive the edicts which fixed the price of each dish and the number of dishes per meal. This caused a great stir in the town. Tacitus writes, "They were afraid that by his austere measures he would hark back to the rigours of the old frugality." Tiberius in his ever-present wisdom made serious jest of the councillors' Spartan enthusiasm, pointing out that Rome had need of her provinces for her very existence and that to sever established relationships would be to expose the State to chaos. How dangerous it was to make laws that are so quickly forgotten or scorned, he advised.

Roman trade had expanded with their conquests, enabling them to know very soon where the best marble could be found, the location of the finest woods, the softest materials and the most delicate foods. Victory gave them all the treasures that kings and their peoples had accumulated down the centuries, so that they found themselves rich all of a sudden, as the Spaniards did after conquering Peru. Then, as has been seen to happen in similar circumstances, people wanted better homes, better clothes and better food. The inheritor of Cincinnatus replaced the thick coarse woollen tunic by one of fine eastern fabric from Miletus dyed in Tyrian purple, and the daughters of the sturdy housewives who crushed the corn and kneaded the family bread, covered their heads, necks and arms with strings of pearls. The little mud or shale houses were replaced by monuments built of marble that radiated the luxury of Ephesus and Antioch, whilst at the table, made of cedar from Mauretania, they served turbot from Ravenna and oysters from Tarentum, snails from Illyria, or Africa and murry from Sicily, wine from the Cyclades and kid from Ambracia, pheasants from the Caucasus and peacock from Persia, flamingo from Egypt and Guinea fowl from Numidia. There were a hundred and one other costly items that came from distant lands, but not so distant as those from which we obtain tea, coffee, sugar, ivory, silk and diamonds. Pliny was put out, because want-

Ships, in a mosaic at Ostia.

Oil jars kept in the store places of a house in Ostia.

ing to have cool drinks, he had to buy snow from the mountain peasants of the Abruzzi to put in his wine.

The Mediterranean coasts were strewn with flourishing cities, for the peoples living on the shores of this great Roman lake exchanged their merchandise, always finding excellent markets. Whilst the ships peacefully plied the gentle sea, goods came in from more distant places overland, thus creating a general sense of well-being. It is not to be wondered that writers, whilst very happy with the present, should appear to regret the simplicity of the ancient past. It was fine to write in praise of austerity, especially as it imposed obligations on no-one, and yet permitted philosophers to write their eulogies of poverty from golden tables. Therefore let us allow writers like Sallust the Epicurean, Varro, Seneca and Pliny the Elder to be shocked, without blaming them, that people chased the length and breadth of land and sea in order to supply the sensuous with momentary pleasures. Because of the all-pervading security, industry and commerce could not help but put a host of products into circulation that one could enjoy without abusing. Many used them to advantage

Roman Mosaics: a bowl of fruit, fish.

under Tiberius' rule, and the freed Pallas of the Claudian period. They amounted to three hundred million sesterces. The fortune of Narcissus in Nero's time was in the region of four hundred million. The wealth of the notorious Apicius only amounted to one quarter of the fortune Narcissus had, and Crassus had one half the amount. At that time the power of money was greater than it is today whilst the masses were poorer, hence the gulf between the majority and the chosen few seemed very much greater. This gave rise to confusion and scandal, but the gulf rapidly diminished. Tacitus

Right: Bakers at work, after a bas-relief and the remains of a bakery in Pompeii: kneading trough, mill and oven.

whilst others did the exact opposite. Such people would go to great excess, wasting their gold on frivolous luxuries, like the foolish man described in Nero's time as having paid four million sesterces for roses on the occasion of a feast. The money naturally went to the peasants of Campania who had developed a rose-growing industry. The period of greatest luxury in Rome was between the time of Lucullus and Nero, or after the conquest of the Asiatic east up to the civil war which followed the extinction of the Caesar dynasty. At this time, the noble families gave way to every kind of extravagance, and intoxicated by their fortunes, they were at a loss as to how to rule their provinces or even to control their wealth. Lucullus and Caesar during the republic and Caligula and Nero under the empire are representative of this new situation of the patriciate.

The largest known fortunes of this period and of any throughout the whole of the Roman era belonged to the augur Lentulus

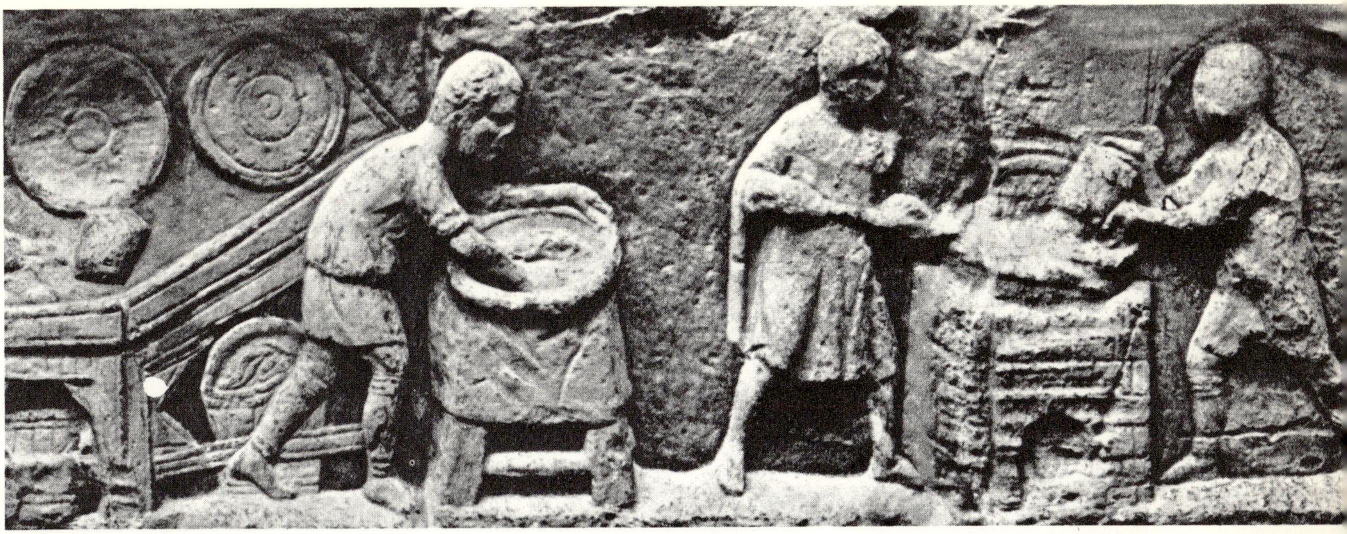

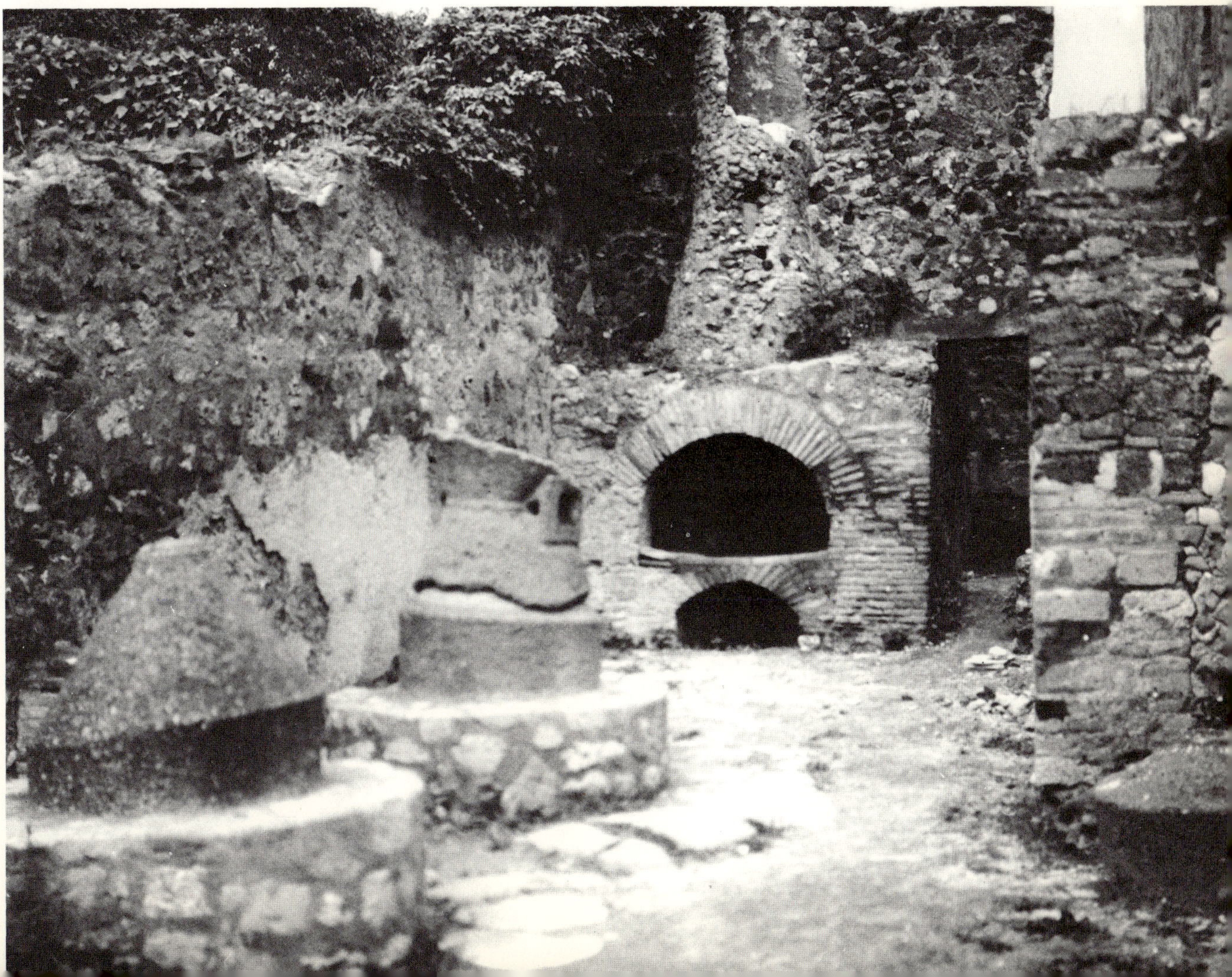

wrote, "Luxury at the table was ardently indulged in for one hundred years, after the battle of Actium until the war which placed Galba at the head of empire." It had been introduced much earlier by people renowned for it like Lucullus, Hortensius, and Philippus, and unusual dishes were prepared well before Augustus. Under the spartan law of Sylla, Macrobus found reference to one thousand dishes considered then very ordinary but no longer known in his time. "Great heavens what a list! Seeing so many kinds of fish and stews unknown today, I cannot help thinking that the breaches of social behaviour must have been extreme during that century." Roman gourmandise had diminished just as luxury had. Varro before Actium, and Pliny from the Nero age, showed that the last republicans and the first senators of the empire could rival each other in gastronomic sensuality. They discovered new foods or new methods of preparing the old ones and they carried out what we think we have invented—fish farms, air-conditioning, tree transplanting, and even replacement of elderly vines. They had greenhouses to grow flowers, fruit and grapes, and "the sterile winters are forced to bear an autumn harvest." They encouraged the breeding of fish from Asian coasts and a large variety of edible shell-fish off the shores of Latium and Campania. They also made nursery ponds to preserve the best species and avoid the risk of losing them all, should there be a heavy sea. The fish beds developed to such a large extent that Lucullus' inheritors obtained forty million sesterces from investments in them, which would seem impossible if a comtemporary, Varro had not said that Hirrius made the annual sum of twelve million sesterces from his nurseries and that on one single occasion he gave Caesar six thousand murry.

The Roman gourmet had discriminating and delicate taste, and turned down ordinary food like lamb and beef. He had a palate for lighter dishes and despite the edicts of the censeurs, aviaries and parks became as big business as the fish nurseries. They bred all manner of bird, animal and shell-fish. We do not eat them any more now. They were for example dormouse, peacock, crane and flamingo. A matron from one of the consular families would sell five thousand plump thrushes a year at three denarii each, and even before the first triumvirate, peacock breeding brought in sixty thousand sesterces a year for Aufidius Lurco. They knew how to enlarge the liver of geese when breeding them, an invention whose honorableness was in question by a consul and a knight.

The patriciate chose to find such things both pleasureable and profitable. Many governors brought home plants and fruit from their Asiatic or African provinces, and then planted them on their own estates, using the labour of the slaves and freed men they had also brought back with them. Since the time of Lucullus, who forty years before Actium had included the cherry tree of Pontus in his share of booty from Mithridates, to the unknown traveller who introduced the melon from the banks of the Oxus to the Naples area in Pliny's time, the importation of new plants into Italy and an attempt to then perfect them, has never ceased.

When speaking of luxury at the Roman table, one has to remember two men who mark its peak: Apicius with his certain type of art, and Vitellius with his brutality. There were several Apicius', of whom the most famous lived during the time of Augustus and Tiberius. He invented dishes, perhaps drew up a treatise on cooking, and had the reputation of being the greatest gourmet on earth. He also had the final distinction of being taken as a model by that fool of an Elgabal. He owned one hundred million sesterces and killed himself when he had only ten million left.

Vitellius had held the dignified position of emperor to those Romans who worshipped their stomachs. They found a method of perpetual eating which they achieved by a disgusting practice. However, he seems to have had to make less effort of the imagination than one would suppose, when he invented his famous shield of Minerva, which was laden with every kind of rare food, if one goes by a feast which the pontiffs and vestals of the republic had prepared for themselves. The menu for the meal and been religiously preserved by the grand pontiff Metellus, for the feasts of the priesthood had been famous in Rome, as everywhere else, for the exquisite fare they provided.

Macrobus wrote: "This is what the feast consisted of on the day when Lentulus celebrated his inauguration as priest (flamen) of Mars:

"First course: Sea urchin, raw oysters, cockles, mussel-type shell fish, thrushes, asparagus, plump chicken on oyster and cockle paté, black and white acorn shells (shell fish, mussels, glycomarides (also shellfish), sea nettles, figeaters, kidneys of the roebuck and wild boar, plump poultry coated in flour, figeaters, murex, and purple-fish (shell-fish).

"Second course: Sow's udder, boar's head, fish paté, paté of sow's udder, duck, boiled teal, hare roast poultry, dishes blended with flour (soups and creams no doubt). Picenum bread of all kinds." It was not necessary for the disciples of Epicurus and Zeno to teach people to emulate sobriety in their schools, because nature, the supreme master, creates its own law. Excess of alcohol is dangerous in the North and in the South it is a vice that kills. The taboo on wine for the followers of Islam is laid down for reasons of health, and this was something that Galenus the physician was already advising the Romans. He used to say, "If you want your health to be good, put water in your wine. In Italy, which is in the

Fresco in the rear room of a tavern in Pompeii showing clients drinking.

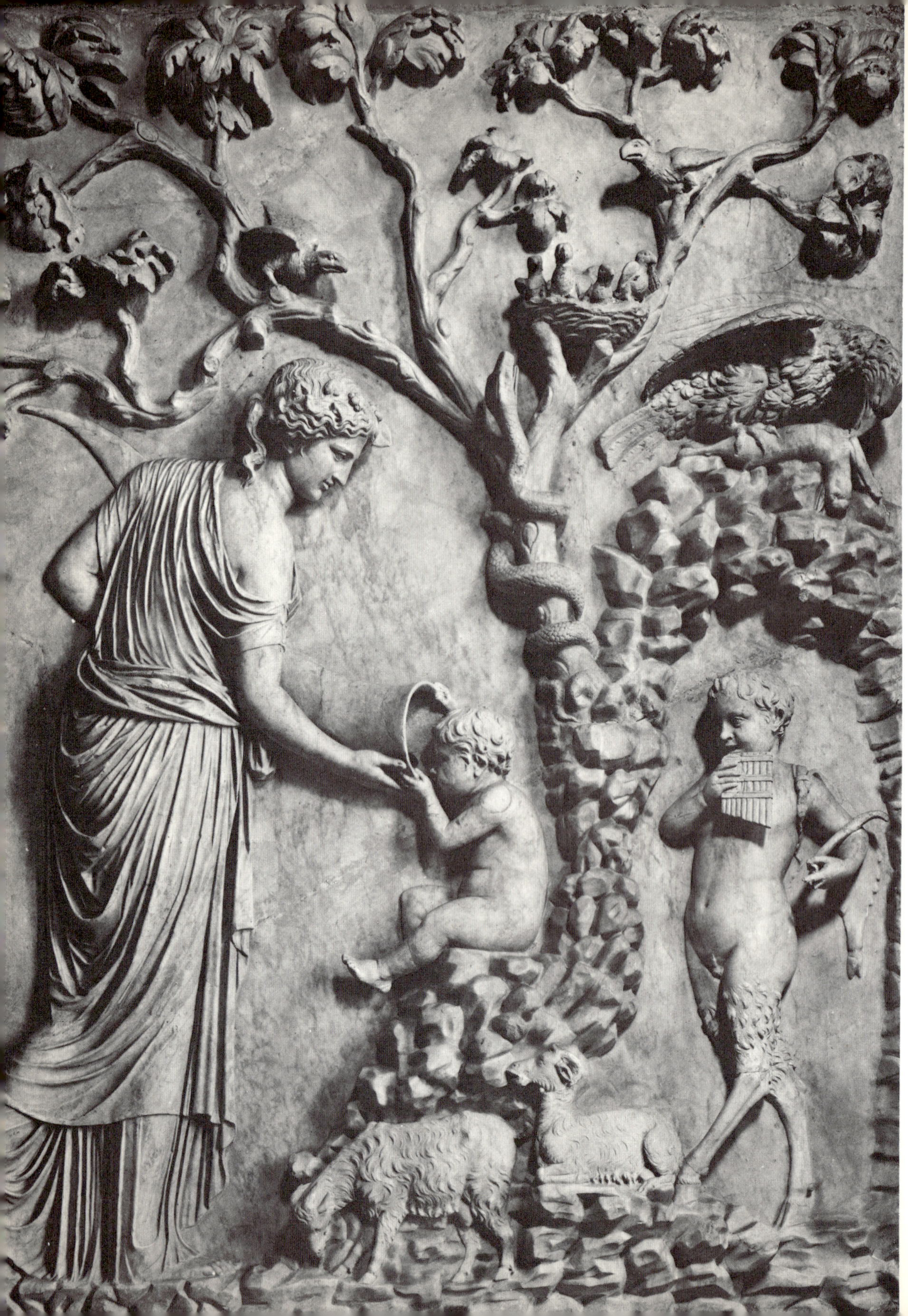

Left: Child of Bacchus. Opposite: in a cellar.

Below: children treading the grapes (sculpture in a tomb).

intermediate zone between the wet regions and the hot countries, wine is made and drunk. When the Saturnalia took place, this being the feast of the multitudes, a number of people could be relied on to get drunk, and some were eager to earn the reputation of heavy drinkers. Mark Antony the triumvir, the son of Cicero, and Novellius Torquatus who had acquired the nickname Three Galloner, (Tricongius), by drinking ten litres at one draught, were typical examples.

Generally speaking, the majority lived soberly. Pliny the Elder ate very little, and Seneca went for a whole year without eating meat; "eventually he gave up drinking wine and the use of perfume, and with other things was moderate to the point of abstinence."

He was fond of repeating Epicurus' words,— "No one is poor who has bread to eat and water to drink, and all can aspire to the supreme happiness of Jove". Having seen one of the Lentulus menus, let us consider one attributed to Pliny the Younger. A friend whom he had invited to dinner was unable to come, and in expressing his regret about it, enumerated to him all the delicacies he had prepared; "Each person has lettuce, three snails, two eggs, a cake, chilled wine with honey, olives from Andalusia, gourds, shallots and many other equally delicate morsels."

Whilst most people were content with little, they liked the games, entertainments and talking and knew exactly how to exploit people who were either extravagant or seekers of popularity with officials of the town. The result was numerous feasts and public eatings, assemblies and group meetings, where southern high-spiritedness made everyone forget the poorness of the scenery and the meagre fare, for the donor would be conceited and at the same time mean. Then, tired or satiated, members of the gathering would go and lie in the sun. "What do you wish to do now?" someone said to a hawker weary of his bowing and scraping. "What do you want?—To sleep."

The southerner is always read to sleep or dream unless passion provokes him to violent action.

Dress.—Roman society on the whole spent even less on clothing than on food. There were the city swells who lived in grand style; they ruined young men of good family and sometimes elderly senators, spreading an unheard-of kind of luxury which is particularly associated with this type of woman. Unfortunately, respectable matrons or others who had discreetly collected a bit of substance behind them, wanted to look just as fine as the courtesan, and spent even more than them on their personal appearance. Toilet materials (mundus muliebris) had already become an arsenal bristling with every means of attack and preservation. There were salves to paint the face with, false teeth, false eyebrows, and even false hair that had been sent for from distant Germany and India. The imperial courtesan Messalina, who was dark-haired, wore a fair wig when she went out with Juvenal, the satirist.

Silenus. A priestess of Bacchus. Aged satyr paying court to a lady.

"You have your hair curled by a hair-dresser in Suburanus street, Gallaï and he also applies your eye-brows. Each evening you remove your teeth as you do your dress. Your looks are enclosed in dozens of little pots, so that your real face does not accompany you to your bed."

Once, clothes were made from local farm wool; gradually however, the use of Egyptian linen came in, along with Indian cottons, Chinese silk, muslins so very fine that they were described as woven air, tunics embossed with gold or embroidered with pearls, precious stones and perfumes of every kind. Pliny noted seeing Lollia Paulina at a private engagement party, who was wearing pearls and emeralds from head to foot, and she was quite ready to prove to him by showing him the receipts, that they were worth forty million sesterces. Agrippina attended a party given by Claudius on Lake Fucino, wearing a cloak woven with gold thread, and Nero burned more incense at the funeral of his favourite, (and then wife) than the whole of prosperous Arabia could produce in one year. Pliny said with bitterness, "Luxuries for the women cost us a hundred million sesterces a year, and Arabia, India, and Eastern Asia put them into their coffers."

Products of the Orient were much more costly than they are now. Caesar gave Servilia a ring which had cost him six million sesterces, Pliny estimated one pound of cinnamon to be worth one thousand five hundred denarii, whilst during the rule of Aurelius, silk was exchanged against its weight in gold.

For men also, clothing covered the body without being tailored to fit it, so that one or two pieces of material swathed around the loins and over the shoulders were quite sufficient. Someone knew how to shape a toga, and on feast days everyone, from the emperor to the most humble citizen was wearing one. The only difference between the togas worn by rich and poor lay in the whiteness and fine quality of the fabric. The owner was smartly dressed if he could drape it well and arrange the folds to hang evenly. He liked to have a well-equipped ward-robe as the climate necessitated changing his clothes often, and it was the height of luxury to have cloaks dyed in various shades of purple. Caesar had banned the purple toga, except for special people and special days. Augustus, Tiberius, and even Nero renewed the ban without further success because during the time of Domitian, Martial speaks of purple robes bought publicly for ten thousand sesterces.

Dwellings.—The true richness of the Romans

Left: Roman lady in traditional dress. Below: bas-relief of a lady and her hairdressers.

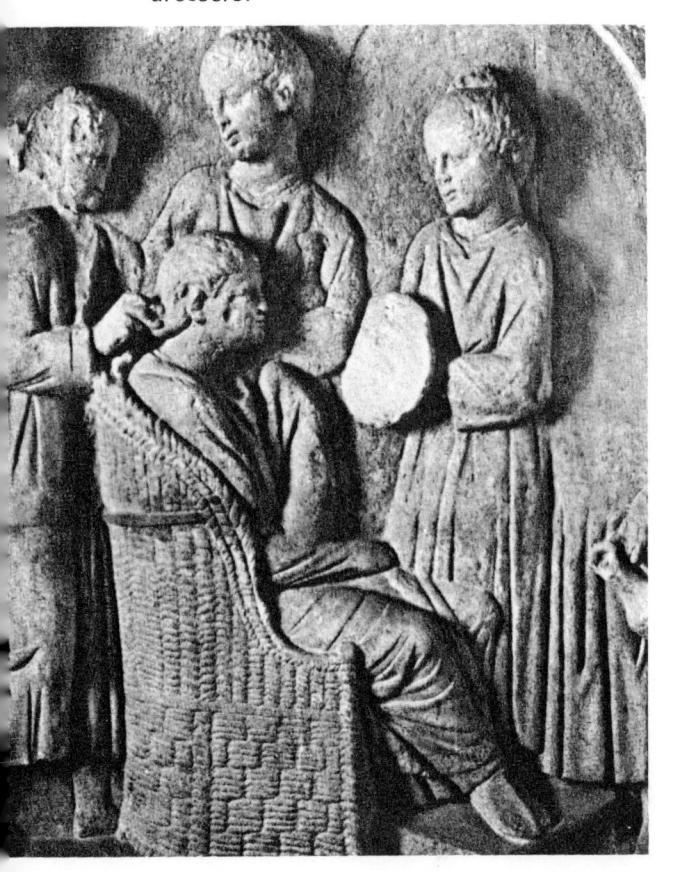

This Roman mural shows that the "bikini" goes back to a very ancient fashion.

of the empire, lay in their building, which they pursued throughout the universe. During each reign, countless works were undertaken by the emperors, beginning with the first. Augustus built for the glory of the gods and for the people, whilst Caligula and Nero erected vast palaces for themselves which disappeared with them. All that is left of Nero's Golden Palace is the description of it by Suetonius and Pliny, yet the modest home of Livy still stands. Ordinary people vied with princes. By the time of the republic, the nobility had adopted the habit of spending the summer in the hills overlooking the countryside around Rome or the shores of Naples Bay, to avoid malaria.

When an imperial decree obliged the senators to give one third of their fortune to an Italian property fund, the whole peninsula became studded with country seats more quickly than any other country in the world, for none can offer better situations or climate for any kind of rural home, whether it is to be on the shore of one of the two seas, by one of the many lakes, or on the mountain slopes which nurture the forests and springs with winter snows beneath a blazing sun. Treasures of Greek art enhance the natural beauty of the landscape with their delights. Every existing kind of marble, stucco, glass, bronze, silver and gold leaf, elegant paintings, fine arabesques that even Raphael did not refrain from imitating, enriched the walls and ceilings, and in order that the eye should be rewarded at every glance, the floors were laid with mosaics, some of very wonderful composition. One has been found in the house of Faunus at Pompeii, representing the battle of Darius and Alexander with the figures almost life-size. Inside, columns of marble from Numidia and Euboea, which a century later will be replaced by porphyrian marble from Egypt, support the airy porticos which give protection against the sun in summer and conserve its warmth in winter. Wherever you turn, there are statues, elaborate vases, works of art and rich hangings. Many rooms have been decorated with especial care. The atrium contained the household gods, images of the family ancestors, and aromatic plants to cleanse the atmosphere. Next to it was the tablinum and the conversation hall for visitors, and further on, the triclinium for guests. There was a room set aside for the women and special accommodation for the slaves. In the courtyards there were cool leaping fountains, and flowers surrounded the marble borders-roses, lilies, violets, anemones and myrtle trained into artistic shapes. If the square allowed, there would be perhaps a fine plane tree to provide shade, offering its smoothe bark, elegant bearing and vigorous growth. The Spanish "patio" freshens their tasteful attraction. There were always two essential parts of a complete habitation:—the library, which was small, although everyone was literate or wished to appear so... and the thermal baths which were complicated and expensive. You passed through many different temperatures and clouds of perfumed

Statue of a faun, Pompeii. On the following pages: a street; roof with rain-water opening above the atrium (impluvium), and the interior of a patrician home.

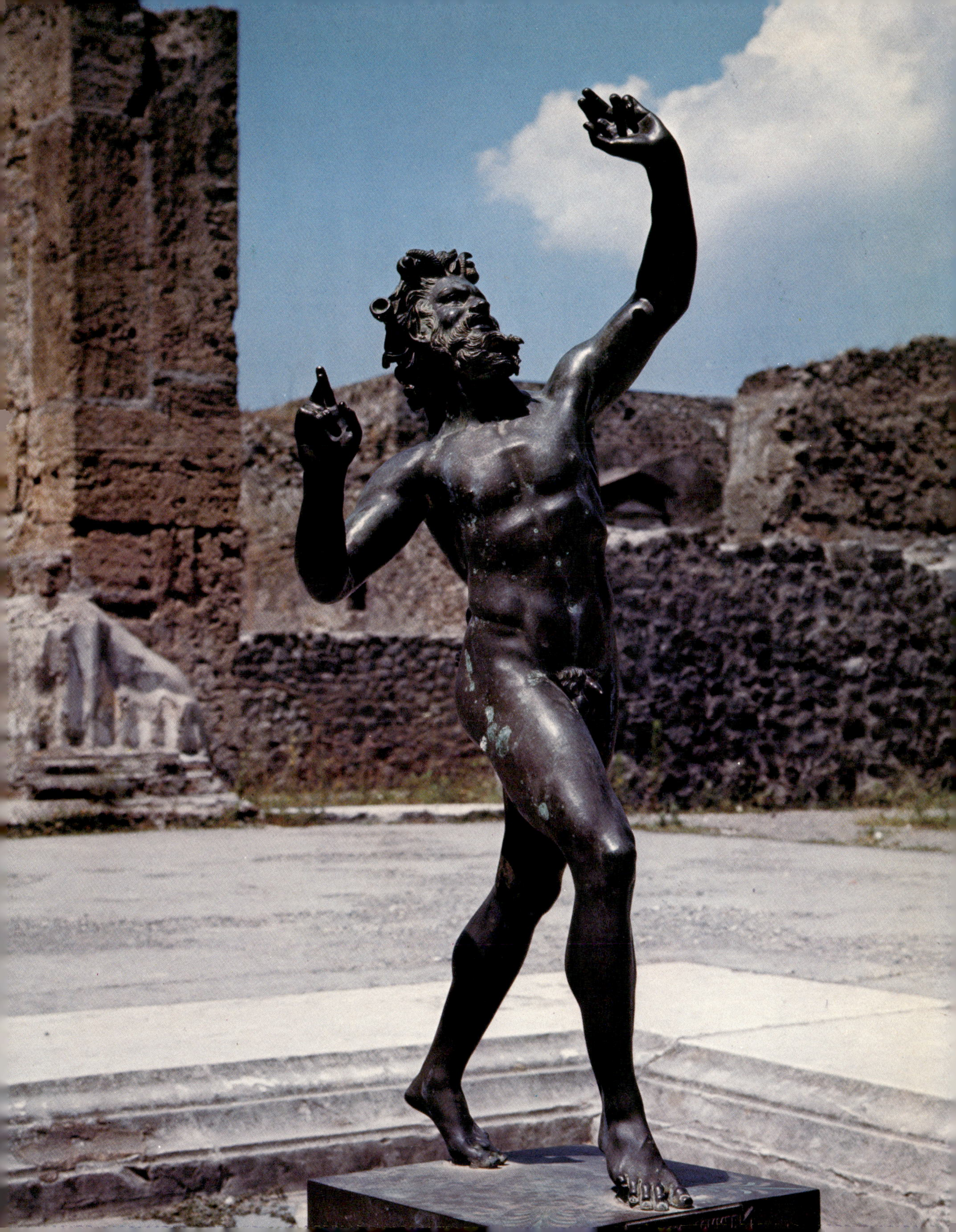

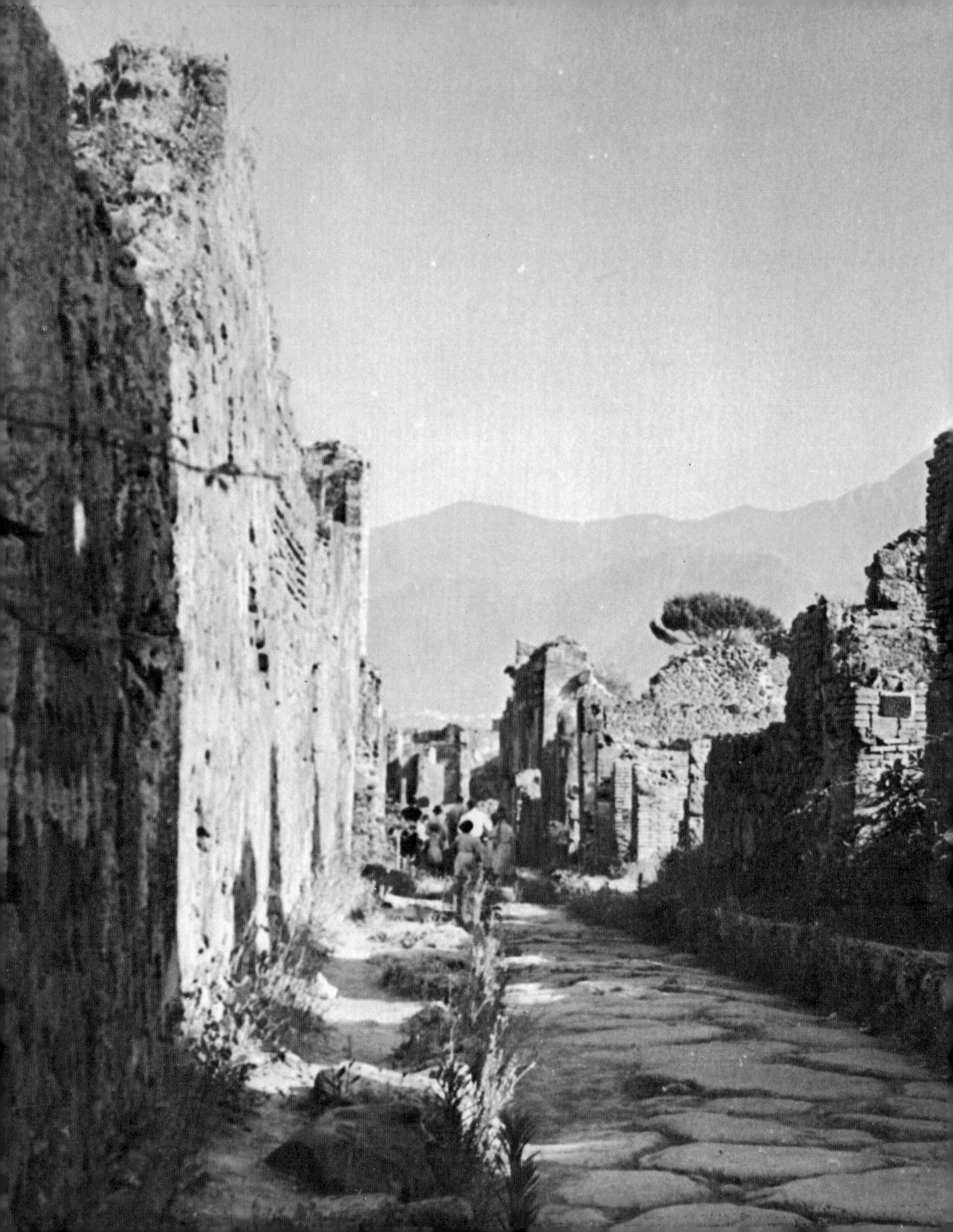

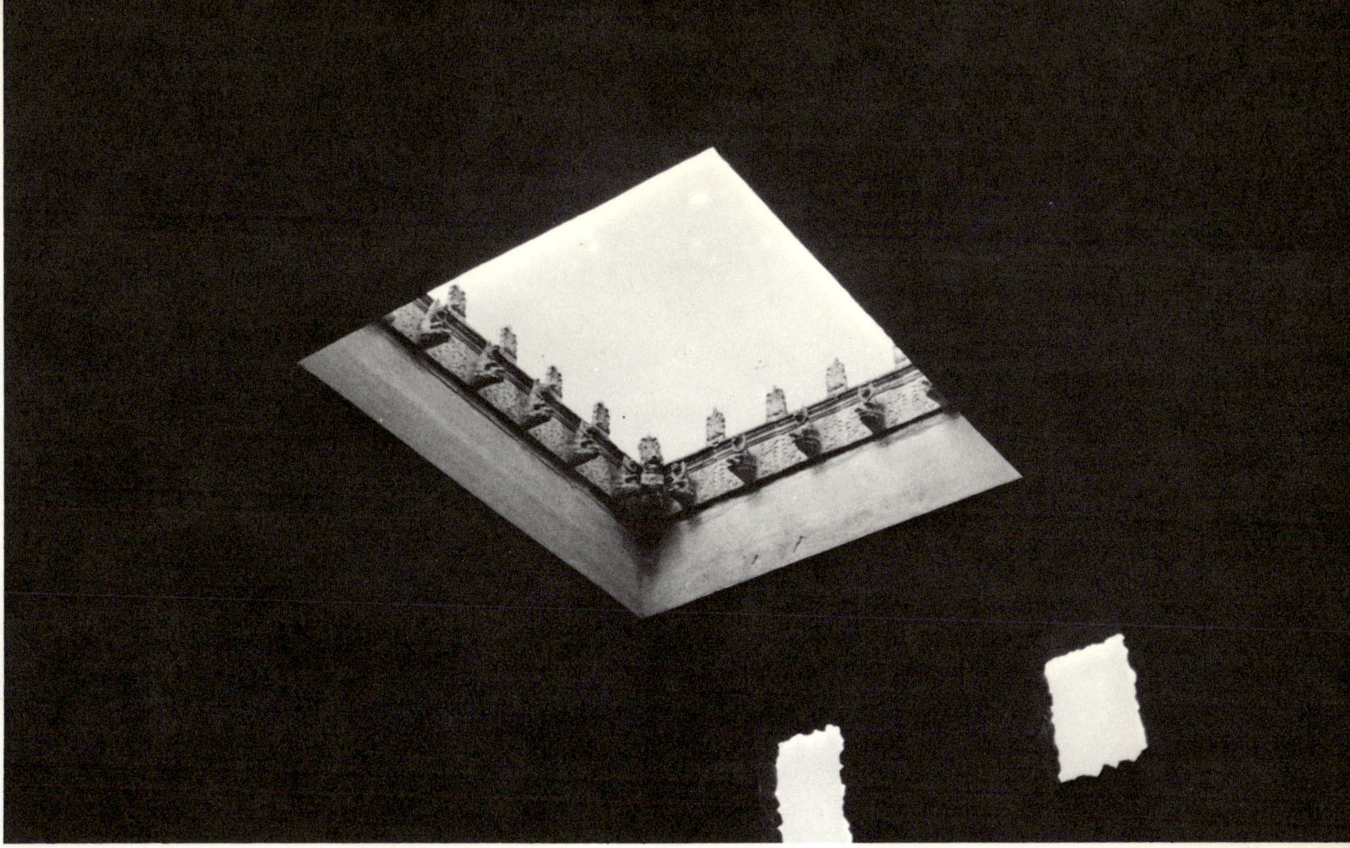

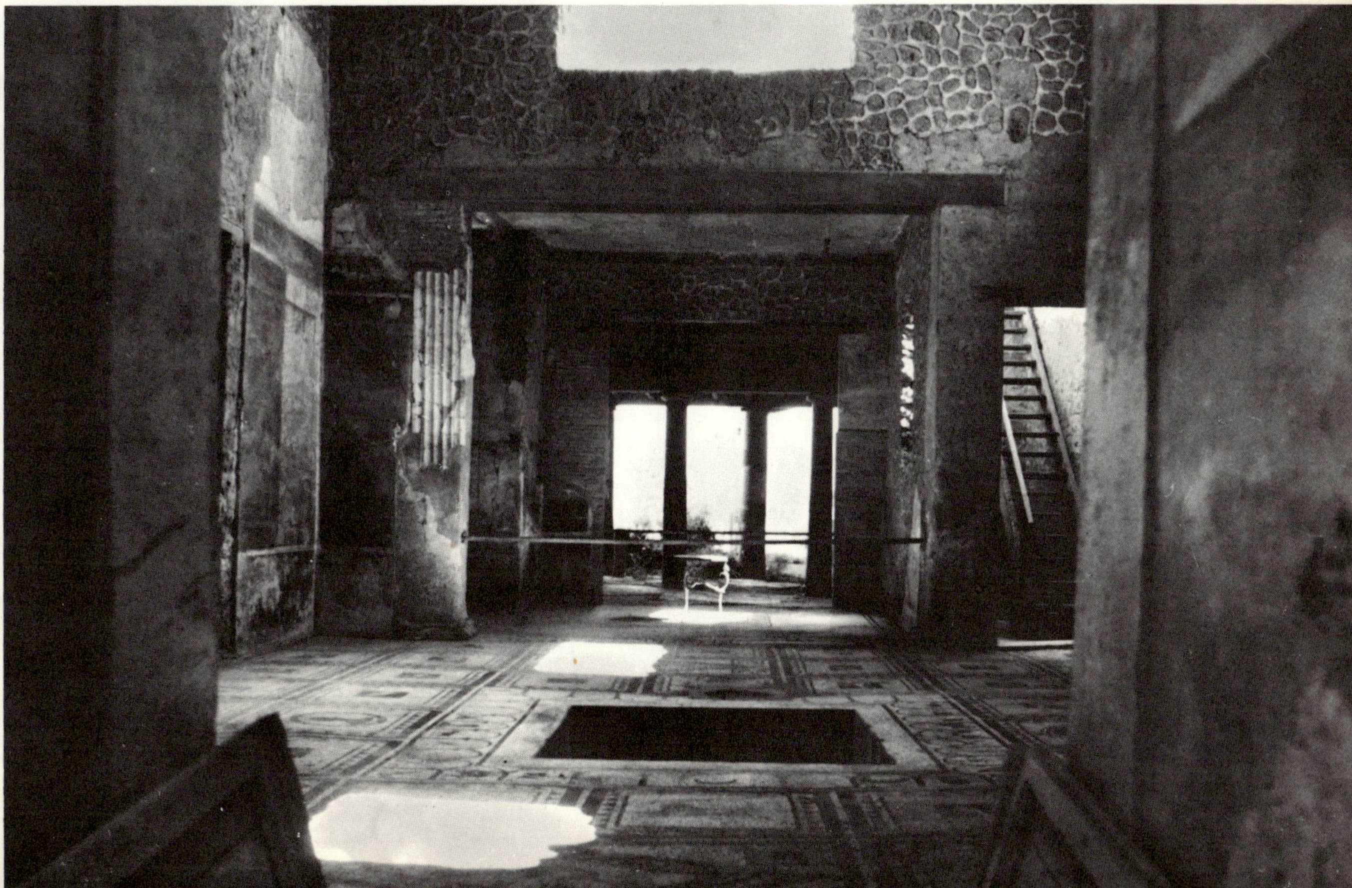

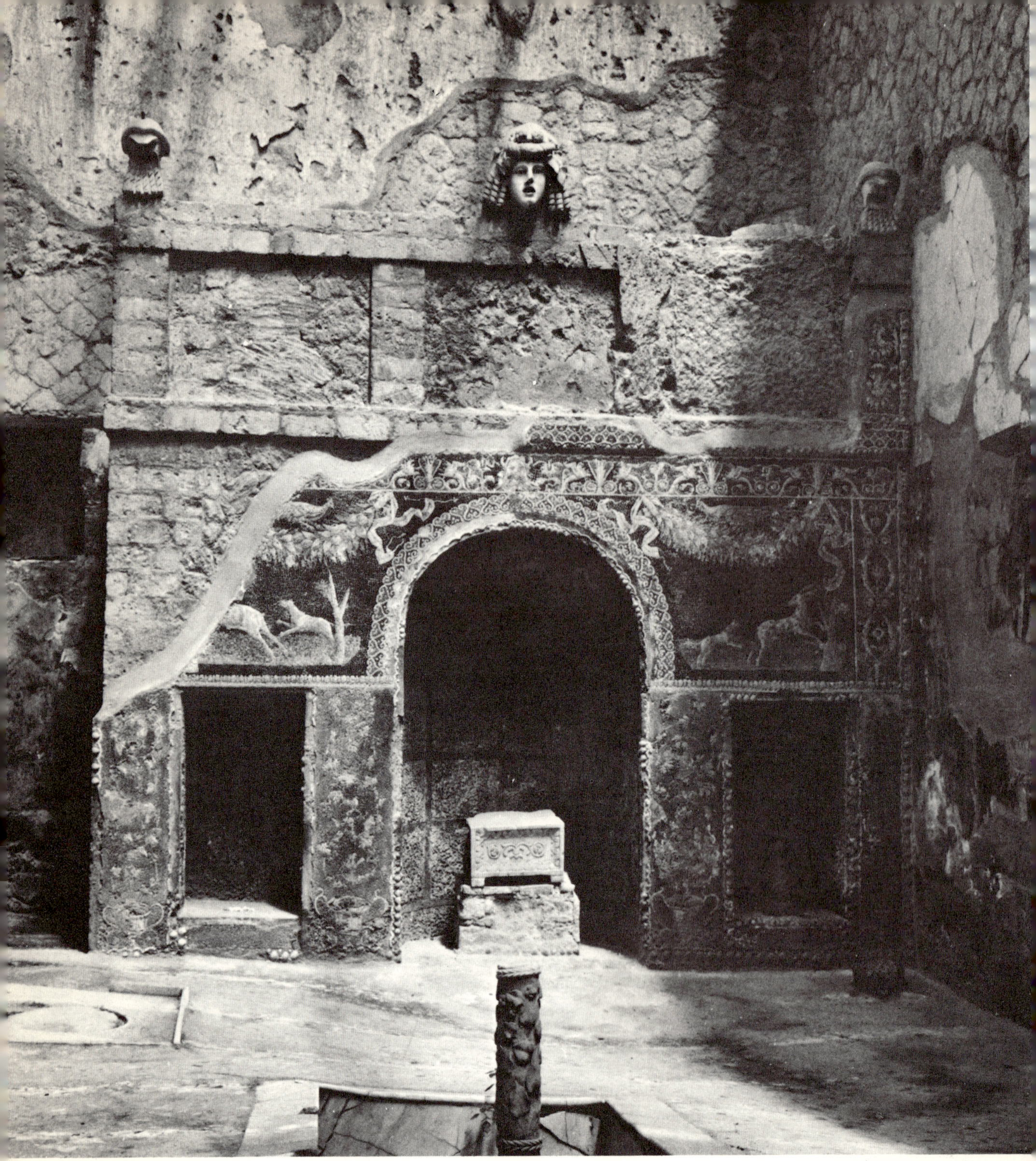

Left: dining-room with couch (triclinium) at Herculaneum. Above: reconstitution of a property in Ostia. Below: peristyle of the House of the Vettii, Pompeii.

Remains of the Roman baths, Fiesole. Below: a fountain at a road junction in Pompeii.

steam until you reached the excercising room to limber up and then invigorate the muscles again. The bath and its accessories always played the key role in preserving the health of the Romans, and not a day passed but what they took one.

However, despite their size and luxury, these mansions were always provided less in view of their comfort and the kind of living they could afford than of their ostentation.

Provincial cities imitated Rome by providing temples, arenas, baths and theatres, basilicas and courts (curia), appropriate to their means. They even used Roman street names.

Every lake and hot spring, or a hill-side offering a view or sunshine, acquired its villa; if need be, nature was made to comply with the taste of the owner. There was a stream where formerly there had been a hill, rocks which used to be bare produced vineyards and woods, and parts of the sea were harnessed to make fish-farms and baths free

Water drainage during the Roman era, Fiesole.

He also claimed to have some money invested in commerce, and although he was very generous towards his native town and his friends, he still received an amount of three million sesterces from Latium. He had a young lady whom he loved, sat at table with the prince, and belonged in rank, relationship and fortune to the highest Roman society.

Accordingly he had to live like one of the most important people in the empire. He has left us a minute description of his two villas near Lavinium by the sea and also of the one at Tifernum in the upper valley of the Tiber. They were built solely for comfort, and any hint at luxury came from their beautiful natural surroundings alone. He does not tell us how many bronze ornaments there were, or pictures, or neo-Greek statues after original masterpieces. Nor does he

Stela of a Greek Arch, Rome: the Romans had a "mania" for horses.

from the damage of storms. Ovid wrote, "The azure seas recoiled before the stout piers." At Antium, the remains of some of these under-water works can still be seen.

Some of the residences were of considerable dimensions. Seneca compares them to towns. Nevertheless the sum total of what we know about the history of ancient Rome, convinces us that by far the greatest number of houses were small and without value. Juvenal said, "You can have an attractive house in Sora, Fabrateria, or Frosinone for the price of the rent of a small pied-a-terre in Rome."

In Pompeii where rich people lived, it is difficult to find two or three houses of any size. The houses are small and the rooms low.

Pliny is an example of a rich man who owned villas near the gates of Rome, in Tuscany, the Beneventine, and in the vicinity of Como. The rent of a single estate was more than four hundred thousand sesterces.

mention rich fabrics or the finery of Calpurnia, but rather the clever arrangement of the rooms in the houses which had a view of the sea and the mountains, sunshine in the autumn, coolness in the summer and peace and tranquillity all the year round. People will say he was a sage, as indeed he was, but at the same time he was like many other men who enjoyed his fortune wisely and knew how to put it to good use.

Reference must be made to the mania for horses, some of which were as famous in Rome as our winners at Longchamps, and they were sold for equally large sums. Caligula wanted to dress up his horse Incitatus as a consul, whilst the popularity of Martial even in his rosiest days of public favour was eclipsed by the passion for the fast horse, Andremon. In Apulia, Calabria, Sicily and Cappadocia there were vast open pastures where the horses were bred. The business was thriving because travellers, and merchants, the rich and those who wanted to become rich, need them for business or pleasure. Cross breeds of Spanish-African stock were considered the best. Antiochus bought some at great cost on the borders of the Tagus and the Guadalquivir. Studies of the Roman Empire are based on the hypothesis that slave labour was at the root of it all. This had been more or less true during the period of war when Rome and Italy were crammed with captives. Crassus had twenty thousand slaves whom he hired to contractors for every kind of trade. War however ceased to stimulate commerce when the army legions were limited to defending the frontiers. Furthermore the lessening of the numbers of slaves through death and acquisition of freedom was hardly surmounted by births in the slave population, slave trading, or claiming children who had been abandoned, stolen, or sold. Therefore there were many opportunities for work available to the free artisan in a situation which was improving every day, to the extent that there grew up whole industries concerned with producing clothes, food, buildings of all kinds, works of artistic merit, and an enormous transport service to sell all the wares of the universe. Saint Paul wanted the bishop and priests to pursue an honest trade and when Chrysostome fled from Rome with nothing except Plato on Phedo and one of the speeches of Demosthenes, he could travel to the four corners of the empire earning his living as he went by work with his hands on the farms in the countryside or in the gardens of the towns.

Already before the days of the empire, Varro pointed out the advantages of having "gardens close to the town so that flowers and fruit can be sold at a good price" to the small proprietor. As proof of what could be done with small means and some skill, he describes two of his former soldiers who were brothers owning an unassuming establishment set in a small field which they had planted with crops attractive to bees. The honey from the hives brought in for them ten

A woman trader. Right: small and larger scale business in Pompeii.

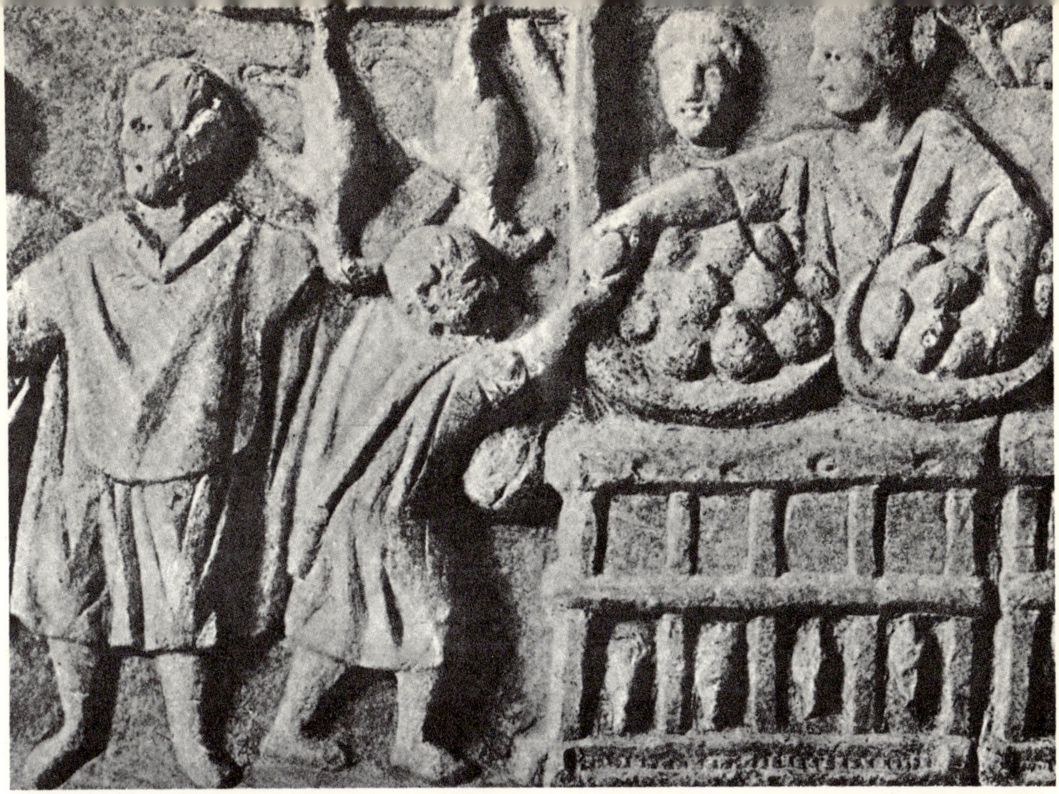

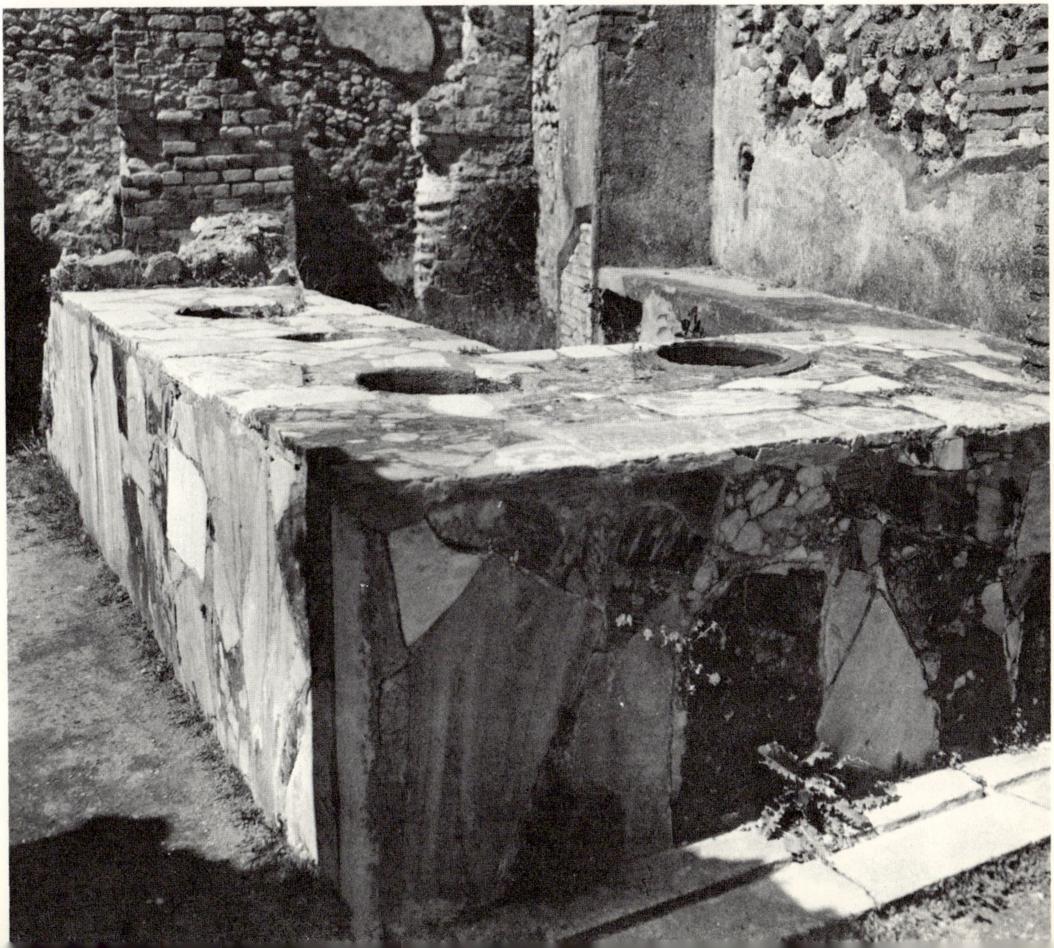

thousand sesterces in an average year. Juvenal's barber acquired fields and houses and Martial saw a shoemaker achieve a fortune such as never came to himself. Small people like this who could rise above their birth through economy, skill and strokes of good fortune were in very large number. When Domitian cleared the stalls from the streets of Rome, Martial said, "Rome is Rome; not long ago it was but a gigantic shop." Pompeii tells us that this was also true of the small towns. Rome, with her fifteen or eighteen hundred thousand inhabitants, produced the same social phenomena as those which exist in our modern towns. There were the small industrialists and above them the big ones, and while the outlet for the small ones was some undersized den, the others transacted in splendid shops.

Official literature, and I mean to say the majority literature which is the only kind that reaches us and lives in the commonplaces of the past, withessed nothing of all this industry and continued to be scornful of the workers, with the exception of Chrysostomus who rated a useful worker above a rhetorician with his brilliant conceited oratory. Yet inscriptions, shop signs, ruined remains full of significance and all those other things which were at one time neglected by history, give evidence of the transformation. The agricultural society of Cato the Elder became the industrial society of the empire. It was nothing less than an economic revolution and consequently a social one too.

It is making an exception to say that the Romans indulged in foolish expenditure, when in fact a section of the assets of the State and of some of the citizens was allocated to building programmes which served the general interests of the empire,... for example

Ancient Rome reconstituted: the Forum, the Palatine, the Circus, the Colosseum, the thermal baths of Trajan.

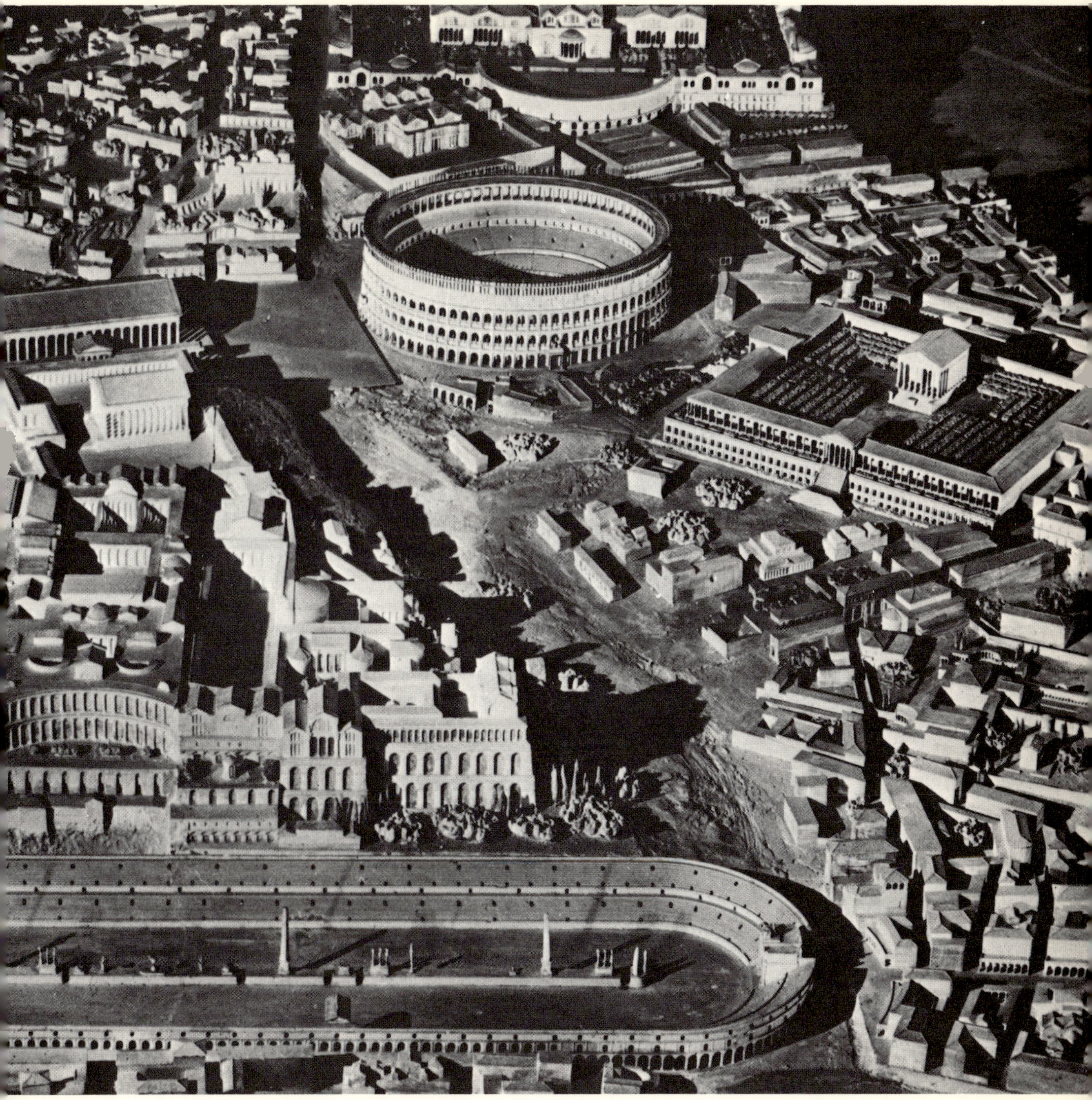

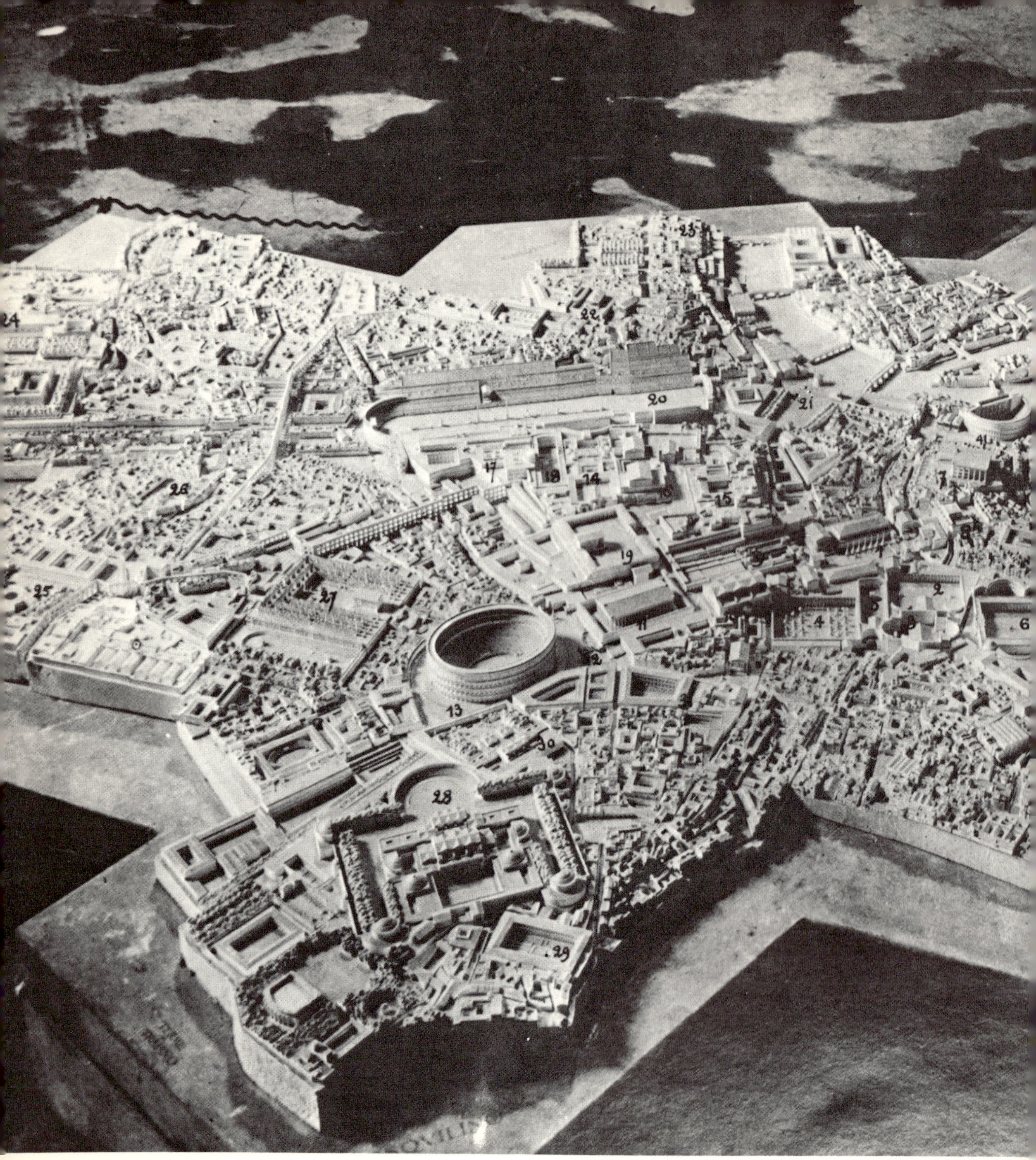
23
24
22
20
21
41
17
18
14
15
26
19
25
27
2
4
6
11
13
30
28
29

This model represents the whole of Imperial Rome.

roads, bridges, arsenals and harbours,... or the beliefs, leisure and well-being of the masses, in the form of temples and basilicas, baths and porticos, or circuses and theatres. The old names which continued to exist in Rome as well as in the provincial towns, lingering from the days of the republic and the sovereignty of the people, compelled the prince on the banks of the Tiber, the rich men of the borough and so on, to pay the poor a ransom for their power and position in many different forms. Augustus gave an example of this. He boasted that he had made Rome a city of marble, and Vespasian, the most careful of the emperors, did not flinch from the gigantic expense of constructing the most enormous edifice which the Romans called the Colosseum. Even among the least of the princes, there were few who did not leave some constructional undertaking

Horse and car and Roman flagstones.

Original Thermal Baths of Caracalla and photograph of a room in the baths at Ostia.

intended for the benefit of the public. What modern capital has made available to all without cost, monuments comparable to the theatre of Marcellus, the baths of Caracalla, or Vespasian's Colosseum, with porticos for walking to take the air, or for shelter from the sun and rain, and what is more, walk for several kilometres surrounded by masterpieces of the Greek culture?

In the lands of the south, water is a commodity of prime necessity, since the baths are indispensable to health. The view was that it was very democratic to provide it free, and so means were found to take it everywhere.

Theatres and Amphitheatres.—If the theatres were more dangerous than useful, it was not the fault of those who built them. It was the poets who wrote bad plays and the spectators who wanted licentious ones who were to blame. When the people's feasts still retained something of their primitive character common to religious mysteries, the audience liked to laugh at coarseness and obscenities that the more severe republicans scorned at the Floral games. What became of these customs when embraced by a population of former slaves? The answer would be to go to the Far East where you would see lascivious performances at the dancing festivals of India or Egypt, which were evoked to some extent by the presentation of mimes in Rome.

Now there you would see realism carried out in the plays to the extent that spectators of drama by Euripides saw it,—a woman insulted before their eyes, or in "The dying Hercules" a real stake, real flames, and in their midst, a living man being consumed by them.

When it came to the circus, the Romans understood it less completely than the Greeks. Only the most noble and the very courageous took part in the Olympic arena events; this meant that everything that went on in the stadium lent a dignity to the games which the Romans could never achieve in theirs. Nor did the Greeks ever have any liking for

A combatant from a mosaic at Ostia. Small statue of a pygmy contestant.

Below: reproduction of a bas-relief showing two contestants at the beginning of their bout.

Circus games... animal fighting, chariot racing and contests.

Right: the Colosseum. On the following page: a view from the circular wall.

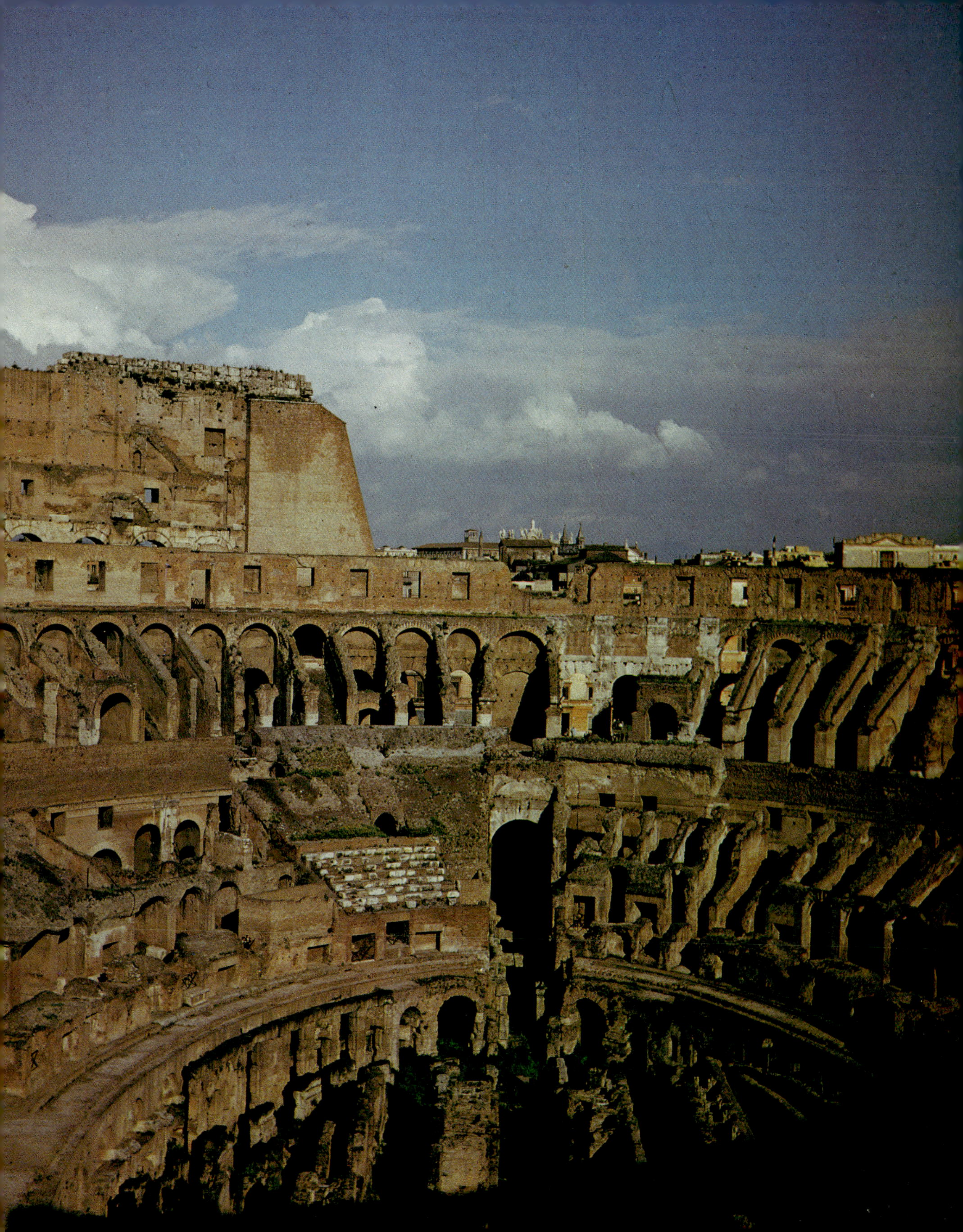

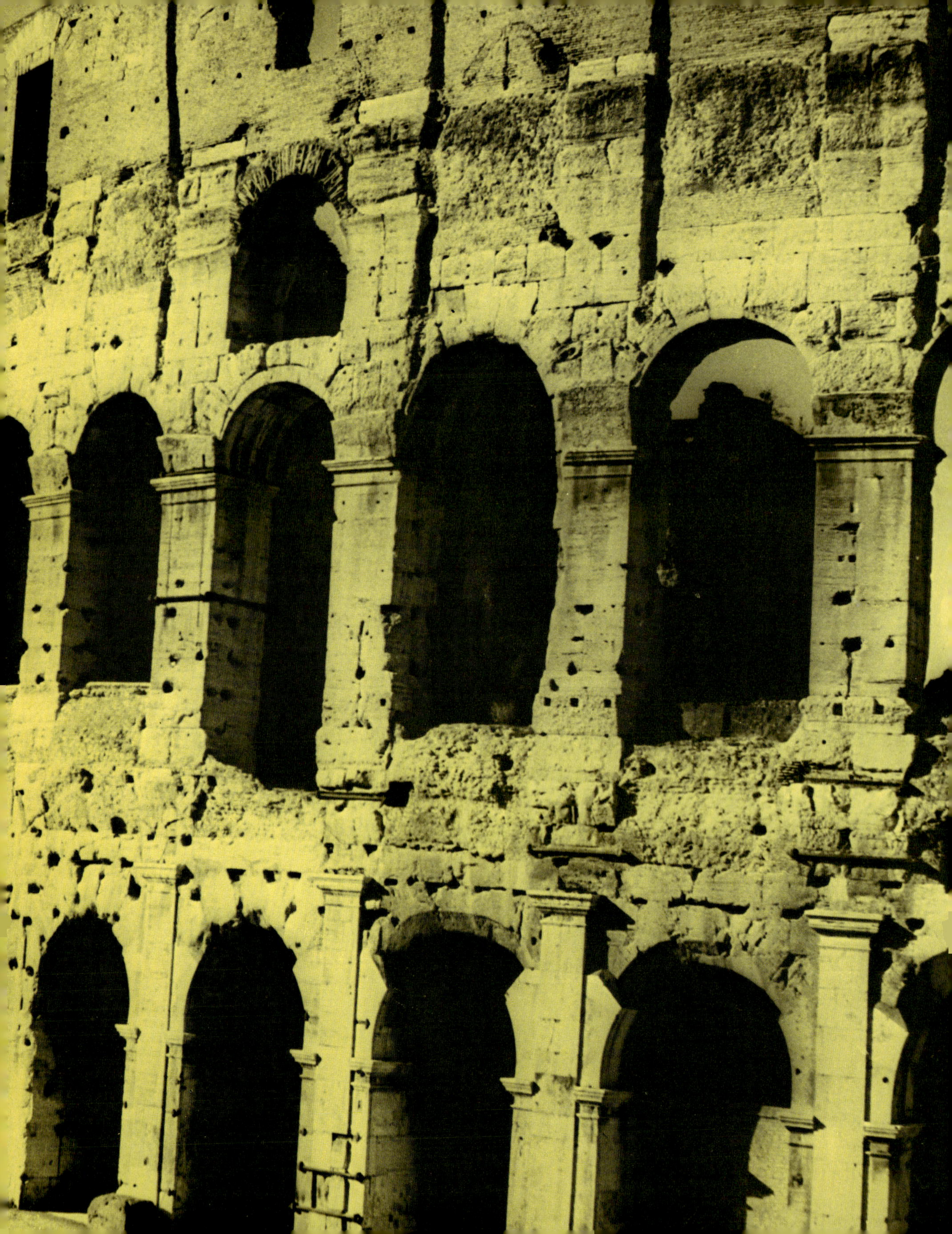

Gladiators. Above, gladiatorial barracks at Pompeii.

Gladiators fight two lions. One of the men is on the ground.

gory spectacles of men being torn to pieces by wild animals before an audience consisting of the whole town. They did not like to see prisoners, volunteers, free men and senators cut each other's throats for money, or applause, or for the sake of a smile from the prince. Trajan, who was the best of all the emperors, arranged contests between ten thousand captives for a festival of games which lasted for one hundred and twenty three days. Claudius was seen to assemble twice as many for the naval battle he arranged on Lake Fucino, and because these poor unfortunates were not all dedicated to certain death, the legions of the army with catapults and engines of war were released against them to coerce them into combat.

Others on the contrary took up their swords joyfully as a way of escaping either life or servitude while some were actors skilled in the games involving blood-shed, who would bring artistry to their movements and elegance to their bearing in face of giving or receiving the death blow. Even as they fell, they would be studying their posture in order to die gracefully. Sometimes too a noble captive would not consent to a degrading contest such as this, but confronted a lion or a panther instead, his head high and his arms folded.

When the games were over, slaves would remove the bodies from the arena with drag-hooks and toss them into the spoliarum, a kind of pit under the steps of the amphitheatre. At this point, two men would chance to arrive, known as Mercury and

Charon. Mercury would test the bodies with a hot iron to see whether there was still life in them, and those which had received wounds rather than the infliction of death were handed over to a doctor. Charon's function was to extinguish life in those which were beyond medical help with a mallet. There were two exit doors from the spoliarium, the living bodies passing through one, and the dead bodies through the other... the one... porta sanavivaria... the other... porta mortualis.

Seventy Italian towns possess ruins of amphitheatres. What human butchery in the interest of popular amusement!

There was indeed less than one imagines. Every year, some hundreds or even thousands of men would die in the ring, but some were prisoners of war or old offenders who had been allowed a chance of escape in death, while others, involved in commerce in a particular way, would play off their lives against fortune, like the Spanish toreador.

It needs to be said that religious belief which had been responsible for games of this kind around the tombs had not died out in the time of Commodus, when there was a gladiatorial combat "to greet the prince". Penal laws in Rome were cruel. Sentence of death increased endlessly and the rights of man were such that the conquered was at the mercy of the conqueror. A gladiator cost a lot of money, therefore a criminal with wild animals let loose on him was more economical. Expenses of the games were further kept down by engaging assassins, those who had committed arson, brigands, sacrilegists, soldiers who had mutinied and so on, either to fight each other or to brave wild animals. As for the prisoners of war who were too barbaric to be seconded to domestic service, they shut them up in schools for gladiators, where they were well-fed, nourished, given exercise, and then sent into the arena where some were able to save themselves by their skill or courage. Vast slaughters took place to celebrate triumphant expeditions—under Vespasian when Jerusalem fell—under Trajan after the Dacian campaign, during the time of Aurelius and Probus on their triumphal return. The small skirmishes that were occurring all the time at the frontiers produced captives of a calibre that did not ruffle Roman toughness. They either enlisted or sold the ones who seemed docile, whilst the rest joined the companies of gladiators. Even during an era which was already Christian, the panegyrists of Constantine said:—"The perfidy of the people of Ems has not made it possible to employ them as soldiers, nor their character to sell them as slaves; by casting them to the wild beasts, you have converted the extermination of the enemies of the empire into amusement for the people. This was the greatest triumph imaginable."

Not every gladiator died in the amphitheatre, for there was always a number at each display who survived because they were skiful or because they recovered from their wounds, which was especially likely to happen if Galenus tended them, and some lived to

Mosaic: fight of two gladiators. One of them is dying.

become celebrities. Heroes of the arena were as popular as heroes of the circus ring in Rome. The poets wrote about them, and their performances were depicted by painters and sculptors in palaces, on tombs, and even in the temples. The young noblemen of equestrian and even of senatorial rank were attracted to enter the arena by the appeal of danger, the intoxicating splendour of the spectacle, the applause of the crowd, and the desire to achieve personal distinction amidst such grandeur for a striking performance, inevitably to reap its reward in other spheres. The law defended him and picked upon the gladiator of infamous reputation, yet custom was stronger than the law. Macrin had been a gladiator.

Some participants in these bloody sports became rich; the parsimonious Tiberius offered up to one hundred thousand sesterces to retired gladiators to appear in his games, and Nero gave vast domains to his soldiers.

Seeing men kill or face death courageously, one would be tempted to say that the peoples of the West retained a strength such as the East did not have, for pleasures of this kind were never popular. Hadrian, who re-introduced military discipline, thought that they were useful exercises and cultivated the idea: "gladiatoria quoque arma tractavit"; Titus and Verus did likewise, and if our laws were not against such practices, there would still be voluntary gladiators. A writer of the Constantine period explained the custom to be based on an idea both religious and warlike. At the beginning of a campaign, a gladiator fight would be arranged to accustom the soldier to wounds and to satiate Nemesis with blood. Seneca is perhaps the only writer in Latin literature whose ideas on the subject were modern: "This ruffian has killed", he said to a regular visitor of the amphitheatre, "and it is right that he should suffer as he has made others suffer. But what have you done to deserve the misfortune of beholding such a spectacle? Were their customs in private life more worthy than this aspect of what went on in public? Yes and no, depending on what is observed and to whom one listens. To take Rome, Antioch, and Alexandria as the only examples would be to substantiate every legitimate accusation, because they were hot-beds of moral degeneration and physical diseases that attracted great hordes of men. It would be the same if you hang on the words of the moralists who see everything as black or support the humorous and satirical poets who see everthing as ugly.

Everyday life, which is peaceful and ordinary, of no obvious virtue or vice, the humdrum, which is almost the same anywhere, was no more the subject of their attention than are flat plains to the traveller in search of precipices and scenes of terrible grandeur.

They show only a small part of the picture rather than the whole of it. Seneca however made sport of those who were forever prosecuting their contemporaries. "Standards have vanished! Wickedness triumphs! All virtue and justice are gone! The world is degenerate! So said our fathers, and thus we repeat it today, and so shall be the voice of our children!"

Let us look at an epic for tramps,—the "Satyricon" of Petronius. We find the pearl and the dung-hill, sentiment and filth,—the human comedy of Nero's day, as you might say. I have no objection, as long as it represents the shady backwaters, and unscrupulous ruffians riddled with every kind of immorality to the point of being unaware of their depravity that are the author's heroes. Tacitus and even Suetonius leave their infamies in half-transparent shade. Petronius and Juvenal expose everything. One should look for a moment at the dregs in which all great societies trail some corner of their cloak. Let the reader who wants to explore the side-avenues of Latin civilisation read all these books right through, or go and have another look at the work of an artist who aimed to paint Roman decadence. In one of the magnificent villas built by the rich people of Rome on the spoils seized from all over the world, the sons of Fabricius, and also of Gracchus are making debauched revelry at the foot of the statues of their fathers, and beneath the indignant gaze of two stoic characters who have escaped the rapture of flowers, women and wine. Rome witnessed patrician orgies and sensuous frenzies such as this, just as modern cities do to this day.

Greek Vice—The Romans became infected with the particular type of Greek vice which they contracted from the Orient by way of the hardy race of Latium and also the Sabines. The inclination in this direction stemmed from the isolation in which oriental women were kept, without education and therefore without any intellectual bond between them and their husbands. The destiny of Italian women however was quite different, and yet one is obliged to recognise that aberration of the senses of this kind existed in the country and seemed to offend no-one. During the time of the republic, Cicero, Brutus and Caesar were thought to have known the vice boasted about by Horace and extolled in poetry by Vergil. In addition it must be said that since it had been proffered to on high and given to the master of Olympus, to Apollo, and even to Hercules,

Homely scene.

it came to the town and court without the slightest trace of shame. Vespasian consecrated the statue of Ganymede in one of the temples, Trajan recalled the mimes because Pylades pleased him and Hadrian made a god of Antinous, to whom every town erected a statue upon the walls.

Seeing the old families rapidly disappear and many unions sterile, to the extent that during the two centuries from Caesar to Antonius, none of the emperors had any sons, makes one tempted to believe that Italian blood had become impoverished like the Italian soil. Whilst it is true that generations die out quickly amidst money, luxury and the unhealthy practices of an idle existence, Roman nobles had two particular enemies;—the lictors under the rule of the bad princes, and the Greek vice perpetually present, for despite the laws forbidding it, it strove for survival in unmarried men, and even if it did not kill, at least prevented birth. This cause must immediately be added to the others as leading to the destruction of the old nobility.

Rome was not the whole empire. If you read the satirists and the poets you could forget the ordinary decent people who lived quietly and respectably away from the big cities composing the mass of the populations of the empire, just as they did. The masses formed a solid but colourless background that is indistinct and acts as a back-cloth against which the vices parade in brilliant colours, and likewise passions and unhealthy ambitions, for evil customs always advertise themselves.

"In the far-off cities the old Italy can be found once more in all the severity of its primitive customs", said Tacitus. He describes the provincial who is passing through Rome, the man of note sent on a deputation to the senate, or the ordinary person who has come on his own private business, all of whom blush at the profligacy which was quite new to them,—lasciviae inexperti. He goes on to say, "The new men who were summoned from the provinces to the senate in Rome brought with them the system and order that bound their private lives." Marseille "seems to combine the politeness of Greece with the simplicity of the provinces in felicitous harmony", and before celebrating the exploits of the provincial Agricola, his father-in-law, he paints his virtues in brief words: "He married Domitia Decidiana. The couple lived in complete understanding and mutual tenderness, their love for each other being greater than self-love." One must not be surprised to see Tacitus attribute a change in the customs of the Roman nobility to the introduction of the provincials to important public functions.

Pliny thinks like Tacitus on this subject. His mother came from hithermost Spain. He said, "You know the reputation this province has and how strict its customs are." And elsewhere, "In Brescia very careful guard is kept to preserve modesty, frugality, and frankness as practised by our fathers." "You are also aware of the natural austerity of the Paduans." Even give ear to Martial, the Spanish poet for whom Rome seemed to be the only possible place to live in, for there facile verses opened the doors of the great. When he felt that he was getting old and that his run of luck was petering out, he quitted his old haunts—the Esquiliae and Palatium—to become a rustic. There he pursues a simple restrained provincial life. "Here, I must nourish my lands; there, the land will nourish me." He wants to leave the banks of the Tiber "where even hunger is costly and you wear out four togas in a single summer whilst anywhere else one would do for four autumns in the fields." He hankers after the house where he was born, its table laden with the rich harvest of the family fields which would make him so rich with so little"; and he will end up by going back there.

Tastes, like the fortune of Suetonius whom Pliny often entertained, were very modest if one goes by the property this man wanted to acquire. "The estate is tempting to my dear

Bust of a Roman lady

Suetonius in more than one respect: the proximity of Rome, the good roads, the little cluster of buildings and the land, all of which are sufficient to distract but not to occupy him. Scholars like him need somewhere to take walks, a vineyard to absorb his interest even to every single mushroom, and that number of shrubs that would not be too difficult nor take too long to count." The philosopher Euphrates is unknown to us and I do not know whether we should be sorry to have lost his works or not. Let us at least keep in mind the portrait Pliny draws of him, showing him to be an amiable moralist who is serious, though not gloomy. "Euphrates maintains an extreme refinement which is in exact keeping with his way of life. He has a family of three children and he sees to it that their education lacks nothing. His father-in-law, who is first citizen of his province is recommendable for hundreds of titles, above all because of his preference for the only virtue, as against birth and fortune,—the choice of a son-in-law!

Corellius Rufus possessed all that makes life sweet: candour, an excellent reputation, a wife and a daughter whom he loved dearly, and true friends. He prolonged his life to the age of sixty seven by his integrity, and when an incurable illness made him a burden to others and to himself, he resolved to put an end to his sufferings. People exhorted him in vain not to pursue his fatal intent. "I have pronounced the decision", he said; whereupon he starved himself to death. Titius Aristo did the same thing. Pliny wrote, "You know my admiration and tender feelings for him. No wisdom is greater than his, and his integrity and learning are unsurpassed... His table and clothes have an old-fashioned simplicity, so that when I go to see him, it is like stepping into the life our fathers knew... When he became the victim of a cruel illness, he called a few friends and me to see him, asking us to have serious discussion with his doctors, because he wanted to take a decision;—whether to patiently await his recovery, if it were to come with time, or whether to quit a life of pain, if the disease were incurable." Men like this who calmly weigh up life and death, being laws unto themselves and announcing their own verdict, scarcely bear resemblance to the effeminates of Martial or the leprous characters of Petronius, and could not have lived the kind of life they led.

Where did Juvenal take the women who pose in his profane gallery? To the haunts where they are still, around the theatres and the shady places, in the Tuscan quarter where, Plautus was already saying, people sold themselves; where the ungodly crowds gather" adds Horace, putting it rather mildly. However, Rome saw other customs, even in the imperial palace which was so profane in the time of Caligula and Claudius, Nero and Domitian. Under Augustus there was Livia who indulged her son but was strict on herself, and Octavia; under Tiberius: Antonia and Agrippina, both worthy of public respect; under Trajan: Plotinas, whose virtue was a source of strength to her husband.

Other women evoke the customs of the past. How many of them do we not find in Pliny and Tacitus who, in addition to being the "light of the house" as Heroditus Atticus described his wife, will always be a credit to their sex? Such were Antistia and Servilia who died with their father as they were unable to save him, and also Pomponia Graecina, a woman of renowned birth, whose life is a sad and touching mystery. Bound by an intimate friendship with Julia, daughter of Drusus, whom Messalina drove to suicide, she mourned for forty years and was never seen to smile. Did her dislike of the Roman way of life and its formidable grandeurs predispose her soul to accept the new faith? She at any rate was accused of giving herself up to strange superstitions. Her husband Plautius, conqueror of Brittany, doubtless in an effort to save her, sought the right to try her himself in the presence of his kinsmen, in accordance with the ancient pattern of domestic tribunals. The tribunal declared her innocent, and as this was during the good years of Nero's reign, the findings were accepted. But Graecina retained her grief, and probably the secret yearning for a life in which all noble sentiments of hearts that were delicate and pure could prevail.

The husband of Arria, Caecina Paetus and his son contracted a serious illness. The son died. His mother kept the funeral so quiet that the father knew nothing of it. Each time she came into his room, she would give him news of the dead son: he had not slept badly, or he was beginning to take nourishment, and when she could not restrain her tears any more, she would go out for a moment, and then return, dry-eyed and calm-faced, having abandoned her grief at the door. Later, her husband being involved in Scribonianus' conspiracy, was captured and taken to Rome, where they put him on board ship. Arria besought the soldiers to let her go on board. She said to them, "You cannot refuse one of the consulate the slaves who wait on him, dress him and put on his shoes. I on my own shall perform all these services for him." As they were unrelenting, she hired a fishing boat and followed the ship that was carrying her husband across the Adriatic. In Rome she met the wife of Scribonianus, who wanted to speak with her: "Let me listen to you who have seen your husband killed in your very arms and still lives!" she said. Foreseeing that Paetus would be condemned to death, she decided not to survive him. Thrasea her son-in-law implored her to change her mind. He said, "If I had just died, would you want your daughter to

Previous page and opposite: busts of Roman ladies. The variety of their hair styles will be noticed.

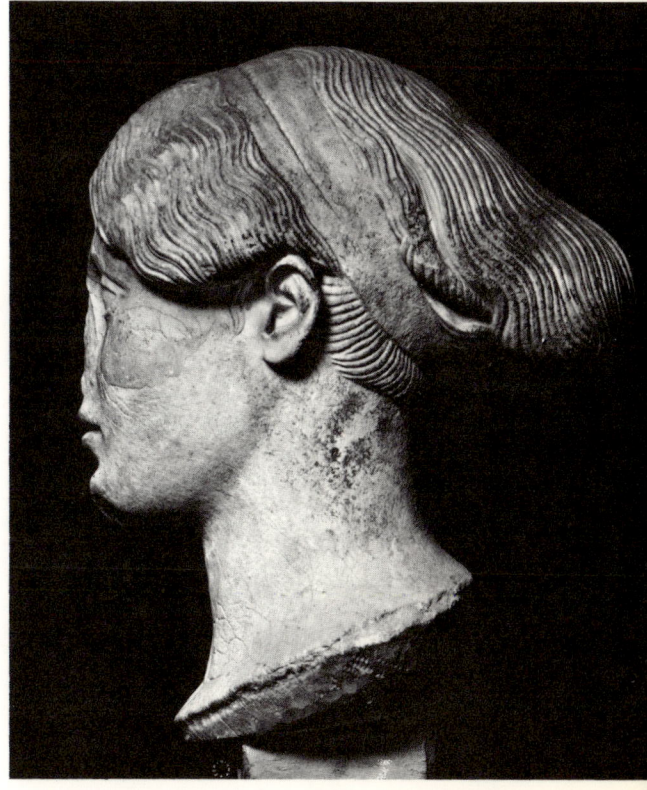

die with me?"—"Yes I would, when she had lived as long and in such perfect union with you as I have with Paetus." Her family kept watch over her movements and doings in order to foil her plan to destroy herself. "You are wasting your time", she said, "you may indeed be able to enforce me to a more painful death but you are powerless to prevent me from dying. At the same time, she rose and ran hurtling her head against the wall so violently that she was apparently dead. When she had come to, she added, "I had warned you that I should find the most difficult means to die if you prevent from using the esiest. So there was no further amazement, that in order to persuade her husband in his reluctance, she stabbed herself with a dagger, and gave it to him saying, "Take it, Paetus, it will do no harm."

Should you prefer more simple affection or more theatrical devotion, then give ear to Pliny: "I was taking a trip on Lake Como recently with one of my friends, an old man, who pointed out to me a house with one room coming right out over the water. A fellow citizen of ours, a woman, threw herself from there with her husband. He suffered a great deal from an ulcer, and when she was convinced that recovery for him was impossible, she exhorted him to take his life, and promised not to survive him. They came out on to that platform, bound themselves together with ropes, and threw themselves into the depths." Her name is not even known, Another woman shows the same proud dignity in not hesitating to do her duty. She had resolved to send a considerable sum of money to one of her friends who had been exiled by Domitian. They told her that the money would inevitably fall into bad hands. "It is of little importance to me that Domitian steals it", she said, "but it matters a great deal to me that I should have sent it."

Paganism despite itself earned many high honours for a virtue that seems to be little associated with the pagan,—chastity. Ceres and Vesta, renowned for their purity and beauty, wished for priestesses in their likeness, and the persons who earned the greatest respect from the Romans were the women consecrated to two chaste goddesses. There was a priestess of Apollo at Agros who must never have known divine love. The vestal virgins would sit in the front places at the festivals, and the reigning empress would take her place amongst them.

These facts and people belong to the great families of the day, but let us look lower down the social scale, as we have already looked outside Rome.

We find a middle class who were committed to work and an economy in their lives, because they were not wealthy, as happens today. Unhappily it is a class that has no history, though one knows that it ploughs the land and seas, yields produce and organises trade, creates the wealth of empire by its industry and spreads tranquillity

Inscription on a tomb.

This engraving shows different tombs on the Appian Way and reconstruction of the same portion of it during the Roman era.

throughout the provinces by its sense of duty. But if you want to know something of the way in which the people thought or felt, you are reduced to reading inscriptions on tomb-stones.

No other race has left so many; in fact one could describe them as some kind of special genre of Roman literature. They are often in verse reflecting every tone and appearing in every form. They contain philosophy and religion, faith and scepticism, banter and bitter regrets, and but faint vestiges of hope. Each one tells a life story and reflects personal feelings.

Primus said of his wife: "She was dearer to me than life": someone else "She has never caused me any grief, unless it were by her death." Yet another: "Her virtues should be written of in golden letters." I begin to distrust such magniloquence. A widow regrets not having preceded her husband to the tomb; a husband states that after having lived with his wife for eighteen years without the slightest misunderstanding, he will never call another to his domestic hearth... It is not certain that he kept his word, but it is something that he gave it.

In Beirut, Rufus Antonianus erects a statue of marble "To the most pious and chaste of women, that she may be an example to others." I prefer the simple words engraved on the tomb-stone of a freed slave: "I await my husband, Virum expecto meum"—the inscription of her surviving partner. It also pleases me to find this inscription in Gaul, yet another that is most certainly sincere; "Oh most holy Spirits, I commend my husband to you. I implore your indulgence to allow me to see him during the hours of darkness." Servilius Fortunatus loved his wife with a similar devotion and brought her remains back from distant Dacia over land and sea to the very foot of Mount Aures.

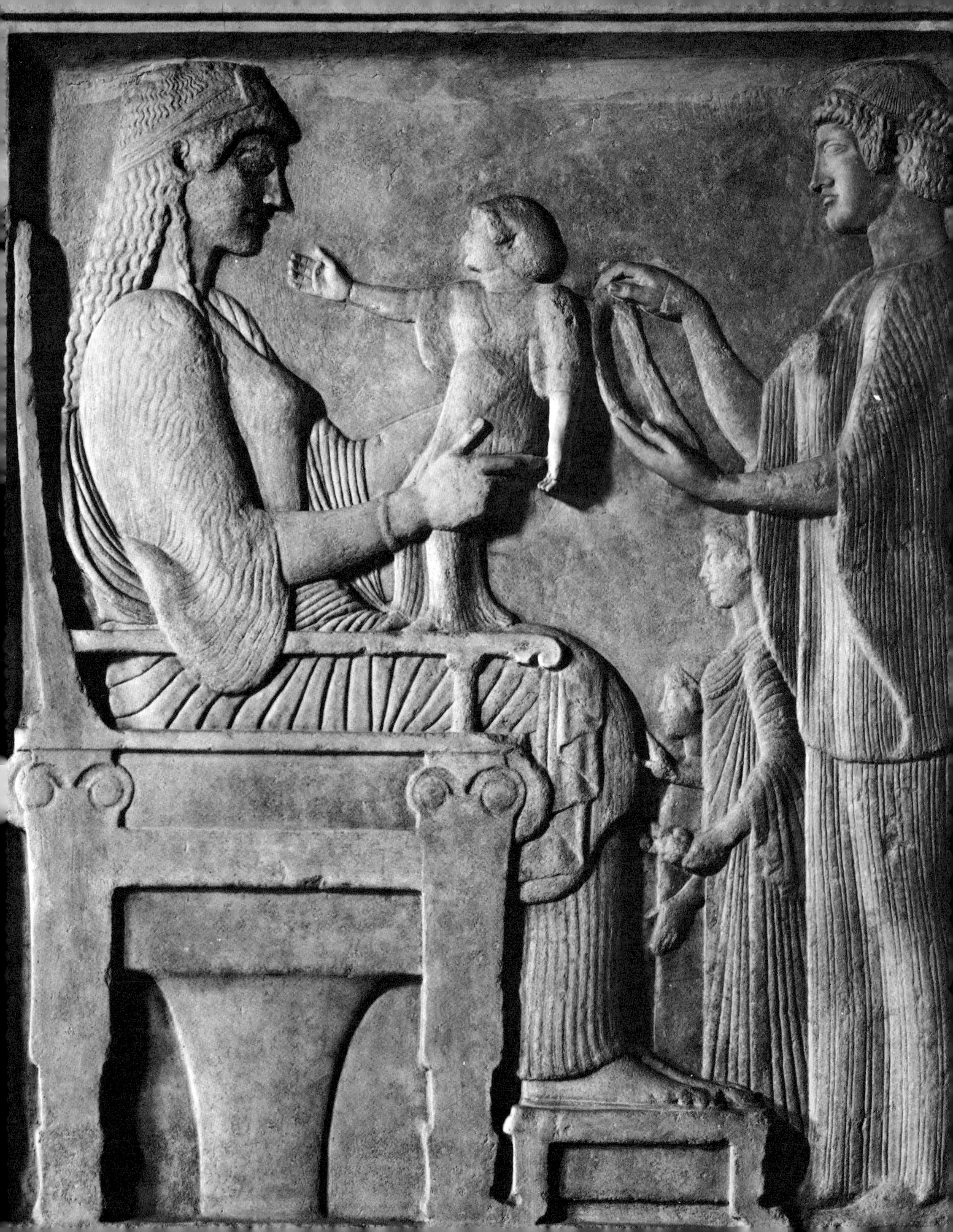

3 - The family

The Romans had not wanted any authority to interpose between father and son and husband and wife. The home was a sacred refuge which was impenetrable even by a representative of the law.

In legitimate unions, the power of the father grips the child at the moment of leaving its mother's womb and controls its right to life or death. The newly-born is placed at the feet of its judge, and if it is picked up, that is to say, recognised, it will live; if it is left on the ground, then the father is rejecting it. It is then carried out and abandoned in some busy thoroughfare where it will quickly die unless a slave dealer chances to pick up the poor little thing to bring it up and sell it one day. The father has motives for violating nature in this way. First there may be doubts of paternity, as in the case of the emperor Claudius who had his daughter cast away at some frontier.

There might also be some trouble, or poverty or an already large family. "Why allow human beings to live if they will know nothing but unhappiness?" said the Miser of the comedy Heautontimorumenos. A feeble constitution or a deformity would mean that they would be condemned. Rome wanted only vigorous soldiers and sturdy husbandmen; and when she was no longer making these demands, the inevitable custom still remained; one meets it again in the second century of our period.

In the absence of the father, judgement was suspended until his return, and the new-born baby was cared for provisionally. Sometimes he gave his consent before leaving the household gods. "Bring up whatever it is in my absence." What a sombre statement! Whatever it is! It was like referring to the young of the herds in the fields. A son was something useful, either as a worker for the family, a soldier for the city, a guarantee of the perpetuity of the race, a pledge that the cult of ancestors was not dying out and that the "sacra gentilitia" would not go short of victims. Hence the expression "auctor filio", or increased by a son.

Since the law of Papia Poppea given by Augustus, paternity gave entitlement to awards and profits. "You have the rights of a father," said Juvenal; "therefore your name is entered on the register of the public treasury; from now on you can inherit, have access to any kind of legacy, even enjoy that amount reserved for the exchequer, "dulce caducum"... if you bring a charge, you will be preferred to your competitors; as a magistrate you will have the right of precedence over your colleagues."

Paternity brings its own special rewards in Rome and the provinces,—and wherever there were citizens,—apart from its natural joys. There was the "jus trium liberorum" which applied to those who had at least

Left and below: two sculptures of different Roman periods on an eternal theme.

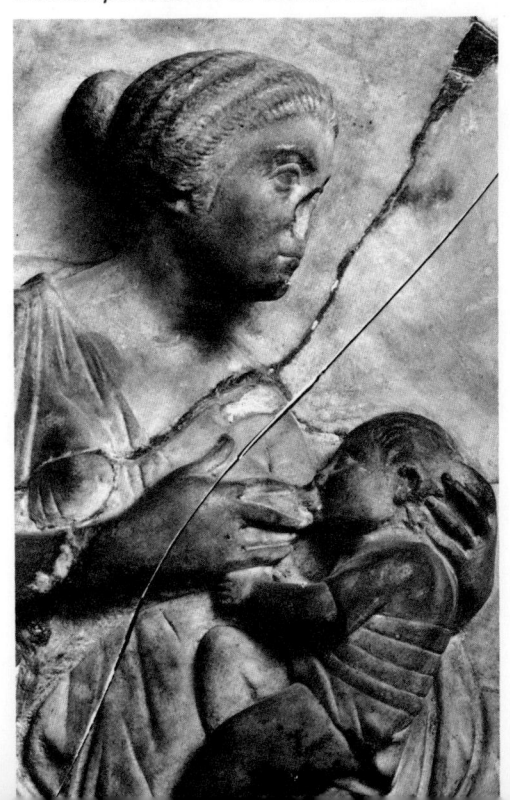

three children or who were considered as if they had by special consent of the prince. Three children, even born out of wedlock, would put the Roman city at their disposal and consequently the right to its benefits.

The birth of a son is an occasion of good fortune that is celebrated joyfully and is a day that is written up as a happy one. The whole house takes on a festive air and the main door is garlanded with fronds of leaves and flowers. Plautus says, "This is the arrival of spring." If the family is in mourning, it abandons the black as the joy of the present obliterates the sorrow of the past. Relations and friends hasten together, and a table is arranged in honour of Juno so that the newly delivered mother will promptly be restored to health. Her bosom is draped with decorative bands that have been embroidered in the temples.

The eighth day is the day of purification for girls and the ninth for boys,—an important occasion which calls for a family reunion and a meal. The eldest of the relatives calls aloud for good wishes for the new-born. Perseus says, "Either grandmother, or a maternal aunt, or a woman who is in awe of the gods—takes the infant from the cradle; first of all she rubs the forehead and the moist lips of the new-born with saliva by means of her middle finger to purify it; then she pats it gently with her two hands."

When this ceremony is over the name of the child is registered on the public rolls.

The child will preserve religious respect for his birthday and will piously celebrate each anniversary. He will invite all members of his family to this annual party. Those who cannot afford to invest in white wear something that is at least newly cleaned and is looking neat and tidy. He is dressed as he was on the day of his birth.

It is also a day of gifts when relatives and friends exchange their presents. If someone is forgotten on this occasion, it is regarded as a breach of politeness and could result in a breach of friendship. Ask Martial and see: he has a rift with Sextus because of an oversight of this kind. He had not given anything to his friend and he does not invite him to the festivities.

In large households, the newly-born is given over to a nurse, who from this day on became an important member of the family

A couple, from a Roman painting.

Couples: on a capital in Pompeii and a wall plaque in Ostia.

Adonis, statue originating from Capua. Right: women, from a fresco. On following pages, couples at a meal and female nude.

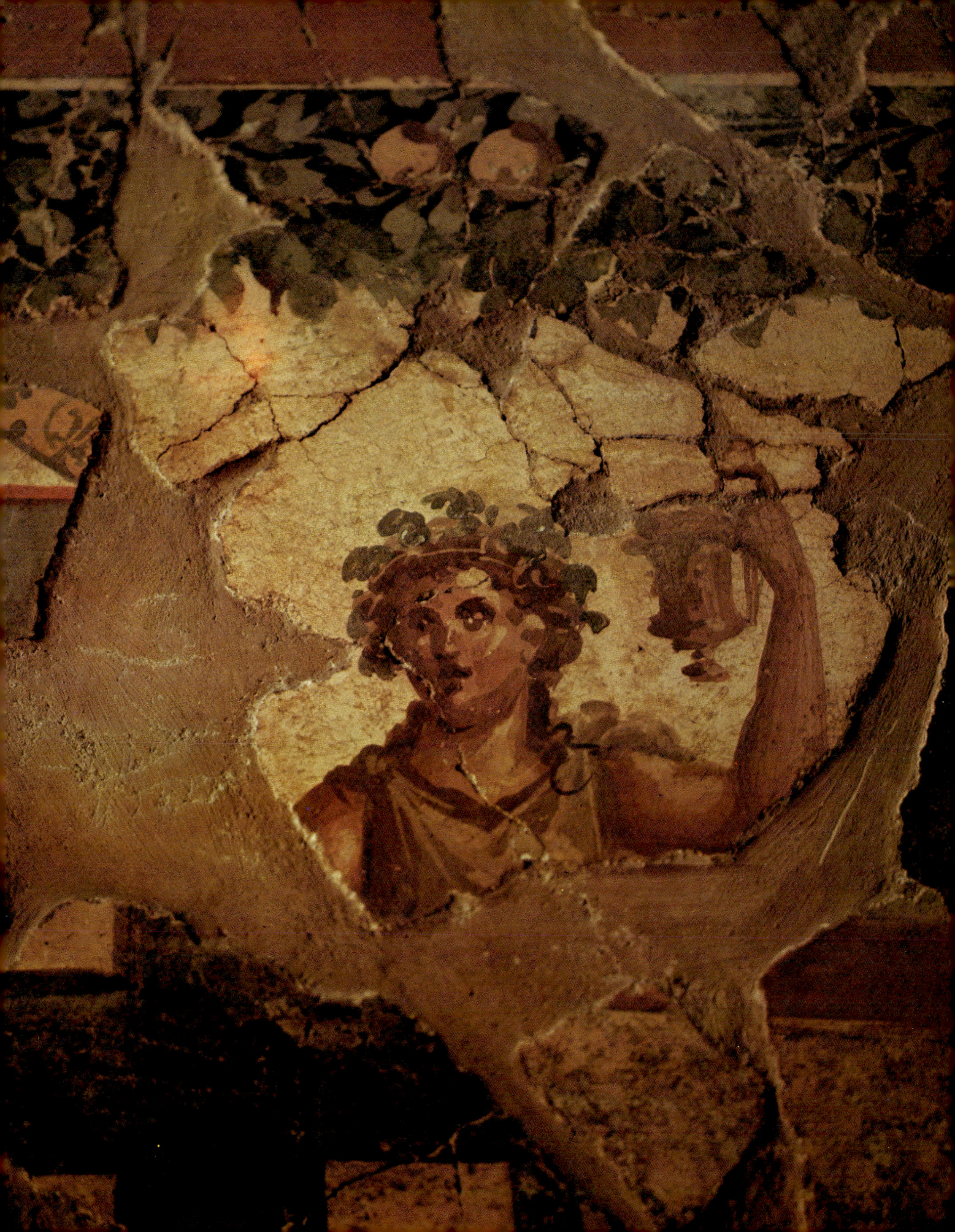

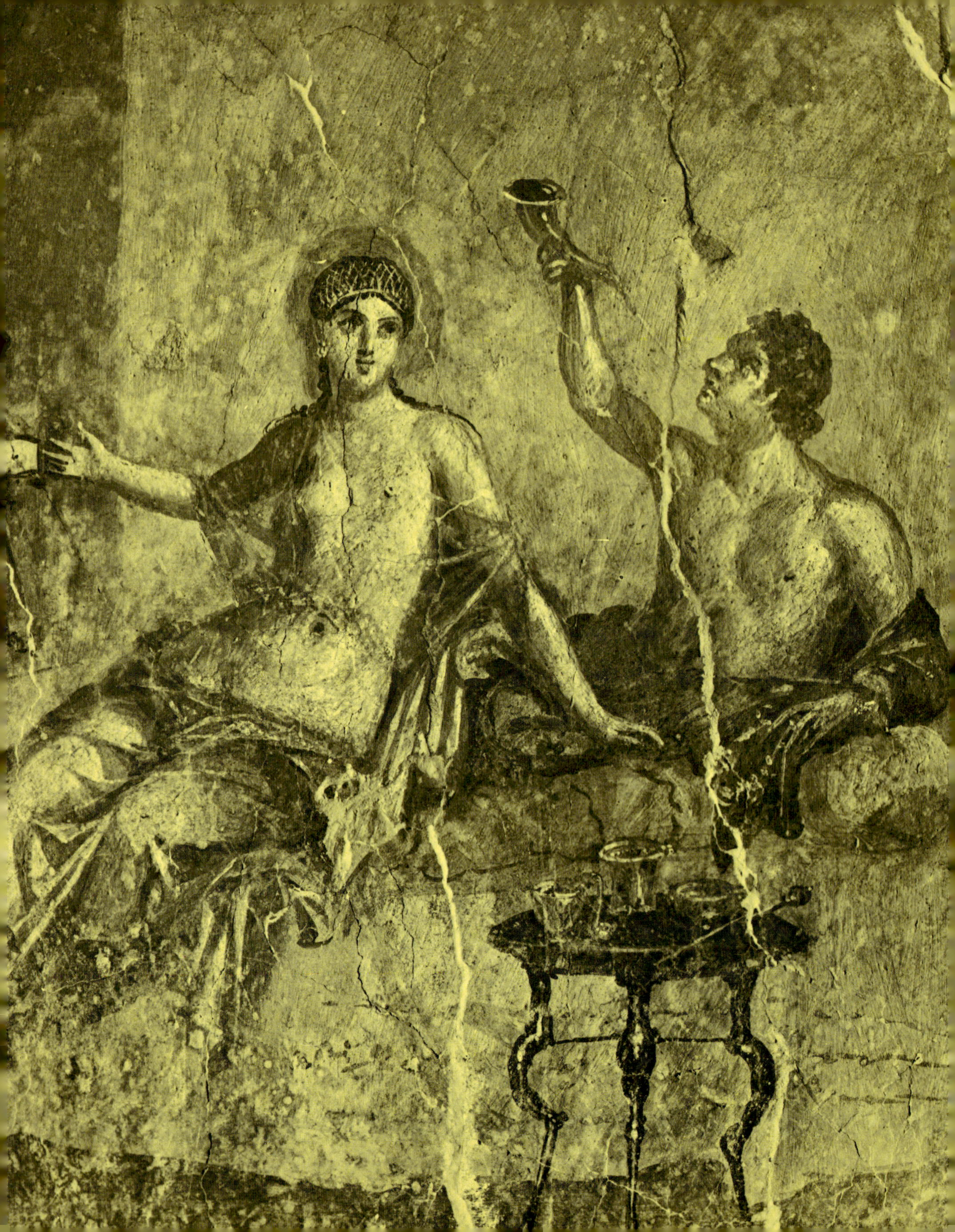

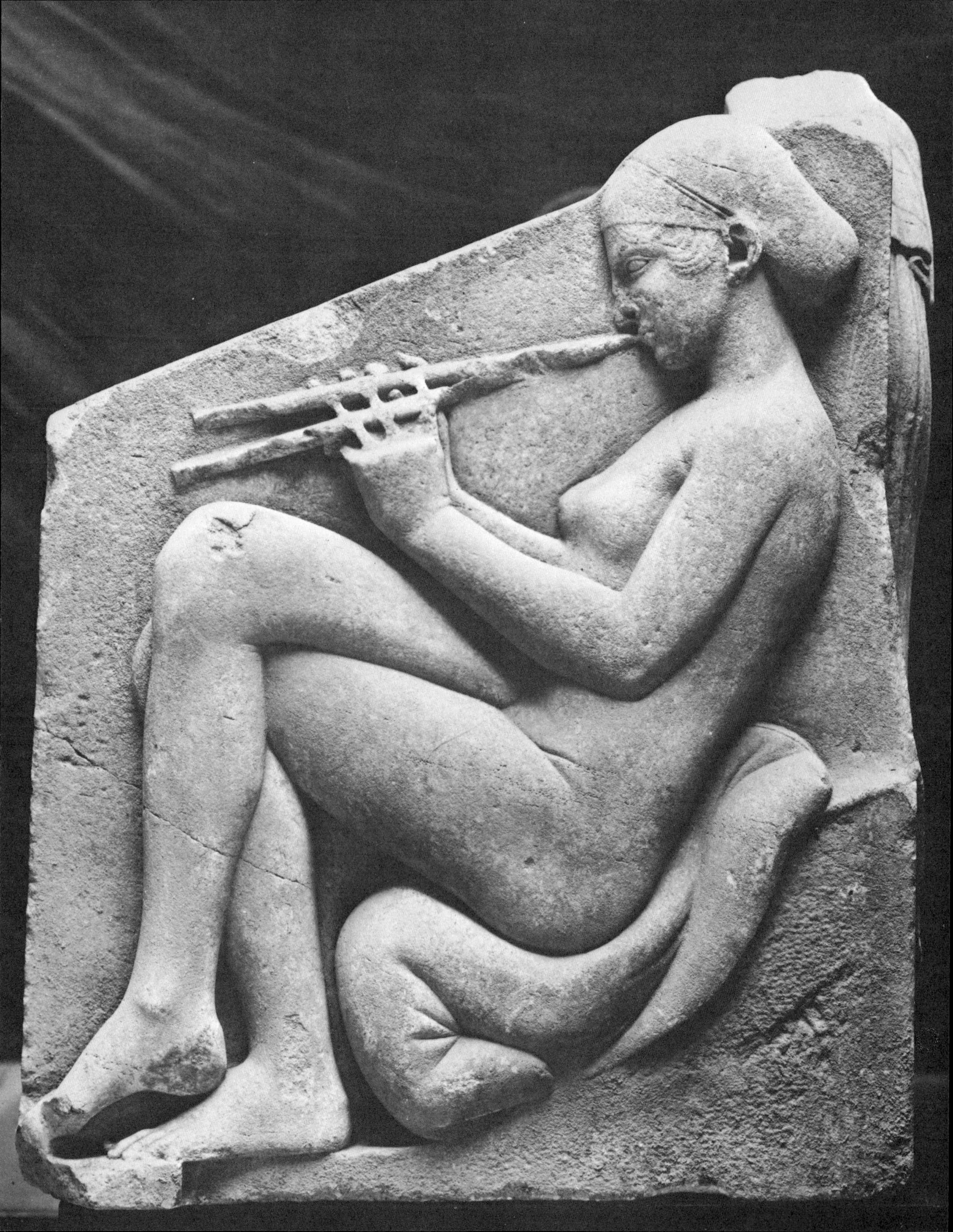

and retained an affection for the child she had nursed, always. Pliny and Dasumius, bequeathed a small house, a field, a few slaves with the herd, implements for the farm, and a little capital to keep things going, to their nurse; Domitian gave his a villa on the Latin way. The nurse, in her turn is preeminently a servant, and she is faithful and devoted until she dies.

No Roman matron would entrust the care of her child to a slave or to a freed slave. Sixteen centuries before Jean-Jacques Rousseau, Favorinus elicited the obligation of the mother to suckle her child.

Puberty cames at the age of sixteen or seventeen when the adolescent puts aside the praetexta, hangs his golden or copper seal around the neck of the lares gods, and puts away his childhood things, the nuts he played with, his clogs, his swing, hoop, and the stick that had been his mount for ten years. He has just started wearing man's clothes, which makes him a citizen. Propertius, Ovid, Perpeus and Seneca count their lives from this day.

The adoption of the male toga takes place each year on the sixteenth day of the calends of March during the Liberalia, or feast of Bacchus, when the god is always young and his name is Liber. "The prestige of religion is accompanied by the imposing importance of a gathering of the whole of the family. In order that everything shall be favourable on the day, the young man has spent the night before, (the last of his childhood) covered in white cloth and saffron veiling like the young fiancee on the eve of her wedding day. Is it not indeed a wedding that is about to take place;—the indissoluble union between the new citizen and the City?

In the morning, the whole family gathers together, and the father or nearest relation places the toga on the adolescent. The toga is white, and therefore pure and has no purple border as the praetexta does. It is free because it removes the constraint of the first stage of his education, and virile because it makes him a man and a citizen. The robe is put on in the presence of the household gods whose favour they evoke; "Ante deos libera sumpta toga" said Propertius. Then everyone goes to the Capitol to make sacrifices to the gods of Rome. Afterwards, the new citizen, flushed with happiness, comes back to the

Roman children; games.

public square with all his party, as if to take up all his rights. Thus the most significant happening in the life of a young Roman is not a religious ceremony but a civic feast. The gods take second place, whilst the city comes first, and the conception of it dominates the entire occasion. Now one of the predominant features of the feast is the offering of a honey cake to Bacchus, his only gift in fact. On the day of the Liberalia the streets of Rome are lined with old women wearing ivy in their hair and selling sacred cakes. Every family buys cakes and the young man himself takes a number of them to the altar of the god who has provided man with honey and the vine, and to honour him still further, the festivities end with long periods of banqueting during which the wine cups are by no means idle.

Paternal authority lasted until the death of the person invested with it and was then passed on to all descendants in direct line. The right of life and death which the father exercises over his children at birth extends to their adulthood and even when they become magistrates. If a crime is committed, he could act as judge instead of the public tribunals. In such cases the severity of their standards of life would guarantee that the guilty one should be punished and at the same time blood ties would prevent unjust penalties. Under Augustus, one father pronounces the sentence of exile on his son and another condemns his to be beaten to death; yet a third appointed himself his son's executioner in the time of Hadrian. The ancient right continues until the time of the Antonys', though already customs are

Below, a family. Right, monument to a child preserved at Ostia.

inconsistent with them, and legislation is following the suit of custom. The people wanted to avenge the first of such murders by killing the murderer; there was nothing more than a riot, and on the occasion of the second, the prince intervened and ordered the deportation of the father. According to an extract of Marcus Ulpius, the father in the third century possessed no more than the right to bring his son before the public judge. If he wrongfully refused marriage to him or neglected the business of it, one of the laws among Caesar's reforms authorised the magistrate to oblige it to be made, and an amendment made by Antony prevented him from breaking the new family up by withdrawing his right to drive his son to reject his wife. Finally Trajan compelled anyone who maltreated his son to let him go free. The right to reprimand however still remained.

If the father had had the right to kill, he had greater reason for the right to sell, so paternal power ceased only after three successive transactions, whilst for girls one was sufficient. Nevertheless the father who consented to his son's marriage was regarded as having no more power over him.

The situation of the son will give an understanding of the situation of the mother. "Look what poor straits I am in", the miser of Plautus proclaims sadly, "I have a strapping daughter on my hands with no dowry and I cannot persuade anyone to take her." You hear moans of this kind very often in Rome. Money is behind many marriages, as in all societies where there is the most talk about sentiment. Horace gets angry about this and complains that when "Queen Wealth" offers a well-endowed bride she would appear to offer simultaneously, beauty, nobility, friends, and faithfulness in marriage..." A young girl who is penniless can remain in her father's house for a long time unless some unselfish young man is attracted by her good looks. Such a thing is rare though not without precedent and Venus is much honoured by anxious mothers.

Counting a sum of money.

They address beseeching prayers to her from as far away as they can see her temple, asking her to bestow seductive charms upon their daughters, and they tax their ingenuity in countless ways to help the goddess in her tasks of making them more beautiful. Chaerea says, "Look how the mothers spend all their time in getting their daughters to keep their shoulders down and to control their bosoms so that they look slim. If a girl has a tendency to plumpness, her mother proclaims at once: "She is an athlete! She immediately cuts down her food until she has made her as thin as a rake despite her constitution".

However, if a husband is still nowhere in sight all friends of the household are put to the search with that phrase which is as old as the hills and will live as long as them. "Please find me a husband for my daughter." The daughter may be hardly thirteen of course, but as the Roman institutions authorise marriage after the age of twelve, maternal anxieties begin as from the year prescribed by the law. At last a husband presents himself, being neigher a relation of the prohibited group nor a foreigner, which are the two obstacles by order, even though the first one did not prevent Claudius marrying his niece Agrippina. The committee convened for this prince even maintained the force of law.

The best time of day for the celebration of a betrothal was considered to be the first or second hour—that is to say, six or seven o'clock in the morning. The family and friends have been assembled in the paternal home since dawn, when the intended bridegroom renews the request to his father. His father consents in their presence, and as he does so in front of so many witnesses, it has the weight of a decree. The young man who wanted to retract afterwards, could be sued by the girl's parents. Nevertheless, a contract is drawn up more often than not, signed by those present. From that moment on the marriage is assured and the terms son-in-law and father-in-law are already brought into use. All the interested parties have given their consent, for the girl has been asked whether she sees anything standing in the way of the contract, and her silence has been taken to mean consent. The future couple have been betrothed. As a pledge of his love and faithfulness, the young man offers the girl a plain iron ring which is the symbol of austerity in the marriage bond. His fiancée wears it on the last finger but one on her left hand, which is supposed to communicate directly with the heart.

Now that the preliminary contract has been signed and the provisional agreements made, the wedding day is fixed; it is normal for the time span between the engagement and the marriage to be quite long. On the eve of the wedding day, the final contract is drawn up, involving the consignment of the dowry and terms of payment. Generally speaking the girl from a good home would receive one million sesterces. When the contract or marriage settlement has been accepted and the consent of the couple and their relations has been given, the marriage is legally concluded; no civil or religious authority can intervene, except in a patrician marriage when the high pontiff consecrates it by offering a sacrifice. By dint of the law, the wife has

"Nascita di Venere".

recognised in her husband a master.

The wedding day is a day of joy, when the door of the house is draped with white hangings garlanded with leaves and flowers. Inside, pictures of family ancestors are displayed and lighted torches illuminate the rooms. The costume of the bride is truly allegorical. She has a flame-coloured bridal veil covering her head, leaving only her face visible. This is normally worn by the wife of a flamen (priest) to whom divorce is forbidden. She also has a white tunic to represent virginity, and her hair is coiled on the top of ther head and stuck through with a pin to indicate submissiveness to her husband. Her coronet of verbena signifies fertility whilst the woollen girdle about her waist is a symbol of her chastity.

The bride is set upon a seat covered with the skin of a sacrificial ewe in her array and her husband is seated beside her on another seat like it.

On arriving at the home they will have together, the husband at the threshold formally asks her who she is, to which she replies, "Wherever you are bridegroom I shall be bride." She is given purified water and a lighted torch, whereupon she throws some drops of the water on herself as a sort of purification, and touches the torch, which then has to be put rapidly in a safe place before mischief makers get up to tricks of witchcraft with it. Before she goes inside, she rubs a little pork fat on the door jambs to keep away unlucky spells. Her female friends then lift her in their arms lest she tread on the threshold which is consecrated to Vesta, the virgin goddess, and the husband tosses nuts to the children signifying that he has renounced children's games. The girl has also said farewell to her virgin status by dedicating her dolls and toys to the divinities that had protected her in her childhood. Representations of their ancestors and gods of the household are placed around the hearth. The couple make a sacrifice there and break the special cake made of the

Erotica in sculpture.

A student and his young wife.

finest flour for their meal together. From then on, the wife is associated with the domestic cult of her husband, or according to that beautiful expression of a Roman lawyer, she enters into a partnership of all things divine and human with him.

Some of the older women then escort the bride to the marriage bed which is surrounded by six statues or images of gods and goddesses. The next day is also a feast day, and all the family once again gather to eat and drink together. From then on the couple are left alone with the hazards of their private lives. Will they be happy? One hopes so, but to believe they will be in advance would be very risky for anyone who has seen something of the private life of certain families in Rome between the time of the Gracchi and Vespasian. A widow was forbidden to marry again before ten months had passed lest her father or her new husband should be disgraced,—or indeed she herself, when disgrace applied to women. Despite all the encouragement given to second marriages by the laws of Julia and Papia Poppea, widows who did not remarry earned particular esteem.

A last feature of custom was that the wife was obliged to mourn her husband, "elugere virum", and she was forbidden to do certain things during mourning. The husband however was not expected to do the reciprocal thing.

Concubinage was permitted by law side by side with marriage, no doubt since the time of Augustus, but it was a state that did not produce children capable of succession. It usually took place between people who were not permitted to contract in lawful marriage, and as a rule, the concubine was usually low class, and often a freed slave.

Plautus describes a young wife who complains to her father that she is scorned and forsaken for courtesans, to which the father replies: "Haven't I told you to be submissive to your husband and not to pry into his affairs, what he does or where he goes?—But he is the lover of a courtesan who lives nearby.—He is right to behave so, and I hope his love for her increases in order to punish you." Again two matrons, one of whom has a grievance, and the other consoles

82

and encourages her: "Take my word for it, you should not conflict with your husband; let him have an affair, let him do as he pleases, because you lack nothing at home; beware of that terrible order. Get out, woman! Sempronius Sophus rejected his wife, said Valerius Maximus, because she went to the circus games without telling him. While she was in desgrace, her husband stole her cloak to put it on his mistress. This astonishes you, but the poet says, "He did as others do."

"Here is another household where the roles are reversed for it is the wife who rules in this case. She is haughty and imperious and makes everyone bow to her authority; she is also extravagant and indulgent and goes around in a carriage with the result that her home is full of dealers and creditors. The husband has to pay in silence. If he remonstrates, she says: "It is I who made you rich isn't it? My dowry made your fortune. It is only fair that I should do some things to my liking isn't it?"

Incompatibility was the usual reason given for separations. In other respects, no problem: the couple have grown tired of living together and so they part. What could be more simple? Each takes his own fortune and goes to live as he likes. There is a story of how long ago there was a little temple dedicated to Viriplaca, reconciler of marriages, where couples who had had differences used to go and explain all to the benevolent goddess, and more often than not they would become reconciled. People gradually forgot Viriplaca and her temple became deserted, while many turned to the praetor to have their marriage dissolved, an occasion they celebrated as fervently as their engagement day. However, it sometimes happens that just when the magistrate is about to announce the separation, the husband experiences a return of tenderness and lets go the marriage tablets he was about to break, confessing himself defeated. So the young man, a new Alcibiades, takes a look at his wife as she goes to the praetor—

he having sent her there—then runs up to her, kisses her and says, "Your beauty wins! Maecenas behaved like this and used to reject Terentia daily, and then would take her back again so that she appeared to have been married dozens of times, when in fact he had only one wife.

A divorce is completed in the presence of seven witnesses who must have reached the age of puberty and become Roman citizens, and the tablets bearing the contract are broken before them. Rejection is a less serious affair and is peacefully kept within the family. The husband gathers his friends together and pours out his troubles to them which they note. Then he announces his intention to the magistrate affirming on oath that his reasons are legitimate. Next he calls his wife before his friends, asks her to hand over the keys of the house, and says to her: "Farewell! Take your fourtune with you and give me my own." Why, Proculeia,

A sculpture from the tomb of a certain Cornelius Statius.

do you abandon your husband like this in the month of January? writes Martial against a miserly woman who was unwilling to give her husband a new cloak as a new-year gift. For you it is not a divorce but a good bit of business." But we know where Martial liked to live and whom he liked to see. This kind of evil, like many others kinds that the empire inherited had begun with the republic. Cicero spoke already of the "Women of many marriages", and the early emperors attacked the scandal it had become by reducing the means of obtaining a divorce. One of Caesar's laws prevented remarriage until six months after a separation, and Augustus tripled this period.

In order to avoid the penalties Augustus imposed on bachelors, they would take a woman for a short time, and then dismiss her straight away. Thus they would find that they escaped the asperities of the law for a year. But although Juvenal thought that a good wife was more rare than a white crow, and that like Pliny, the bachelor life made way for fortune and power, the determined enemies of marriage were very few.

In Rome, they did not bring out ancestral mummies on the feast days as they did in Egypt. They thought a great deal about death nevertheless and took every possible trouble over funerals, appointing the spot for the tomb and often building a final dwelling place there. We shall see that the members of the most common corporate groups under the empire were able to call themselves "the fraternity of the dead", since the object of the colleges they founded was to ensure a tomb for members, and if he were a sufficiently rich one, also a "regular service" after his death when his survivors would celebrate with a sacrifice or a funeral breakfast to his memory. According to Roman belief, the souls of those whose remains had not received the last rites would wander in wretchedness along the banks of the Styx for a thousand years. It followed that no kind of dead body was more feared

A woman has just died. Left: another dies in child-birth.

than the one found floating on the water.

Those who no longer feared the Styx at least wished to have a friendly hand to close their eyes. Near relatives would gather around the dying person, as though he were a man about to go on a long journey, whilst he experienced his last moment of pride when a large number of the family were present during his final hour. Inscriptions such as this would be put on his tomb; "I had five sons and five daughters; they have all closed my eyes."

When the closest relative had put his lips on those of the dying man to receive his last breath, and his eyelids had been closed, they called to him aloud three times, and when he did not reply, they would go to the temple of Libitina to announce his death. If the family did things well, the dead man would have a bed of ivory with covers of precious material, and the house would be draped in black. A cypress tree would be planted by the door, being the tree dedicated to Pluto which would never grow again if it were once cut.

The lying in state lasts for seven days, and on the eigth day a public crier summons the people to the funeral; "It is time for those who can follow the funeral procession to come."

The procession sets out by the light of torches even though the ceremony is carried out in broad daylight. This is a relic of the ancient custom of holding funerals during the night. The person officiating (rather like our master of ceremonies), followed by the lictors, arranges the gathering in order. The procession is headed by a flautist who plays a funereal air and walk behind, the mourners and slaves of the goddess of death, who beat their breasts, utter heartrending cries and appear to tear their hair.

The funeral cortege of important people

This reproduction of an engraved plaque depicts a funeral chariot and the traditional followers.

would stop at the Forum, where a close relative would read the funeral oration, and from thence to the pyre or altar, made of resinous wood and strewn with funereal tree branches. This was always outside the town. The body would be placed on the pyre wrapped in a shroud of amianth and sprinkled with perfume, to the accompaniment of a lament on trumpets. The closest relations set light to it with a torch turning their head and eyes away as they do so: "Aversi tenuere facem", said Vergil. Once, they were careful to open the dead man's eyes so that he should see the light for the last time and know the glory of his funeral feast. They would remove his ring, and his mother, wife or son would place a last kiss on his icy lips. Pliny said, "The custom of burning corpses does not go very far back in the Town. It originated during the war waged in other countries. As they used to exhume our dead, we decided to burn the bodies."

Because the Romans thought that the nature of the soul was that of fire, they believed that by some mysterious connection, the flames would help it to flee the body, and so they only accorded the honour of the funeral pyre to those whom they thought to have some sort of intelligence and sensitivy.

When the body was consumed, the flames were extinguished with wine. The nearest relative would gather the still burning bones and wash them "In old wine or milk and dry them with a linen cloth". The remains were then placed in an urn along with roses and aromatic plants. All the members of the funeral procession would say a last farewell to the dead man. "Farewell for ever! we shall all follow you in the order that nature wishes". Finally one of the mourners, or perhaps someone else, would dismiss the gathering with these words: "I, licet", and all would be free to go.

The urn was enclosed in a tomb which bore an inscription recording the dead man's name, birth, and the public services he had given (cursus honorum). Sometimes there would be a few philosophical lines written to those who had passed on: "I shall not disclose my name, nor that of my father, nor my achievements. I am silent for eternity. I am but ashes, and shall be nothing more; so shall you be also." There are others: "Whilst I lived, I lived well. My drama is over, as yours will finish soon. Applaud." Also we find, "When the gods gave you light, they prepared this resting place for you."

A tomb, preserved at Ostia.

Relations and friends would arrange a funeral feast for the day after the funeral. If the dead man was wealthy, they would put on scenic plays and arrange a public feast (silicernium), or a distribution of fresh meat. (visceratio). On the ninth day all the family would meet over another feast, and on the tenth the house would be purified. The presence of the dead had polluted it and so it was swept with branches of verbena. None of the relatives could be summoned to a court during these ten days. A poor person, a "consumer of pulses", would die as he had lived with far less stir, and his corpse would await little. Four grave diggers bear it in a hired coffin at nightfall to a point away from the city and cast it into one of the communal graves or "puticuli" where it would decompose rapidly.

Those who set a sum of money aside for their funeral are at least honoured by burning. A pyre is made and when they have piled materials that burn easily on it, they put the bodies there, including one female to every ten male corpses. Macrobus said, "This was a common practice, as though the woman's body would burn more readily,— the woman being warmer by nature and easily inflamed."

It is conceivable that there are no feasts and celebrations for relatives and public at a pauper's funeral, and that just as no one makes it a joyful occasion, no one beats his breast in the funeral procession either.

The rich man on the other hand, would leave a will, and when he felt death approaching, he would place his ring on the finger of his inheritor. "Uti pater familias legassit, ita jus esto" said the law of the Twelve Tablets. Every citizen was free to leave his estate to another citizen, and his wishes were carried out to the full if they were set out in the form of a will.

During the Roman Empire, you were either born a slave or you became one. Slavery renewed itself by self-generation, commerce, and war. Once, a creditor would

Altar in a house, Pompeii.

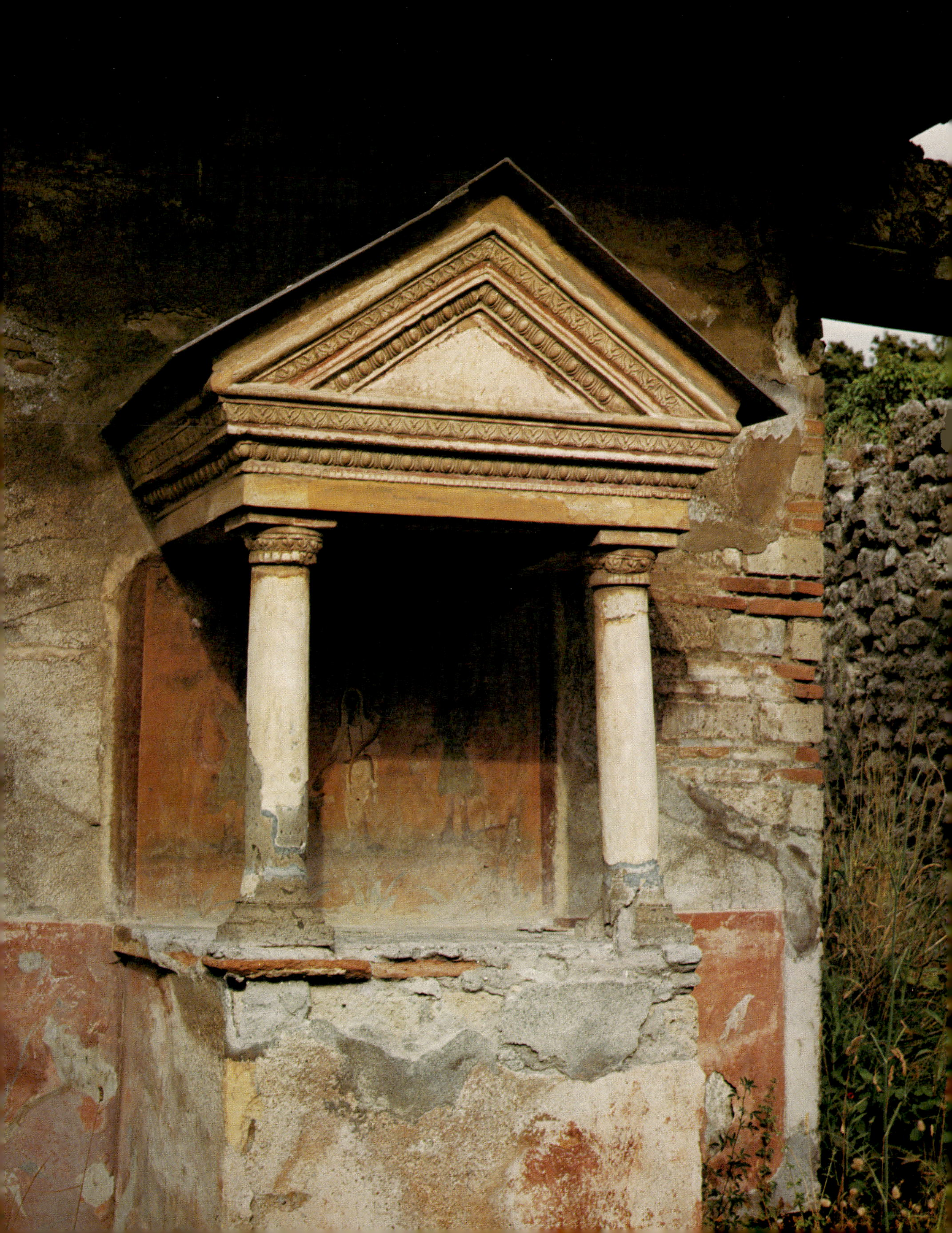

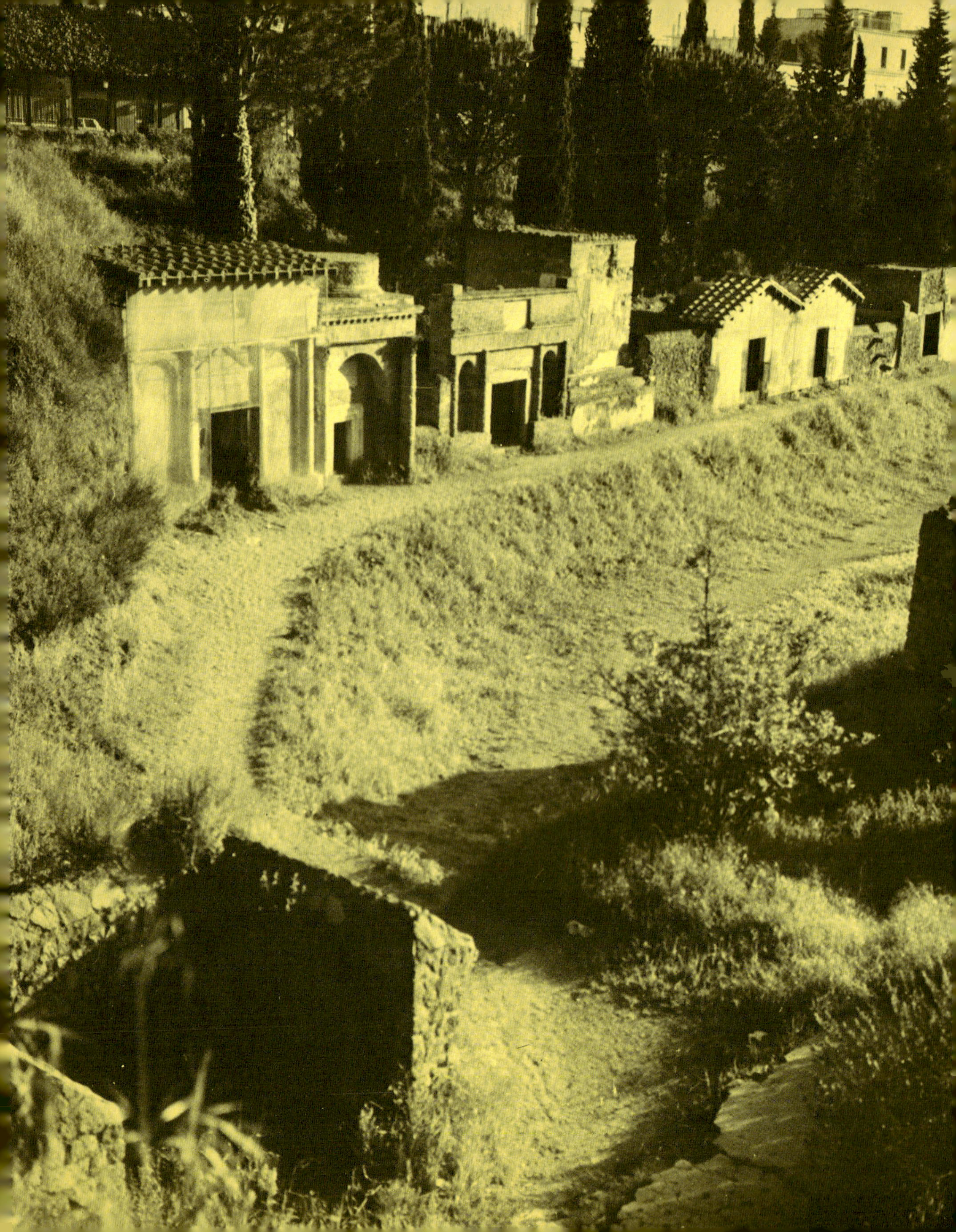

Left, necropolis view, Pompeii. Opposite, Virgil's tomb, Naples.

sell an insolvent debtor, a magistrate the citizen who refused to undertake military service, and a father could sell his son. Sources of slavery like these became less common as customs became more gentle, without however disappearing altogether. You have to look at the period of Caracalla and Diocletian to find imperial rescripts which protect the child and the insolvent debtor against slavery which could be imposed upon them by father and creditor. According to the rigour of primitive law, the slave belonged to his master like an inanimate object. He had no will of his own and was not really a person, with the consequence that he did not come under the protection of civil law. He did not enter into marriage, though he had a real relationship or "contubernium", and his offspring would fall to the master. However at the feast of the Saturnalia, he enjoyed a few moments of freedom, and at the Compitalia, he would offer sacrifices like the free men.

But imperious logic yielded gradually before humanity, and although the emperors did not get at the principle of slavery which was one of the bases on which ancient society was founded, they gradually reduced its severity.

The incurable slave would be cast into the street. Claudius decided that if a master abandonned one of his slaves who had serious weaknesses, he should go free and that if he were to kill him, he would be prosecuted as a murderer. Antony specified that he should be punished as if he had killed the slave of someone else.

Indeed history reveals a number of people of servile status who held positions of trust in rich families under their masters, or who were officers of the governors concerned with administration in the provinces, or even in the service of the emperor to perform the innumerable functions of the palace, and some who enjoyed excellent credit or household services that were the envy of the most noble patricians. For example, a slave of Tiberius who was a treasurer of the imperial exchequer in Lyon, travelled to Rome with a princely escort consisting of doctor, three secretaries, a business man, a treasurer, valet, two cooks, two financial advisers and two lackeys. In Pompéii, another one kept the accounts for a banker and on the receipts that were made out in the name of the duumvirs, he had his own seal side by side with the city magistrates".

The freed slave became a citizen yet did not enjoy the full rights of the born Roman. He was obliged to consider his former master as his father, took his name and was still attached to his family.

Emancipation often took place under onerous conditions. For example, the freed slave would make undertaking either on oath, or in the form of a written stipulation, to give presents in certain circumstances, and either to give honorary services (officiales) useful services (fabriles).

A Roman.

4 - Arts and sciences

The Romans produced nothing in the sciences. "All they knew", said Strabo, "they owed to the Greeks without adding the slightest thing, and in those spheres where knowledge was incomplete, do not aspire to thinking that they made any contribution to it." Martianus Capella went one better: "If you exclude Varro and one or two other famous people, there is not a single son of Romulus who has admitted science across his threshold." Science indeed was only admitted as a fleeting and distracted guest because it did not bring out any spirit of discovery. Vitruvius did not add to Archimedes' geometry any more than Celsus furthered the medicine of Hippocrates; Nigidius who carried out studies in mathematics and natural history in the time of Caesar, is known particularly for a treatise on astrology which was a theory of foretelling the future. By virtue of his being a senator, he could concern himself with mysteries and not degrade himself; as for pure science, that was for the freedman. The king Juba who was brought up in Rome and regarded as one of the most scientifically minded men in the court of Augustus, firmly believed that a dead man had been brought back to life by the powers of a certain plant from Arabia.

So the mathematicians failed but astrologers spread far and wide. Everyone, even Varro, consulted them, Varro asking his friend Tarutius for a horoscope for Rome;— Augustus even, who firmly believed in his star since he knew that his future greatness had been predicted in accordance with its legend at his birth. Doctors were very numerous, for Martial and Celsus report that there was one to tend every part of the body and every

Astrological altar. The twelve divinities of Olympus. The circumference of the table (which unfortunately cannot be seen on the photograph below) is engraved with the twelve signs of the Zodiac: so each divinity presides over one month of the year.

At the oculist's. From a design in a tomb.

type of disease. Even women practiced, a custom that has persisted in Italy for a long time, but whether male or female the attitude to medicine was the same as the mathematicians to astronomy, and the sick were treated at random or according to preconceived ideas. Asclepiades of Bithynia, a friend of Cicero and all the dignitaries in Rome, and the most famous physician of them all was one of these well-known charlatans. However, he did state a very important half-truth: "Nature is the physician"; he wanted to cure people "pleasantly", jucunde, by dieting. Musa eclipsed his reputation after having saved the life of Augustus with cold baths in the year 23 B.C. The sole merits of the medical anthology compiled by Celsus were that it preserved a great deal of Greek scientific information and gave an important place to anatomy. Surgery was more advanced than medicine; cutting, trepanning and obstetrical operations, and the removal of cataract were all known. In order to attract doctors to Rome, Caesar had extended the freedom of the city to them, and Augustus immunity from taxation. "But this art was not taken seriously by the Romans", said Pliny. The Greeks exploited this lucrative profession alone. If there were any doctors who did not come from Peloponesia on the Asiatic coast, they were well advised to learn the language of the Greeks as well as their prescriptions. In the art field, the Romans, rich parvenus that they were, expressed their taste in painting and sculpture through Mummius, and they wanted his work everywhere. But I suspect that they were as incapable of sculpting a Venus de Milo as they were of understanding her chaste beauty. When you see Scaurus collect three thousand statues together for a one-day theatre, and the city to have perhaps seventy thousand statues, you cannot help thinking that they believed in quantity above all.

There is no doubt at all however, that sculptors produced very fine work during the Roman period, from the statue of Agrippina the elder that can be seen at the Capitol, an exquisite study in nobility and pride, to the one of Antinous that Hadrian had copied throughout the empire. But it was the hands of the Greeks that created them. Painting was even less Roman if that were possible. The great pictures to be seen in Rome were the spoils of war, except for some that were purchased.

An art which is still much sought after by the Romans today is mosaic, which covers the pavements of Italian and provincial villas. Examples of it have been found everywhere, and they are most beautiful. The "Battle of Issus" discovered in Pompeii at the house of Faunus is justifiably famous.

There is a science in which the Romans have no rivals—namely law—and an art form, architecture, to which they have given a new form on the basis of old elements. But one of these two glories of Rome is anonymous, because whilst we have great monuments, we do not know of any great designers responsible for their construction, with the single exception of Apollodorus, architect

Frescoes decorating the walls of a patrician household. (House of the Vettii, Pompeii.)

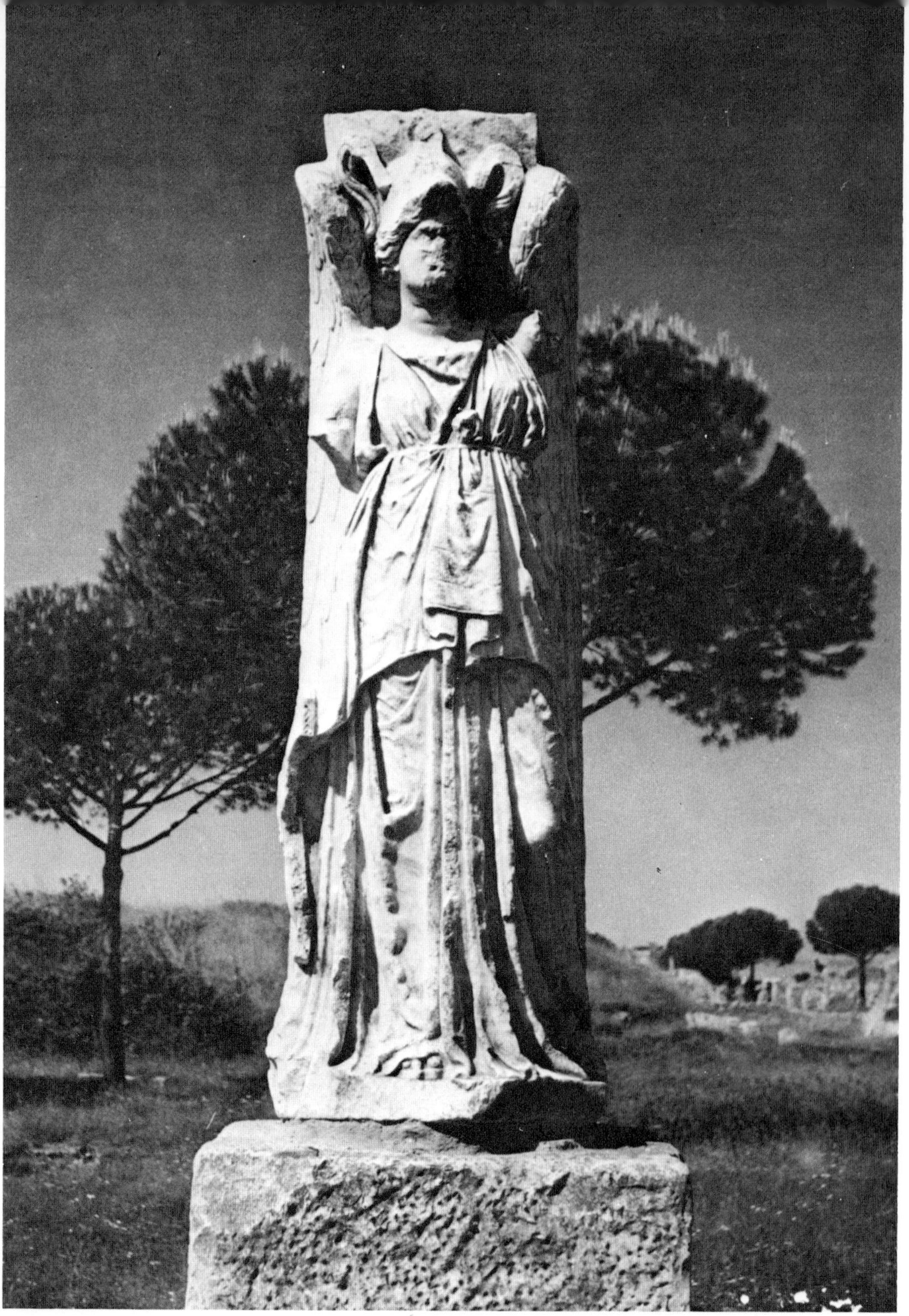

Left, statue of the Marine Victory, Ostia. Another photograph of this statue taken from a different angle will be seen on page 143.

Above, mosaic from the Thermal Baths of Caracalla.

Opposite: mosaic decoration... with swastikas... on the floor of a house in Pompeii.

to Trajan and Hadrian; the other is connected with many names and has no bearing on any book. Architecture and law share the characteristic of having expressed Roman genius more effectively than literature.

Roma has only a few large buildings if one excepts the wall of Servius, the Cloaca Maxima, the aqueducts, the military ways, the temple of Jupiter at the Capitol, the theatre, the Portico, Pompey's curia, and the strange tomb of Caecilia Metella (Capi di Bove) on the Appian Way. Caesar instigated monumental Rome with his forum and temple of Venus Genitrix, a Julian ancestor, the basilica that Augustus completed, and above all with his vast Circus, six hundred and fifty metres long, nearly three hundred metres wide and having a two storey portico where there were two obelisks. The were discovered in 1587 twenty four feet below the ground. He had sent eight million (sesterces) from Gaul to Aemilius Paulus to complete a basilica with five naves decorated by an enormous number of Phrygian marble columns, and he had helped Curius to build two theatres side by side which were turned with their spectators by a powerful mechanism to convert into an arena for amphitheatre contests. Augustus gave immense scope to all constructional work. He said in his Testament, "I have built sixteen new temples, a curia, the Julian basilica, the forum which is named after me, the theatre of Marcellus, the Tiber naumachia and two porticos. I have restored the Capitol and Pompey's theatre at great expense, yet I have not inscribed my name anywhere. I have completed the Julian forum and the basilica between the temple of Castor and the temple of Saturnus which had been begun by my father; as this basilica had been destroyed by fire, I had it rebuilt much bigger, and I also repaired eighty two temples."

Many people following the example of Augustus spent the remainder of the fortune acquired as proconsul or of gifts made by the prince on decorating the town in order

Impressions of a crane and a scene of construction in progress (Rome Trajan's Column).

A bust of Maecenas.

to gain his good graces. Maecenas cleared the Esquiliae and built a palace there set in wonderful gardens; when the emperor had added a wood and a basilica with spacious galleries, the site which was once the scene of the punishment and burial of slaves became one of the most beautiful walks in Rome.

Agrippa's Pantheon remains intact. Inside this round temple one is stunned by the daring of its roof, which seems to rest on the ground just as the vault of the sky seems to rest on the earth at the extremities of the horizon. At the top it opens into an orifice twenty seven feet in diameter, so that the enormous mass seems to hold together by a miracle of equilibrium and the entire temple has no source of light other than the light coming down from above. Agrippa obviously wanted the first monument of the new Rome to be a symbol of the Universe, of which the Augustan empire formed the best part. The elevation of this single eye in the vaulted

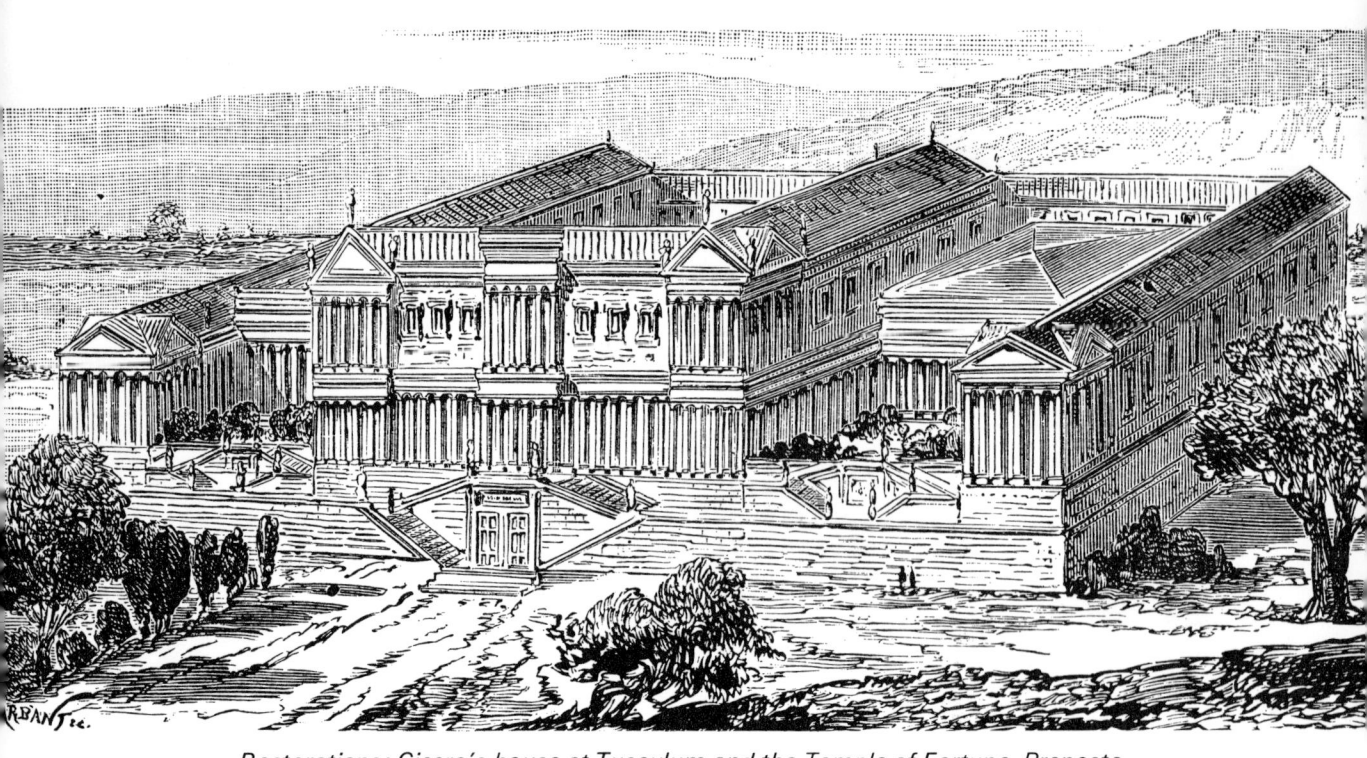

Restorations: Cicero's house at Tusculum and the Temple of Fortune, Preneste.

The famous tomb of Cecilia Metella on the Appian Way and old fragments recessed into the wall of a nearby house.

Dome interior, Pantheon. Right, a vault in the Temple of Venus, Rome.

Below, restoration of the villa of the Quintilii, on the Appian Way.

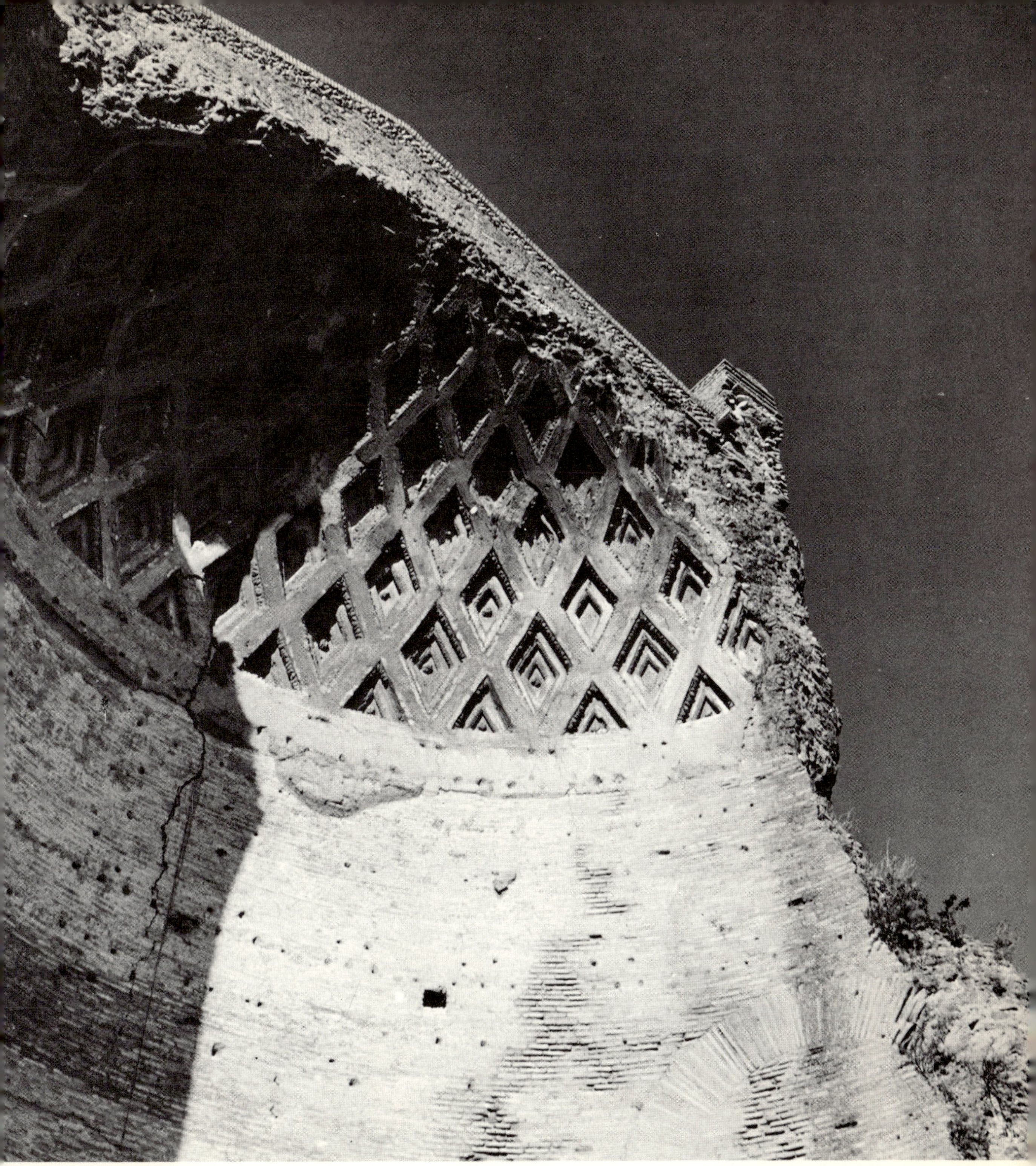

roof is such that despite its huge aperture, the temperature does not change.

The Romans were not restricted anywhere in their building because stone was available everywhere for facing, or at least ragstone for belting courses, rubble for in-fill, earth for bricks, lime for their durable cement, and the hands to shift it all. The outcome of it was first of all that with materials that were so easy to use and yet so resistant, nothing prevented them from creating monuments of gigantic proportions, not always a condition of beauty, but one under which the artist can obtain powerful effects.

So the great appeal of the Roman countryside rests especially in the huge viaducts which descend from the Tivoli and Albano hills and span the Latin plain with infinite grace and majesty. So the ruined baths of Caracalla in their bareness have an imposing grandeur, and the Coliseum built of bricks and stone from Tibur makes a more profound impression than the pyramids of Ghizeh.

Like people, like art; the domination by Rome is made apparent by the roads which forge dead straight ahead, like the Roman will, without deviating to avoid obstacles, and also by the massive constructions, devoid of grace, and I was about to say, devoid of art, which demonstrate such great strength, tower so high and weigh so heavily upon the ground that supports them.

The architecture of the Romans, adapting itself to all the needs of civil life, has spread as their language, laws and customs did throughout the whole of the West where all have left their eternal mark.

Plunder of the world enabled Rome to lavish the most rare marbles on her buildings of the Martian Fields and on the Forum and all the marble quarries of the empire were worked for her. One of them, a rich deposit on the Ostia road, has been rediscovered. Individual people, provincial cities, and Rome herself, often used to build in rough stone chippings and bricks.

Preparing bricks at the base of the temple of Venus.

5 - Beliefs and changes in ideas

We know the gods of the ancient Romans. The most revered were first, Janus, the great national divinity whose name headed every solemn invocation, the god of two demeanours because he opens and closes, begins and ends; then Jovis or Jupiter, the god of light who is the father and preserver of all things; Saturnus who protects the grain in the earth; Minerva who warns the ploughman in time to carry out his work; Mars the symbol of life renewing itself in the spring and of virile strength which no obstacle can resist; Quirinus who was mistaken for Romulus and one day will descend to the rank of demi-god; Vesta, whose altar indicated the centre of domestic life in the home and political life in the city; Vulcan, the other god of fire, both of the fire that consumes and destroys and the fire that tames iron and constrains the hardest metals to submit to the needs of man.

During a period of refined philosophy, Plutarch explained that the Fortune cult completed the Destiny cult; this was to say that the goddess with rapid wings arranged fortuitous events whilst "the son of necessity" watched over the enforcement of the immutable laws of the universe and the carrying out of decisions incontestably made by the supreme god. The Romans did not work out as much philosophy as this, but they vaguely thought everything in life did not obey the laws of fate. Out of custom they had created a divinity which satisfied their feeling on this point—Fortuna,—an ancient Italian goddess whom Servius was reputed to have imported to Rome and who had certainly come alone. She was very much revered at Praeneste and Antium (sortes), and one day she will have more worshippers than the mighty gods of the Capitol. The ordinary people and the slaves celebrated the one who could give them

At Pompeii: the Propylaea of the Triangular Forum; right, the Street of Mercury and Caligula's Arch; Vesuvius in the background. On the following pages, the Basilica and view of the Forum.

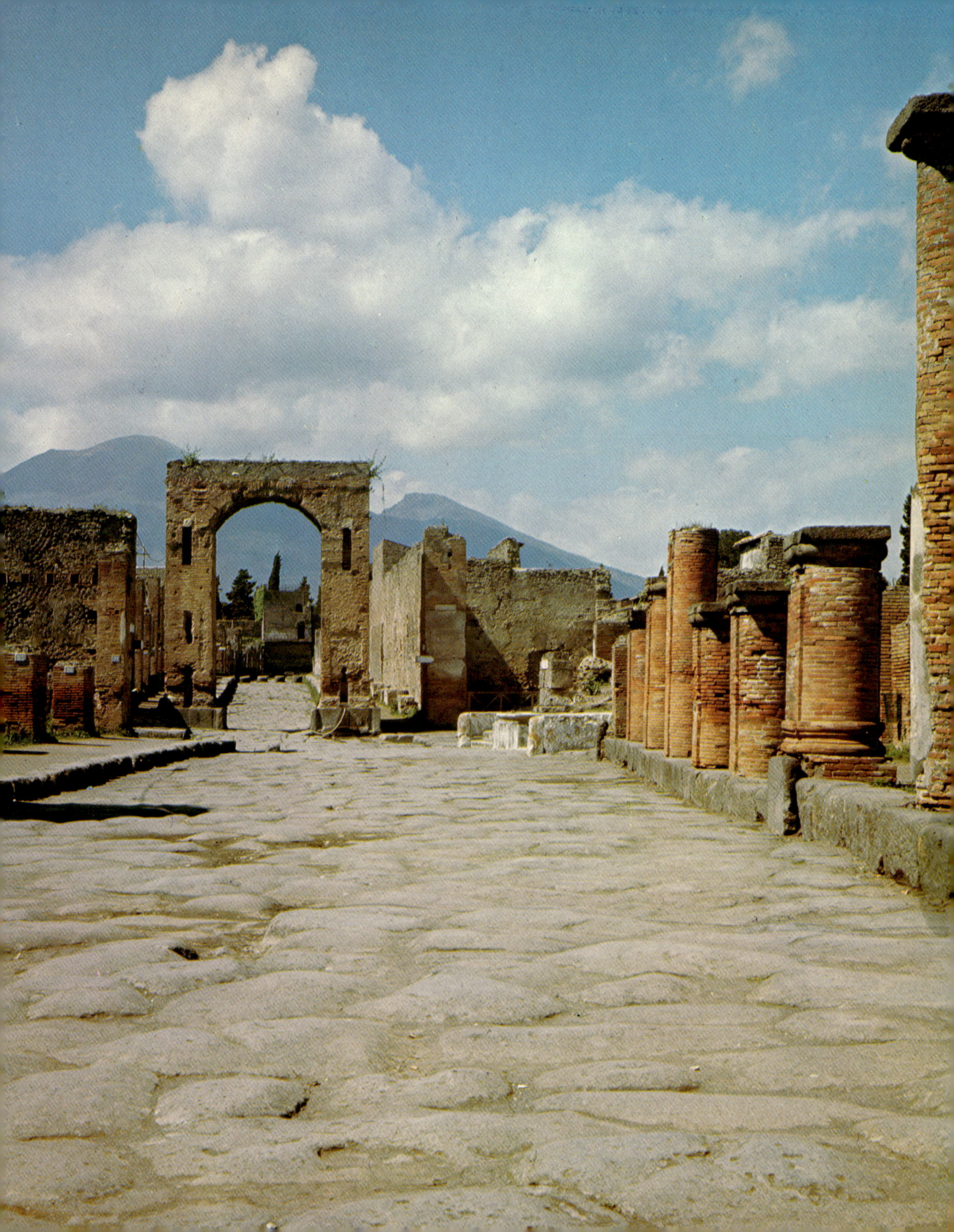

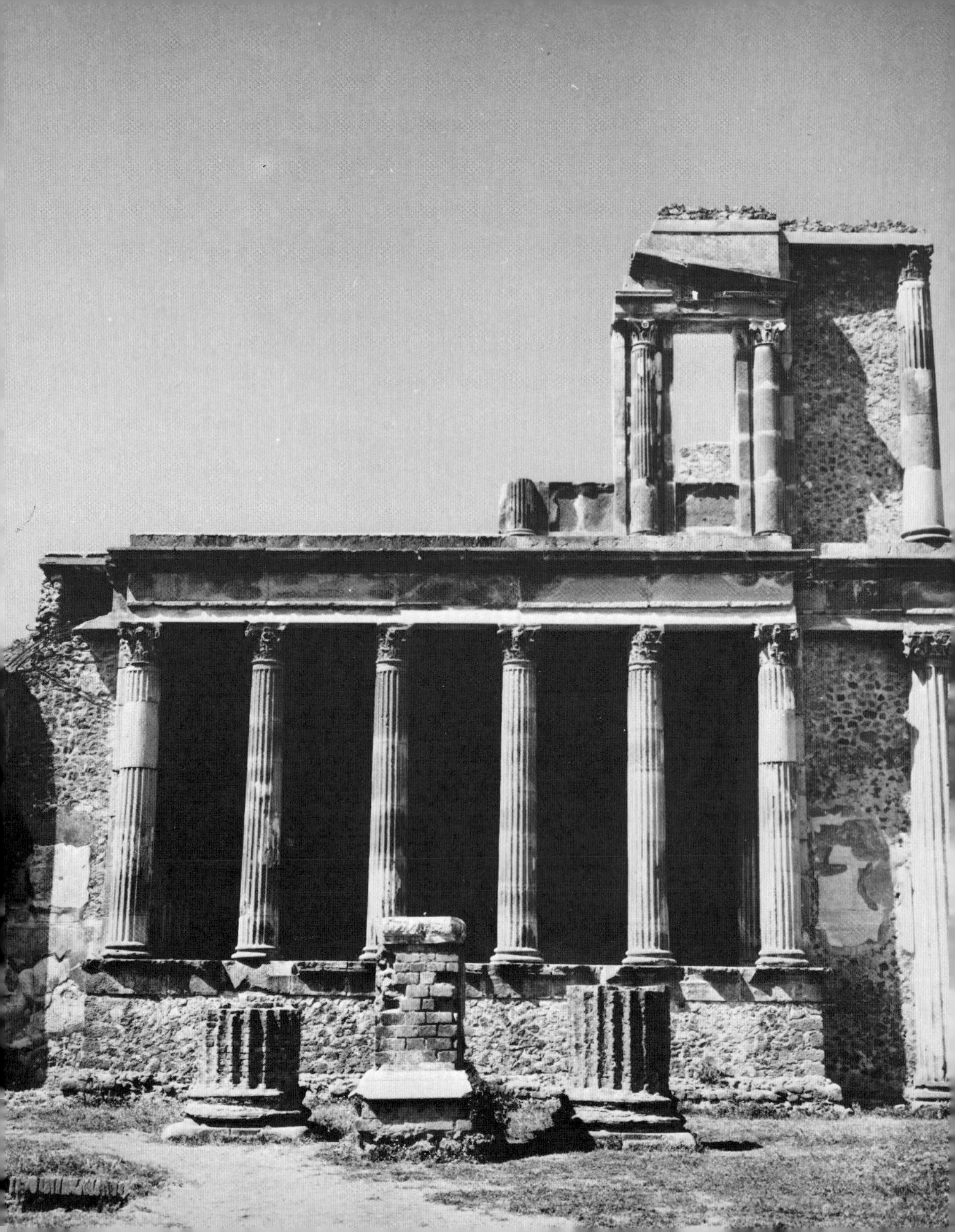

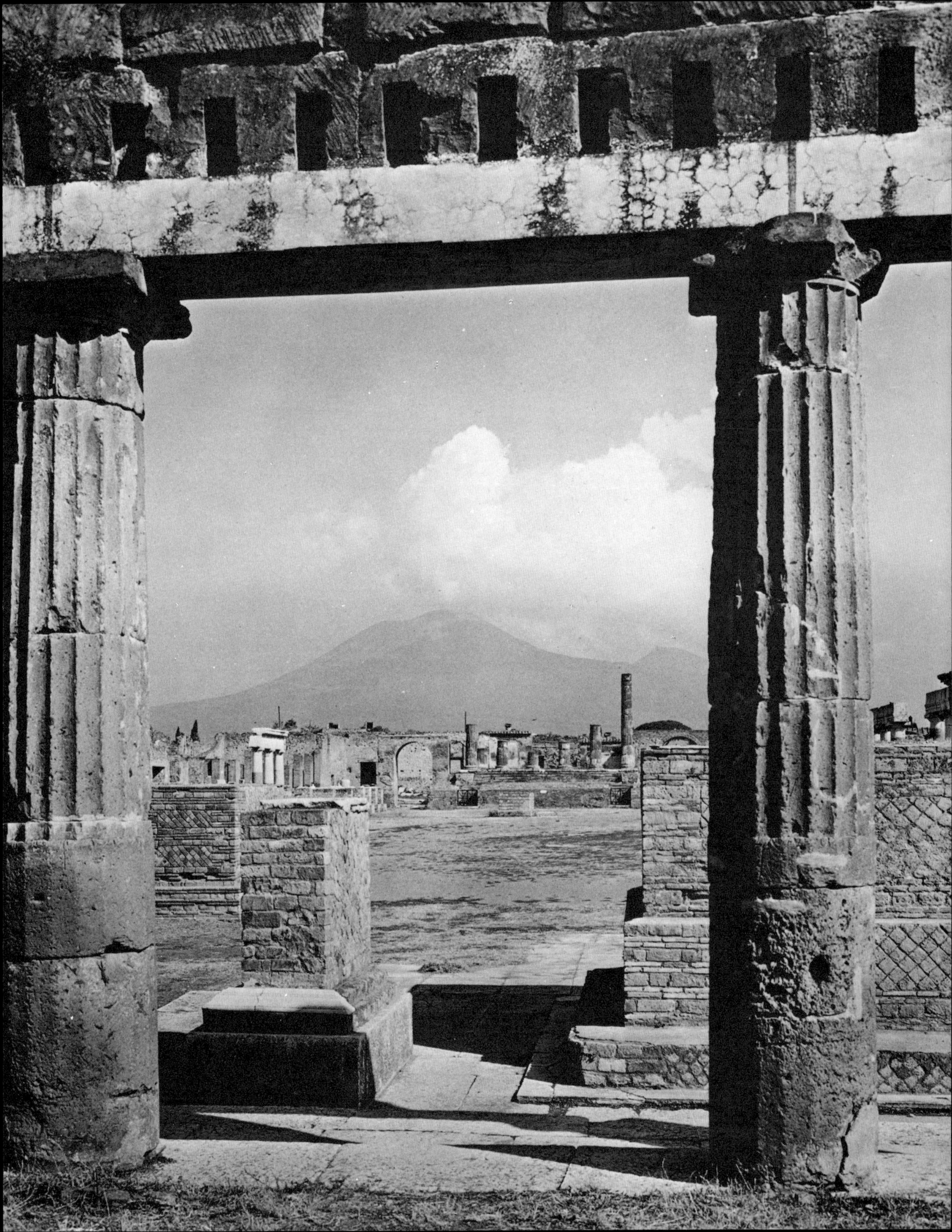

freedom or wealth every year on the 24th. of June.

She earned innumerable other names and consequently acquired innumerable temples, for each epithet they gave her expressing the particular favour from her, there seemed to be as many goddesses of Fortune as there were reasons for imploring Lady Luck. The Romans divided their deity like this according to the functions they gave her to fulfil, and all their gods had more than one personage.

The gods of the world underground, Tellus, Terra-Mater, Ceres, Dis-Pater and so on, were responsible for the germination of the seeds in the bosom of the silent earth and watched over the dead. The gods of the sea who were so numerous with the Greeks, a people who spent half their life at sea, could not claim a following from a people without a fleet. But in the middle area there lived the gods of the earth, "Medioxumi", gods of the fields and forests, of the harvests of corn and vine, of springs and rivers, popular gods who were cherished more than the great deities who lived too far away. There lived Bona Dea or Maia, the Earth which provides all things necessary to life, and for which reason they called the Great Mother, "Mater Magna". There was also Saturnus "the good sower", Faunus, Silvanus and Pales, gods of the woods and fields who protected the farm, the farm-yard and garden that were situated in a clearing in the forest and kept away wolves and fatal diseases. In days gone by Italy was a country of large pasture lands as she still is, and the Roman countryside still preserves the wild shepherds mentioned by Vergil if only for their festive occasions. Their main feast, the "Palilia", was celebrated on the day of the founding of Rome, April 21st... Above the naiads, nymphs and all the host of water spirits ran Pater Tiberinus, the powerful river which did not wish to be shackled by a stone bridge and which only tolerated the "pons Sublicius" for a long time. It was a wooden bridge constructed entirely without iron.

Furthermore, in order to ward off the wrath of the god, the pontiffs had undertaken to construct it themselves, and they directed repairs to it which were carried out only during religious ceremonies. In the distant past, the Tiber had taken its toll of human victims; it was now appeased by twenty four dummies made of osiers which were thrown on to the river bed from the top of the Sublicius bridge by the vestal priestesses on the 13th. May every year.

Some of the divinities that can be described as official and that had their own temples, priests and public recognition with a mass following, were also honoured in a special way in the "gentes, sacra gentilitia". Each of the great families had its own god of protection, just as our guilds of the middle ages would choose a divine patron, and the cult of this deity would bind all the members of the "gens" into a close unity. To cease to worship was to perish; the "gens" would not survive unprotected by its ancient altar. Titus Livius says that the Politii who handed over the worship of Hercules to the State, he having been their special god, all died within the year.

Each house no matter how poor, also had its domestic gods. They were humble modest gods, some invisible, like the Spirits and Ghosts, others, the Penates and Lares, were represented by crudely made earthen figures that were not properly moulded or hardened in the kiln, but were honoured as much as the Russian peasant honours his holy icons today. They were uneasily distinguished one

Left, small statue representing Ceres. Below, frescoes depicting the cult of the goddess.

from the other, because they all represented the idea of supernatural protection in a more or less clear way. They were guardians from the heart of the invisible world who continued to watch over the house where they had lived.

The Penates or gods of the interior whom Vergil calls the paternal gods, were the spirits of the house in which they preserved abundance, "penus". All the dear and loving memories of the household were connected with the Lares or Lords, the spirits of ancestors. The Lares shared the joys and sorrows of the family, and were associated with both its good fortune and ill luck. There was no festival in which they did not have their part, and on every joyful occasion, they were decorated with flowers and leaves, and when the young man wore male dress for the first time, he would dedicate the seal he had borne to them. No meal was eaten without a portion being set aside for them first. This was a kind of communion with the god and was fulfilled by the whole city if things were serious. The city would then invite its various divinities to the solemn feast of the "lectisternium".

The worship of the domestic fire was associated with the cult of the Lares, and one can say that the two foundations of Roman society were the hearth stone and the tomb stone. The family had grown up around one and in spite of the painful separation, it was being perpetuated around the other. Those who had no penates would wander through life like a person wandering after death if he had no tomb. The hearth is a sacred place moreover. It is festooned with a coronet of flowers at the calends, the ides, the nones, and on each festival day, and when the father of the family enters the house, he greets the Lares of the hearth before anything else.

The lofty Vesta reigned over the public foyer as a "living flame which neither gives nor receives any source of life"; she is therefore an immortal virgin who wishes only for virgins as her companions. Each house also

Altar of the "Villa of Mysteries", Pompeii and three bronzes representing the Lares gods.

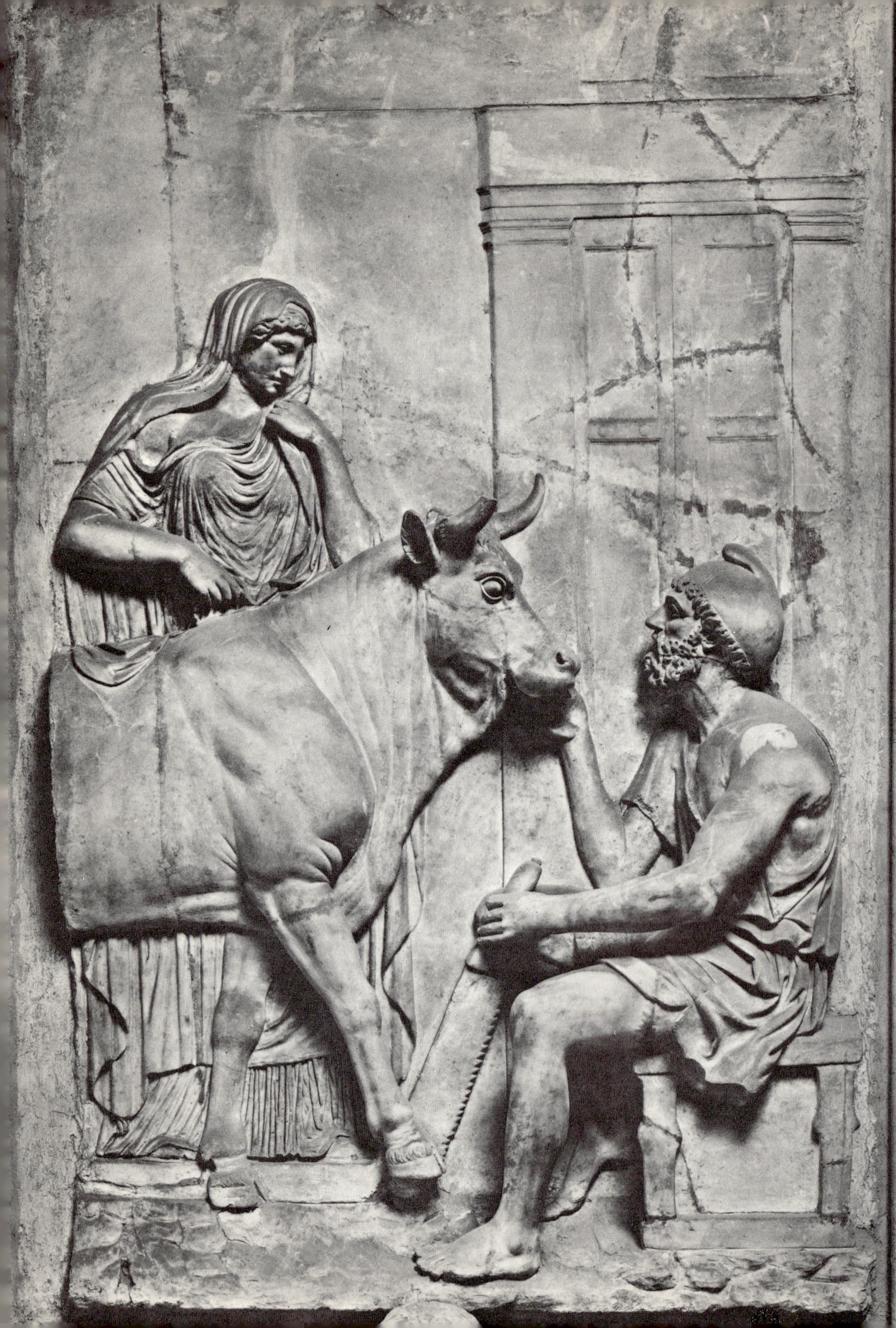

The bull; often offered as a sacrifice, as shown in the bas-relief above.

has a domestic Vesta. The hearth is her altar and the fire burning on it is a god; this god tends the life of the house just as the sun looks after nature; he is the god who cooks the bread, makes tools, and helps everyone in his work; in addition he is the purifier and is himself pure; he receives sacrifices and conveys the prayers of mortals to other gods, as the flames quickened with oil, incense and the fat of victims glow brightly and leap to the ceiling.

The spirits of the dead, or "Lemures", were of two kinds;—the wicked ones or "Larves" and the good ones or "Manes". The Manes or "pure beings" were the dead who had been cleansed by the funeral rites to become protectors of those whom they had left behind in life. They did not believe that the dead were completely dead in Rome in the same way that people everywhere believe it. The dead man had his dwelling like the living; his hearth was his tomb where he would embark on a second life, which though sad, was a peaceful one if he had had full funeral rites. If funeral honours had not been accorded to him, he would be anxious and unhappy. Once separated from his mortal remains the human being would not quit the earth to ascend to the ethereal spheres nor to descend into hell. He would maintain an invisible presence among those he had loved to inspire them with thoughts of wisdom, protect their fortune and their home, but always on condition that the living

Minerva, the subject of an ornamental disc on a wall in Pompeii. Below, restoration of the Temple of Concord, Rome. Right, a priestess.

extended ancestor worship to him. Originally they were cruel rites, at least on the funeral day itself, for it was believed that the Manes liked blood. They would sacrifice wife, slaves, war horse or captives of a king on his tomb, a custom which gave rise to the gladiatorial combats, first and foremost acts of devotion like the auto-da-fe in Spain. But at anniversaries, the Manes were satisfied if relatives came to place leafy garlands on their tomb as we would place flowers, to leave flower cakes and honey there, and make libations from wine, milk and the blood of a modest victim.

No especial knowledge or particular vocation were necessary for people who wanted to become priests. If Rome had clergy, she had no priest class owning great riches or levying tithes, and there was no religious interest as distinct from State interest. The augurs could take auspices only by permission of the magistrates, and it was forbidden to reveal a prophecy to the people unless the senate had authorised it. "Our ancestors", said Cicero, "were never wiser or more inspired by the gods than when they established that the same people should preside over both religion and the government of the republic. In this way, magistrates and pontiffs preserve the State by mutual understanding." There was no dependence of one power upon the other. The State and religion were one.

The most revered priests were the three flamines, or lighters of the altars of Jupiter, Mars and Quirinus, who could not appear in public or in the open air, unless it were the court-yard of their home, without the special hat or apex, the symbol of their priesthood; the three augurs, sacred interpreters of omens come next; then the vestals or guardians of the public hearth where the fire must never be allowed to go out; the twelve salians or dancers, guardians of the "ancilia" or shields, who would dance a war dance in March each year and as soon as war was declared, would enter simultaneously with the "god who kills" to beat their shields of bronze with

Bust of a Vestal Virgin. Right, the Temple of Vesta and restoration of the Temple of the Sun, Rome.

pikes shouting; "Mars, awake!" then the twelve Arvales brothers or brothers of the fields, priests of Dea-Dia, an earth goddess; finally the four pontiffs who were free of any authority, and were not answerable to the senate or to the people who kept watch over the preservation of laws and religious institutions under the presidency of the high pontiff, and who fixed the calendar and the holidays and rest days making the administration of justice and the holding of meetings dependent on them to some degree. The day when the golden sickle of the new moon appeared, one of the pontiffs would convene the people at the Capitol and advise them how many days to count from the calends to the nones. On the nones, another one would announce the feasts that were to be celebrated during the month. Initially there were four vestals, two for each tribe; then after the association of the Luceres, there were six. When a vacancy occurred at the college, the king, as high pontiff would select twenty young patrician girls of about ten years who had no physical defect and were promising in looks. Fate, representing divine will, designated the one to be dedicated to the office. This done, the pontiff would take the hand of the appointed saying: "I take you, you shall be the priestess of Vesta and you shall fulfil the sacred rites for the safety of the Roman people"; then he would escort her to the "regia" or priestess' home, where her hair would fall to the scissors and her sisters would dress her in white.

The Vestal Virgins would take it in turns to keep the fire on the altar burning night and day. If it came to the point of going out, it was a terrible omen for Rome, and the person who had committed the negligence was beaten with rods by the high pontiff in some obscure spot; the pontiff would light the fire again at once by rubbing together two pieces of wood taken from a lucky tree, "felix arbor" though later the method was to direct the sun's rays on to a metal urn. They had to prepare libations, sacrifices, and a strange operation that doubtless had some connection with their vow of virginity. When the pontiffs sacrificed thirty cows in calf on the 15th. April, the embryos taken from their mothers' womb were handed to the senior vestal who burned them and carefuly preserved the ashes, which she distributed to the people on the day of the Palilia so that they could make sacrificial offerings of them. Each morning they would wash the temple with water drawn from the fountain of Egeria into a pot with a wide opening and pointed at the bottom (futile) so that it was impossible to place it on the ground without all the water spilling out.

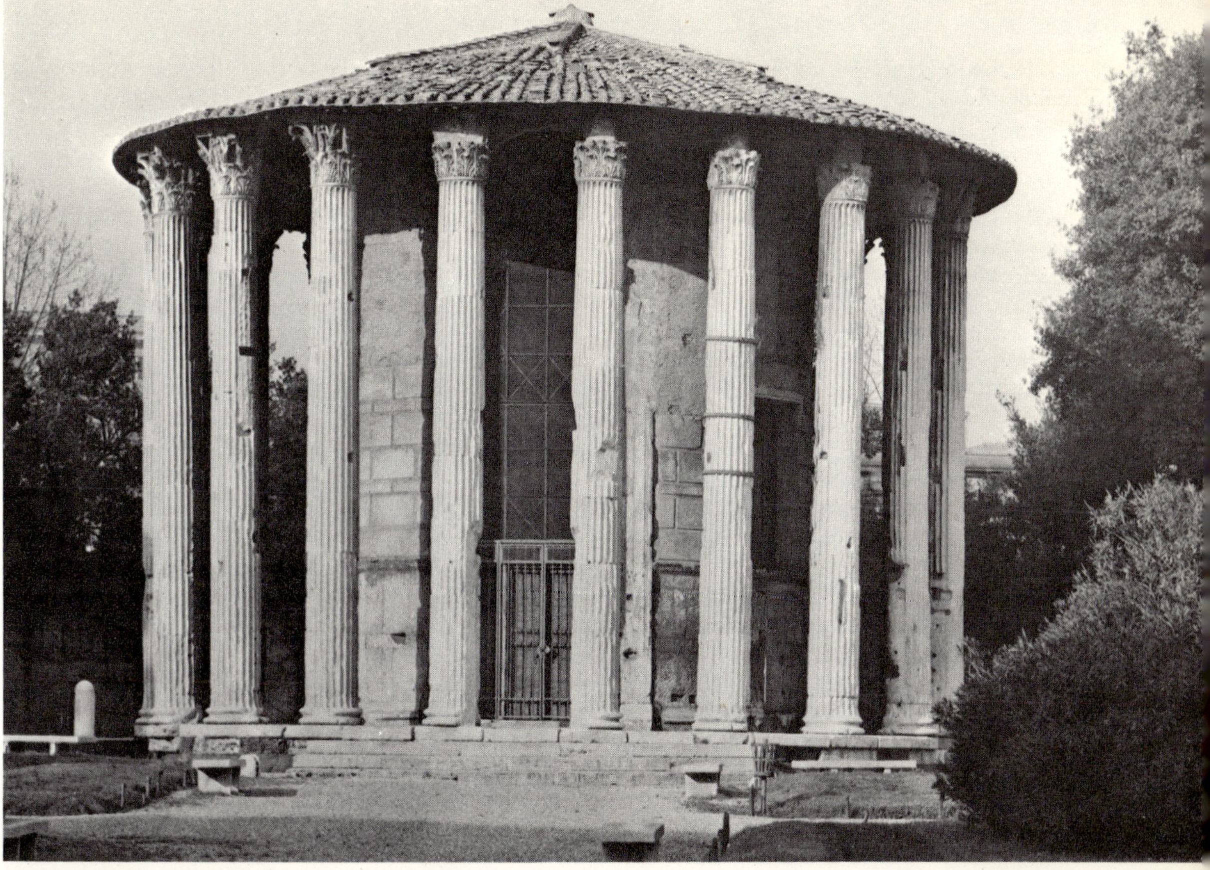

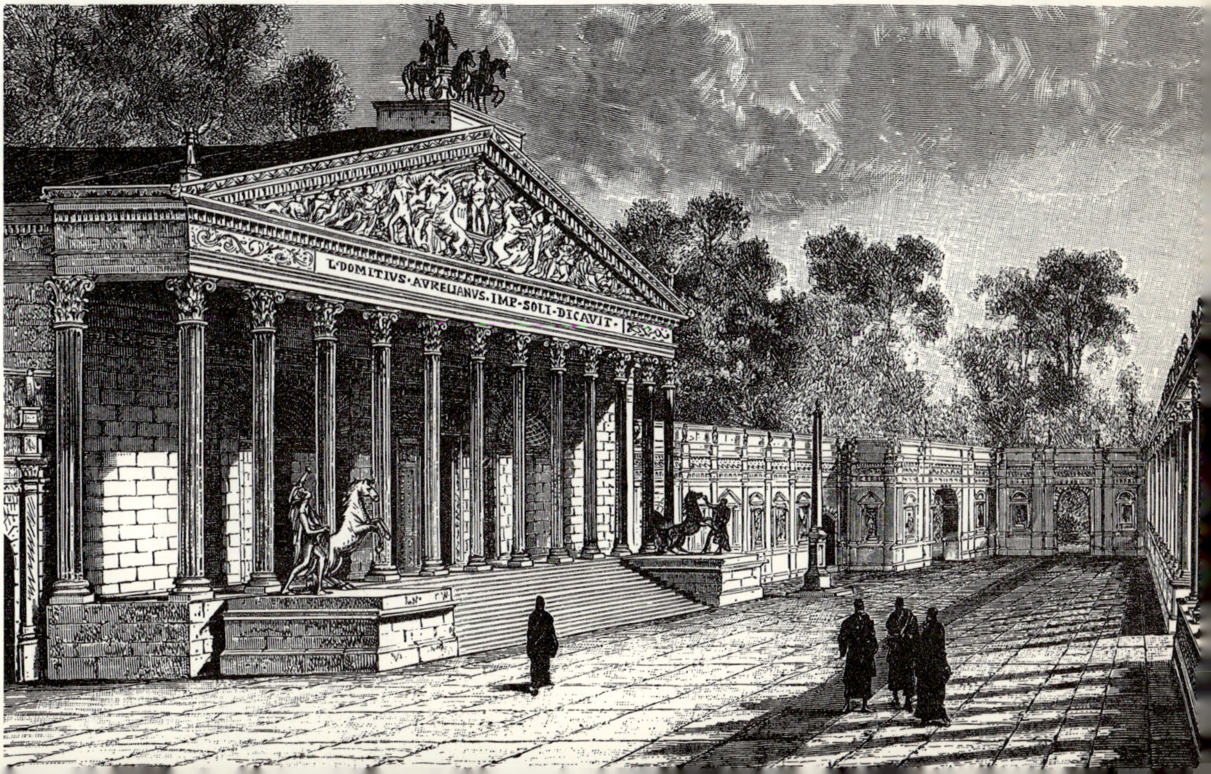
L·DOMITIVS·AVRELIANVS·IMP·SOLI·DICAVIT

The vestals served for thirty years, and then they could return to the world, and even marry. Few of them took advantage of the privilege and spent the rest of their lives close to the goddess to whom they had made their vow of virginity. In compensation for the sacrifice they were making, they were highly respected and great honours were accorded them. They are not affected by bonds of relationship, which means that they are safe from paternal power, "patria potestas", and the protection of family kinsmen, and so can accept legacies and bequeath their goods by making a will. They could give evidence in the law courts without being under oath. The magistrate would have the fasces lowered before them and the criminal under escort to his punishment was set free, provided that they said they felt fortuitously about his release. But if the vestals broke their vow, what a horrible death they faced. On the Quirinal Hill between the Colline Gate and the famous gardens of Sallust, was "the field of unhappiness", campus Sceleratus. They dug a subterranean chamber in which they buried the guilty priestess alive. They would put her on a stretcher for the dead swathed in heavy covers to stifle her cries, and carry her with grim ceremony across the Forum and through the silent crowd to the vault where they had placed a bed, a lighted lamp, bread, water, milk and oil. A day's provisions for eternal imprisonment and mocking succour from dutiful worship which did not want to inform Vesta of the murder of one of her virgins! When the funeral cortege had reached the scene of punishment, the high priest would say secret prayers; then the stretcher was uncovered, and wrapped round in thin white cotton like a shroud, she would go down into the tomb by a ladder and slaves would quickly fill in the opening. The soil was carefully levelled so that nothing gave away the spot where the vestal was atoning for sacrilege that she had perhaps never committed, in the darkness and cold of the tomb. No one came to make libations such as the poorest person would offer to the Manes and so she was simultaneously cut off from the world of the living and the dead. When the murder was over, the crowd would disperse slowly. Some would be deeply moved by the terrible end of a beautiful and noble young girl who had taken her vows in an awe-inspiring order when under age. By far the greatest number would be convinced that the evils with which Rome had been threatened were now averted by a necessary sacrifice.

Feasts were as innumerable as the gods, for the Italian of all time has liked religious pomp which formed a diversion to the monotony of ordinary life, was an occasion of pious ceremonies, noisy games and feasts on which the very poorest would spend a whole week's savings.

Statue of Ceres. (Monte-Pincio, Rome.)

Augustus will protect religion on the score of its utility. Before even having become high pontiff, he will purify its sources by choosing oracles which were spread amongst the public, and more than two thousand volumes of predictions in both Greek and Latin will be burned. Magicians who were turned out of Rome under the republic returned and increased their influence, as happens with any profession that speculates on the vices and follies of mankind. Augustus will forbid them to predict the future against penalty of death, because their forecasts are not generally favourable to current policy.

A philosophical movement had developed amongst forward-looking groups through contact with the Greeks. Freedom of thought introduced many new notions. Pacuvius said, "I for one hate men who spend their lives philosophising and not acting". This was the Roman conscience speaking. Cato, who considered Socrates garrulous and had condemned him twice for having wanted to modify traditional habits and customs, had said to his son: "Remember this clearly, and accept it as the word of the oracle: when the philosophers invade us with their literature, Rome will be lost." He was most certainly one of the members of the famous senatorial committee of 161 who had instigated the banishment of philosophy. Six years later the exile returned to Rome.

The ancient Romans respected the signs that the priests interpreted as a divine revelation, constantly renewed by the gods who were always in the midst of their people. Statesmen too, whilst giving a free rein to poets and men of letters, perpetuated this old institution by their show of respect. Pontiff Aurelius Cotta said: "It is not easy to deny the existence of the gods in public, though in private it is a different matter": —and he did not hesitate to exploit the fact.

Polybius, a friend of Cato, adviser to Scipio Emilius, and the most reasoning man of his time, disgusted by popular religion, which for some had become a school for scandal and for others a barbarous superstition, banished Providence from history and replaced it by an austere sense of individual and public duty. He denied that there were punishments lined up for the wicked, but laid down a rigorous code of responsibility to one's conscience and to society; lastly, with that superb disdain for crowds that superior intellects often have, he did not consider religion to be anything more than a useful rein with which to control the masses. When one sees that Cato, augur and censor, did not understand how two soothsayers could look at one another without laughing, one is no longer amazed that the government allowed the gods to be scorned with impunity, provided that the magistrates were respected.

Clever people like Varro and the high pontiff Scovola for example, escaped difficulties by distinguishing between several different types of theology;—the poets', —good at best for the theatre,—the philosophers', that reason would examine,—and the theology of the people and the State, that the laws had to respect and defend.

Philosophers and rhetoricians were banished from Rome in vain; their influence remained, and Greek education, replacing Etruscan, spread through families and went to the heart of the rising generations who brought scorn upon the ancient customs and ancestor worship.

Expulsion orders only affected famous masters and did not touch the ordinary crowd rushing about in the great city—the Greek element that pervaded everywhere in the persons of slaves, sculptors, painters, preceptors, and parasites,—a treacherous and deceitful lot who were studied for the refinements of their intellect and skill with words. In ancient Greece, the education of children had been one of the most important concerns of the government; the Romans, except for the occasional intervention of the magistrates, abandoned it to private speculation. Terence, enumerating the tastes of up-to-date young men, puts

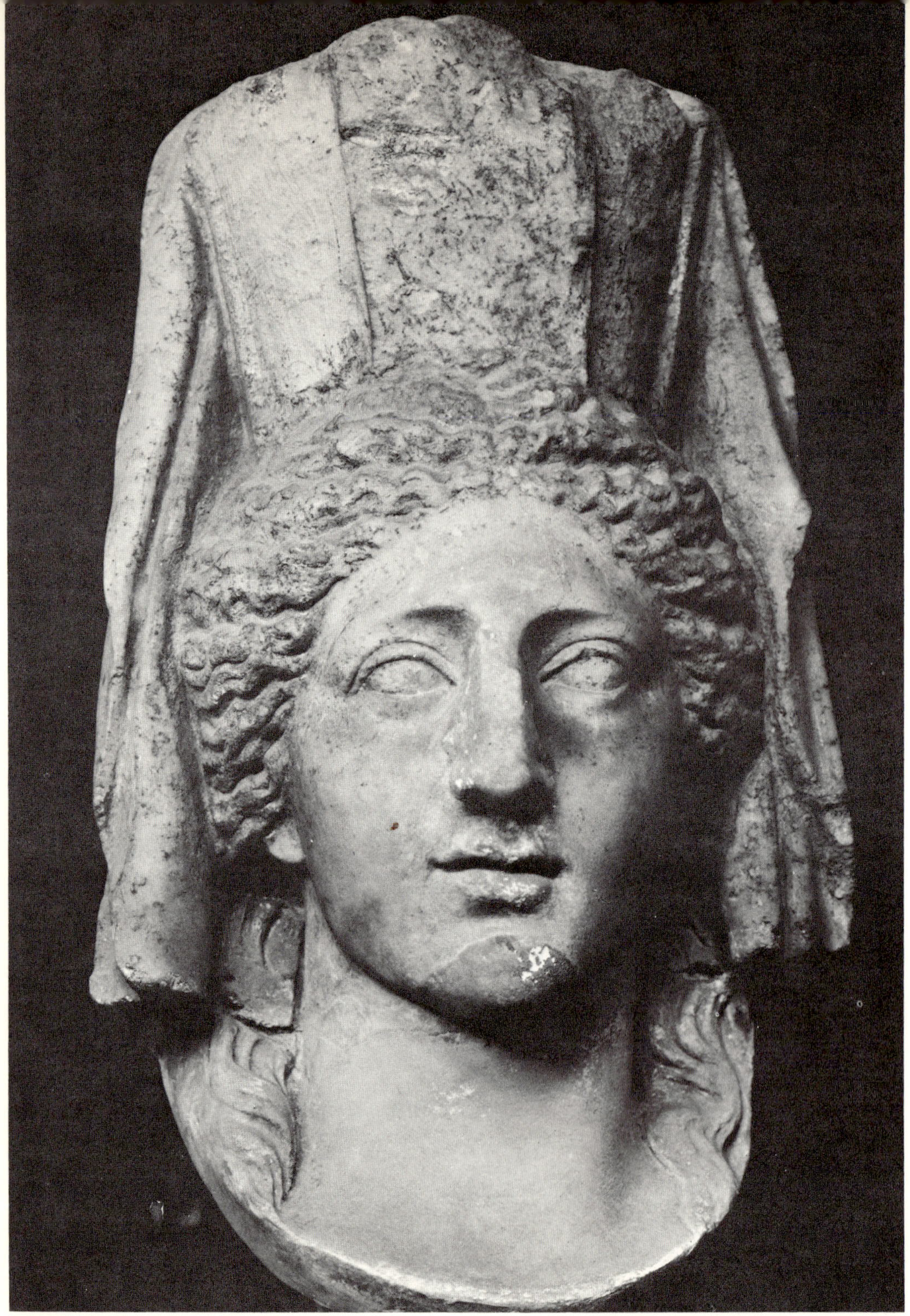

philosophers alongside horses and hounds without any ado. However, the most illustrious Romans of this period, the Scipios, Paulus Emilius, all the nobility, and those who were striving to emulate the proper fashion, surrounded their children with Greek teachers. But how could those who had been conquered, bought as slaves, bring up the sons of the conquerors in the strong traditions of their ancestors?

Some people, after having had doubts, would become believers again after some mishap, for is this not a time-honoured fact? As for the masses, they preserved their lares and penates, their rustic gods, and their faith in Jupiter "the most good and the most great" who reigned from the Capitol and gave Rome power to reign over the world. But many too whose religious feelings were not completely satisfied by the arid formality of national religion, sought new heavens and brought down from them new gods.

However, after the Greek gods, the most dangerous divinities of the Orient slipped into the city; from the year 220, Isis and Serapis had had their own temples, later to be demolished by the senate.

Oriental deities gave a new turn to the religious feeling of these people who had endured a prosaic cult for so long. The Orientals, born in blazing hot climates, liked wild rites and pious debauches. Dramatic spectacles and intoxicating ceremonies deeply moved their slow minds, set alight enthusiasm and inspired divine rapture, so that for the first time the Roman experienced extasy in God which according to his doctrine and the nature of his spirit, produced entirely contrary effects:—the purity of life, or debauchery sanctified by faith. Asiatic slaves who were numerous in Rome certainly contributed by spreading secret propaganda, (as happened later in the beginnings of Christianity,) in this first wave of cults from the Orient. It will be sufficient to describe the rites of two such religions, so that it can be seen along what unexpected path the spiritual life of the Romans travelled. Lucretius portrays the following picture of the feasts of Cybele, in which he does not include the shameful parts.

"When Greek poets praise the Earth, they represent her seated in a chariot drawn by two lions and crown her forehead with a circlet... Disfigured priests follow in her train... drums resound to the beat of their hands, and cymbals and trumpets add their shrilling tones to the Phrygian flute, putting their minds in a frenzy... They carry javelins to spur on the fury and the silent image of the goddess passes through the town without showing her unproclaimed bounty. Silver and bronze coins and flowers strew the route where the procession passes. She and her priests are showered with a cloud of roses. Then a troop of armed men wearing threatening eagle plumes on their heads dance intertwined, sometimes becoming entangled

Left, bust of Cybelle. Below, Juno.

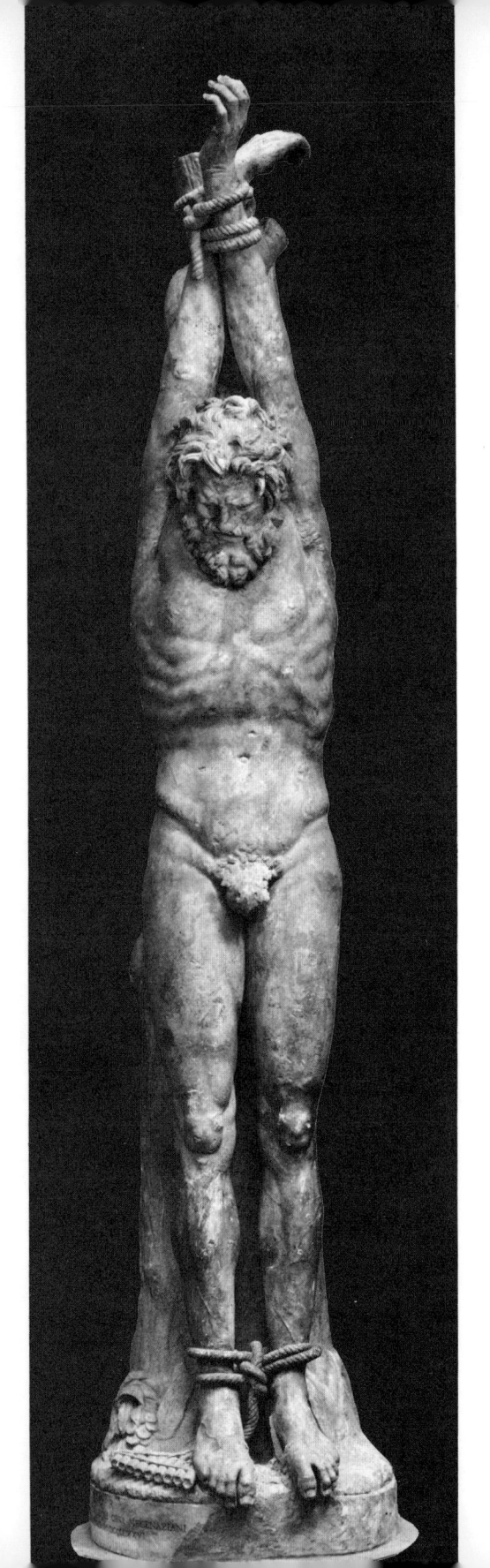

Left, Marsia. Right, fresco preserved at Herculaneum evoking Bacchus. On the following pages: reproduction of another fresco, showing a bacchanalian feast and the fountain of Plenty, Pompeii.

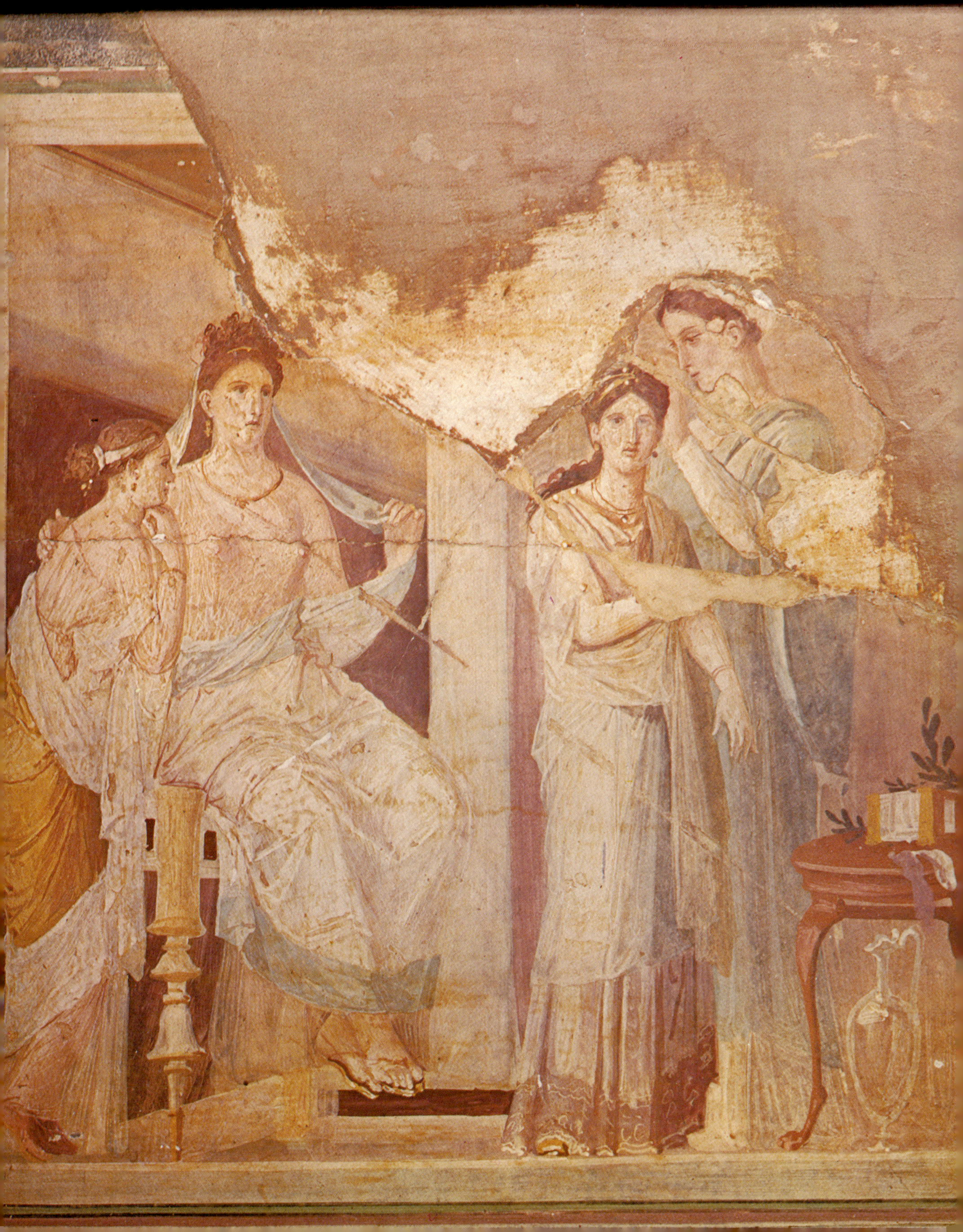

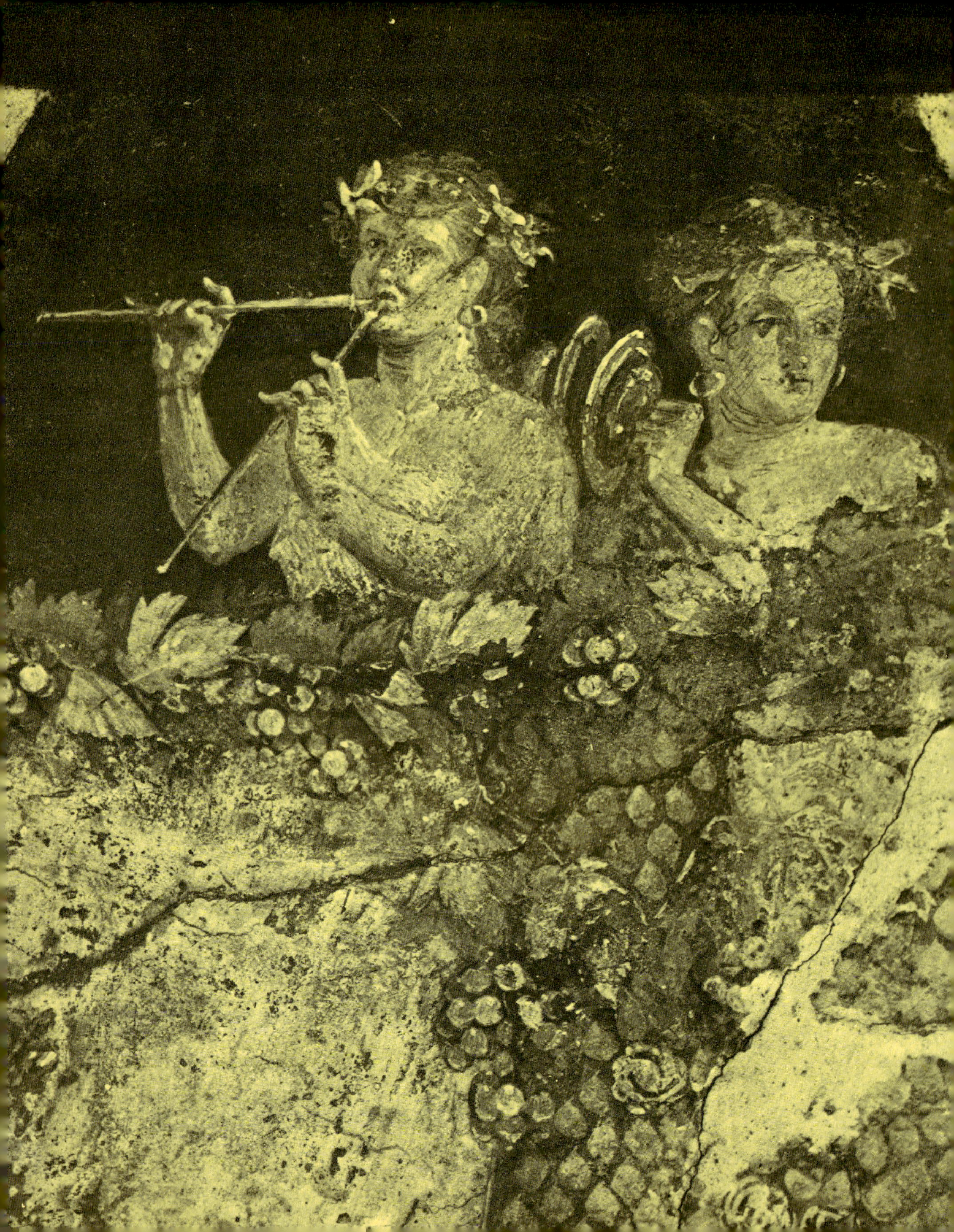

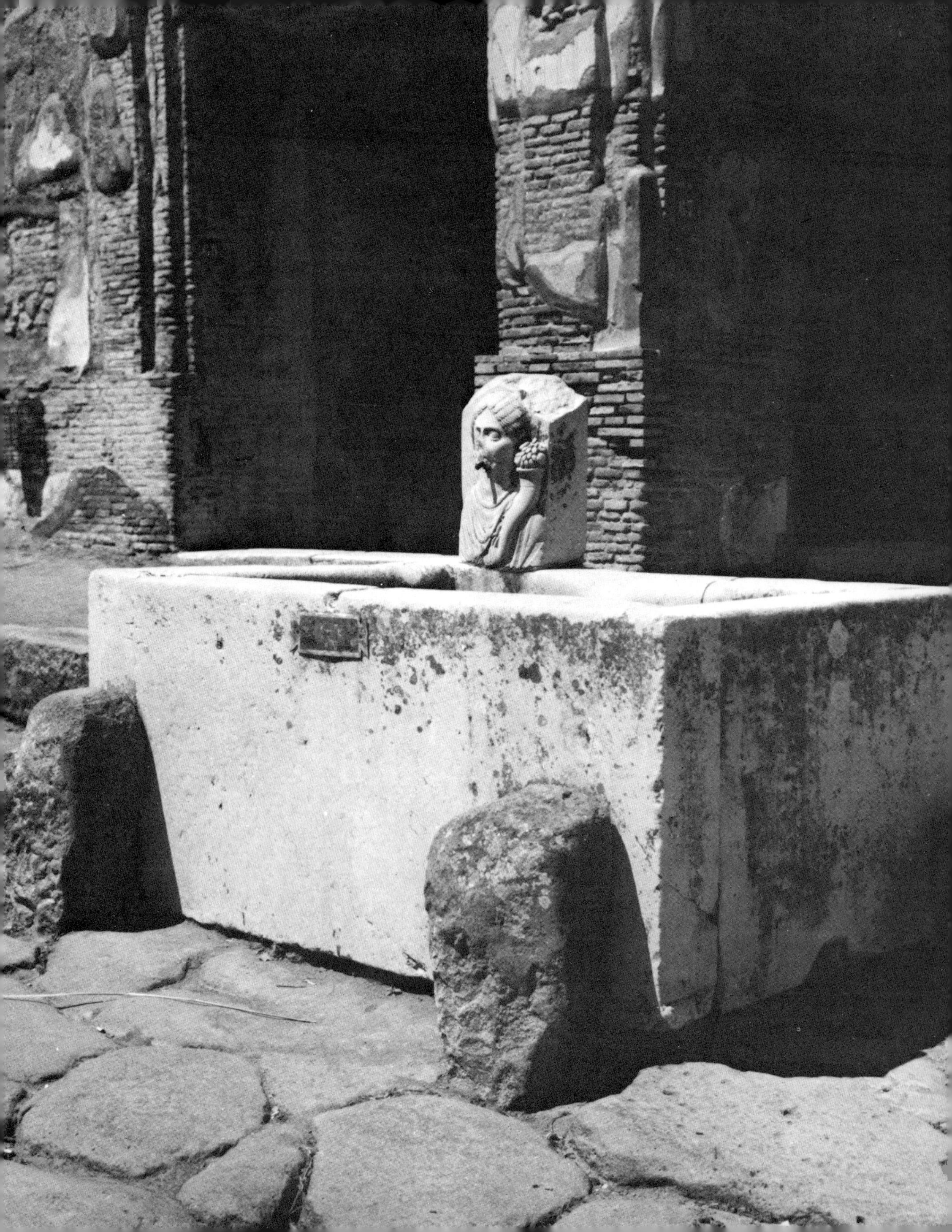

with one another and leaping in time with the beat of the instruments, while the blood flows from the wounds they inflict."

As these strange rites formed part of the public cult, a certain reserve was maintained, but they compensated for the mysteries of Bacchus in secret. Listen to Titus Livy:

"A Greek, a kind of priest and divine, had brought this mysterious religion into Etruria, and by contagion it spread to Rome. A woman from Campania, claiming to have received an order from heaven, increased ceromonies to five per month and arranged them during the night. It was nothing more than a hideous mixture of debauchery and crimes. Bemused with drink and excessive wantonness, men overtaken by convulsive twitchings thought they were inspired by god. Women dressed as priestesses of Bacchus and their hair unbound, would rush to the Tiber to plunge burning torches into the water and withdraw them alight. This was a symbol of god himself, for at the same time, the sun, from time to time plunged into darkness and light, was the living fire and creator who descends, seeming to vanish in the bosom of creation, but there to make seeds fruitful and develop life by its power and radiance. To initiates, who were accepted under the age of twenty, they expounded the oriental doctrine that actions are of no importance and consequently that everything is allowed. Furthermore there arose out of this fraternity false witness, false signatures, faked wills, slanderous accusations murder and poisoning. Those who refused initiation, and the oath of secret or infamous actions, were hurled by a device into dark vaults. Savage roarings and the sound of drums and cymbals muffled the cries of the sacrificed and dishonoured victims. "The sect was already so large as to form a people almost; men and women from the noble houses added their membership."

A decree of the senate of which we possess a copy, decided that there should be no more bacchanalia either in Rome or in Italy, but that the altars and statues formerly consecrated to Bacchus should be preserved. Later, they began to hear talk of Christians. At that time, Christians were confused in the mind of the crowd with the Jews. Followers of the old law and of the new, all prayed in the synagogues on the same feast days and seemed to worship the same god, the god of Abraham, of Isaac, and of Jacob, who had given them all the same sign of being his chosen ones,— the baptims of blood, of which many Christians still bore the mark. In Rome where they were not very plentiful, they lived in the same quarter as the Jews, which was a kind of Ghetto and a centre of small industries and dwellings. However they distinguised themselves from the children of Israel by their faith in Christ and the Resurrection, and by the wider understanding of their doctrine of which Saint Paul had just become theologian by way of his teaching in Rome, and his Epistles. But as they had no canonical books nor decrees of council to define and preserve dogma, their faith, still in the state of orally transmitted legend, had a quality of uncertainty and transitoriness which for this very reason resulted in its spreading more easily than a narrow rigid formula.

The new ideas, either of the Christian or the Jewish faith attracted disciples from time to time, because they fulfilled the secret aspi-

A Christian emblem on a Roman wall.

The Jewish seven-branched chandelier and emblem of Israel figuring in the triumph of Titus after the destruction of Jerusalem. (Rome, bas-relief of the Arch of Titus.)

rations of exalted delicate souls that were otherwise unsatisfied by the religious sterility of the established cult. They even permeated the palace of the prince. Josephus reports that he was introduced to Poppea by a Jewish writer of comedy of whom Nero was very fond. Josephus, of high birth amongst his own race, very scholarly and even more cunning and ingratiating, won the good graces of Poppea. She, like many women of that time and indeed of all times, combined religion with pleasure. He said: "She had a very religious spirit." Let us understand that this heartless woman was nevertheless deeply distressed in her soul by the great problem that was afoot at the time. Former gods were dying; she was looking for a new god and many others did the same. Actaea for example, Nero's first love, did so, and many of her freed slaves seemed to have become Christian, according to the inscriptions on their tombs. A strict matron, Pomponia Graecina, who never abandonned her mourning weeds, who was never seen to smile, and who was accused of strange superstitions, was no doubt either Christian or Jewish too. So in the heart of Roman society, even within the highest ranks, faiths were creeping in which were hostile to the established religion. They made no clamour and remained in the shade but you could feel them noiselessly gaining ground. Some feared the wrath of the gods who must have been vexed by such profane sermons. The Jews and the Christians cursed pagan idolatry in their canticles, and they understood sufficiently to know that Rome, her gods and her empire were the subject of their religious abhorrence. Despite the foreign language, their prophecies of foreboding spread abroad: "I have seen the infidel; he was taller than the cedars of Lebanon; but I passed on; already he was gone.—Jehovah has broken the tyrant's rod; he has whipped the peoples with his wrath.—You have fallen from the heavens a morning Star to be cast down upon the earth, you who commanded all nations!"

Rome had tolerated a cult which was an absolute contradition of its own for political reasons and out of disdain for the common people. But the sect that was newly come from Judea aroused violent hatred with its secret meetings which permitted a belief in criminal practices, and the worship of a man who died on the cross which was a gallows for slaves, and one who seemed to be an incitement to revolution. When more was known about the Christians, Tacitus and Suetonius referred to them only with scorn. "These unfortunate people", said Tacitus, "hated for their profanities, owe their name to Christ, who was crucified under Tiberius. His death momentarily suppressed this execrable superstition. It spread in Judea, where it originated, as far as Rome, where all the vices and crimes of the universe come together and gain ground". After the fire of Rome in Nero's time, some people said: "They are the guilty ones!" The crowd, terrified by a great scourge, needed nothing more to rush upon these men, who were enemies of their gods and whom they never saw at the feasts or sharing their entertainments.

When Nero had captured the victims necessary to him being those whom he was certain no one would defend, he made plans to seal reconciliation with the mob by arranging a great feast in which those he had condemned would play a role. It was not easy to vary the entertainment for the regular visitors to the amphitheatre. The cross, the axe, and red hot tongs were things seen every day. To throw these wretches to the stake would be poaching on the ground of the circus. To bury them alive would be to detract from the

Christians thrown to the lions.

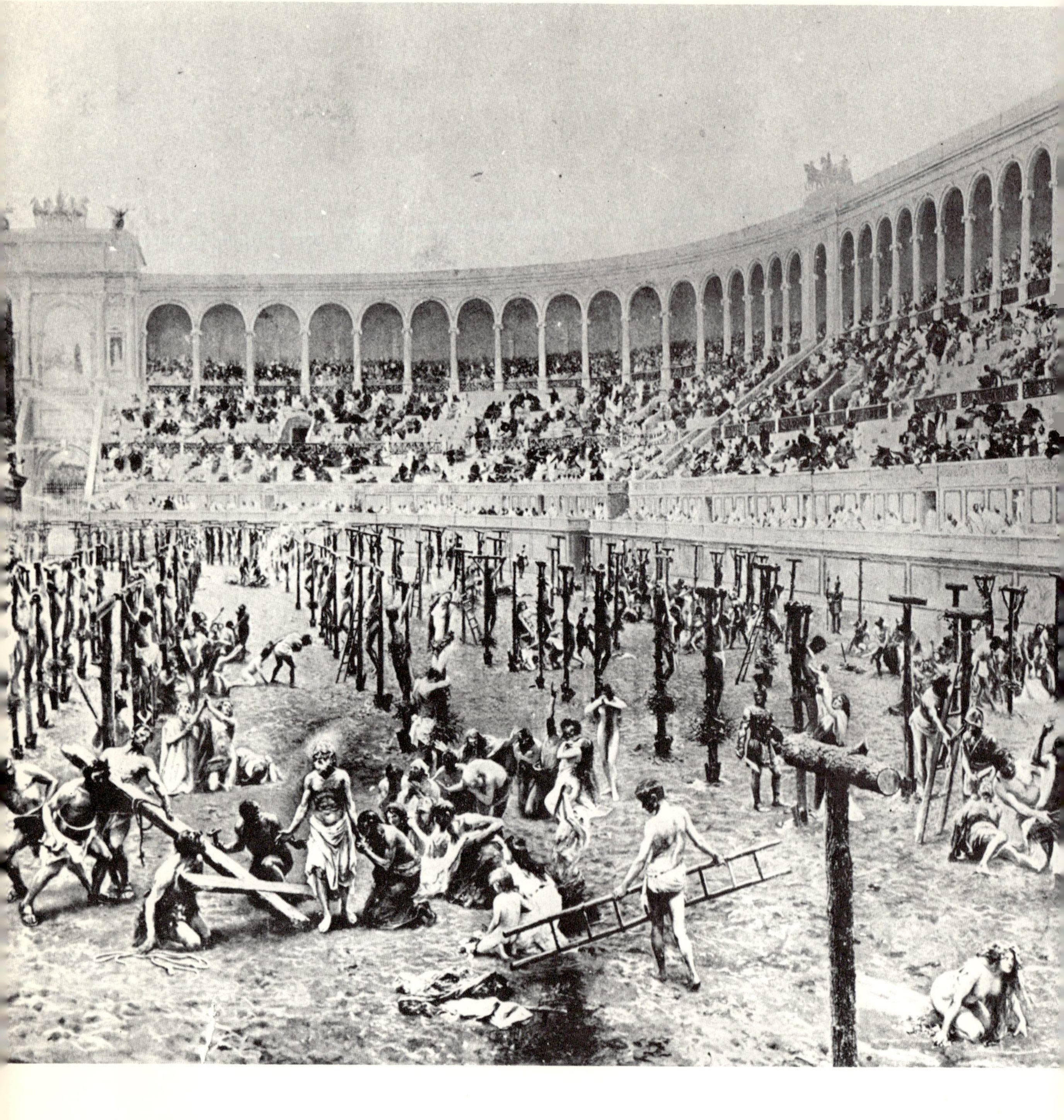

appeal of the spectacle,—the sight of agony, pain and death. They wrapped some of them in animal skins and exposed them to mad dogs who tore them to pieces. That was again reminiscent of the arena; Nero found something better. Those who remained were coated in resin and bound to stakes alive so that they could watch the games that were being put on for the crowd in the palace gardens like this. When evening came, they set fire to them, and they became the

An engraving, which according to contemporary documents, portrays one of the early Christian martyrs. Busts of Nero.

torches that illuminated the orgy. When recounting these cruel pass-times, Tacitus became moved to some measure of pity for the victims despite himself.

Rome had easily got the better of a religion of limited sway, like Druidism; it was strictly nationalistic and powerless to expand. For the reverse reasons, Christianity, which is now spreading amongst the masses inaccessible to the philosophers, will become the most feared enemy for this society, whose head is at the same time master both of things human and things divine, both emperor and sovereign pontiff. It will find strength in its weakness, and life in its burning desire for death; and the magnificent poem that Nero's martyrs have just begun to write will be one of its claims to the conquest of the world. If Seneca is not too sure what he should think about God, Providence, the human soul and the future life, and about all the uncertainties that the theologian does not experience, but which disturb the thoughts of the philosopher, he is well aware of what should be done in the present life... first and foremost for his own improvement.

Tertullian said of Seneca: "He is often one of us." In his treatises and letters you find scorn for wealth, pain and death, in fact. Life is a suffering that we endure; death is delivrance.—We have an ulcer that gnaws at us, sin; we must be cured from it before all else.—The beginning of health is the recognition of one's sin, and the recovery of the soul is the great task of the philosopher. This point is reached through the development of one's spiritual self, and by following the advice of philosophy.

These spiritual preoccupations are marked in the conduct of one's life by a horror of evil and a love of the good, as on a level with some of the refinements and extreme severities of Christianity. The Stoics, and even the Epicureans and Cynics gave counsel like Saint Paul, the celibate; they condemned excesses of the senses, honoured chastity and modesty and held all the rigours of the Church against adultery, and showed complete disdain for the pleasures and pains of the flesh. They delighted in abstinence and fasting; they had to deter Marcus Aurelius from doing it when he was ill. Demonax said: "Happiness belongs only to the free man, and the only person who is free is he who fears nothing and hopes for nothing."

The Cynics wanted no personal possessions and begged in the streets. Others of a more austere character waited for alms, like Demetrius who had refused two hundred thousand sesterces from Caligula and braved the wrath of Nero. Seneca, who sought conversation with him, said of him: "I do not doubt that nature gave him life that he should serve as an example and as a living reproach to our age. When I see him little short of naked and lying on straw, it seems to me that truth has found in him, not an interpreter, but a testimony." He was a "confessor" of philosophy.

The Stoics' only claim to recognition was because they thought they possessed a breath of universal reason or a spark of the divine Word. "Our bodies are like the bodies of the animals", they said, "but our souls are part of the divine spirit. We are the sons of Jupiter and a god is within us."

There were "sermonisers", or clergy of a particular sort, who did not belong to a hierarchy or obey any rules, who had no dogma or theology but who wandered as they pleased according to their inspiration and fancy. Many charlatans joined them as they found it a good way to lead a lazy life. Even fanatics were known, including heretical characters like Peregrinus who climbed on to a pyre on Olympus because he wanted to show off. It is not surprising either that the philosophers inspired Lucian, as the monks inspired Erasmus. Tatian, a Christian who finally led a heresy said of them: "What do your philosophers hold that is so great? I see nothing extraordinary about them, unless it is that they grow their hair, have beards,

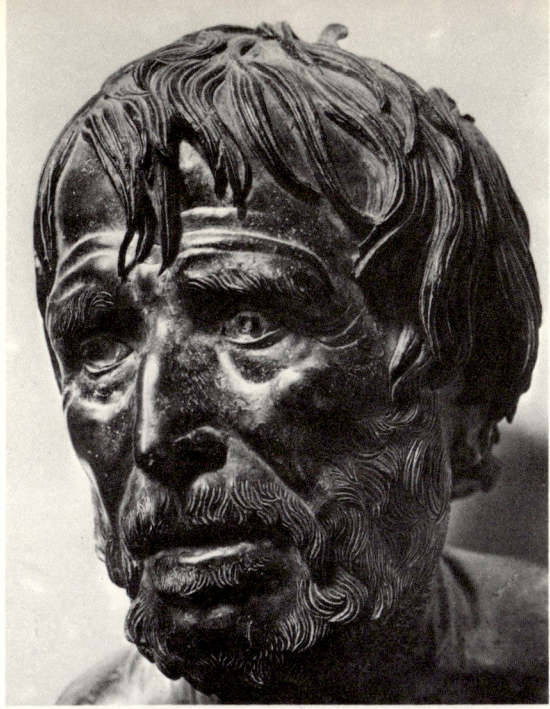

Seneca.

Doves painted by Christians in the catacombs of Saint Sebastian on the Via Appia.

and finger nails as long as animals' claws. They profess to have need of no-one, but yet they need the currier to provide their pouches, a turner to produce their staffs, a tailor to make their cloaks, and plenty of money and a good cook to satisfy their love of food."

It had always been part of the policy, as well as a characteristic of the religion of Rome, to bestow the freedom of the city on the gods of their conquered peoples, even when the senate refused it to their worshippers. Under the empire, the frequency and reliability of communications made it easier to spread this form of religious propaganda and Olympus housed many divinities. Rome, the religious capital of the world, as she was also the political capital, was already referred to as "the most holy city".

The new gods were sought in that part of the world to which everything was leaning. Trade, arts and letters, philosophy, even the preferred language, were all moving towards the Orient. Religious thought was once more following this trend, and the princes themselves encouraged it. Marcus Aurelius filled Rome with foreign cults.

The Oriental religions brought in their train, nevertheless, their habitual incantations, sacrificial purifications, and wild forms of devotion such as Greece and Rome had not known. They were boisterous, theatrical and appealed to the emotions of tragedy, and were going to transform the simple faith of the western provinces. The cults of the two sun gods, Adonis and Atys fitted this description. Death and resurrection, images of the renewal of the seasons and so on, gave place to festivals to which the oriental peoples brought every extreme of joy and grief; there were fasting, funereal lamentations and whippings with boned lashes. There would even be bloodshed, wounds, horrible mutilations or joyful hymns, orgiastic dances and obscene singing. Such also were certain rites of the cults of Cybele and Mithra, well-known for their bull sacrifices.

Prudentius, describing one of these sacrifices to Cybele, the Great Mother, tells of the crowd coming to the celebration from all over, as the person arranging it was lavishing on it everything that he could afford and the clergy were going to provide all their pomp. They dug a pit near the temple, and a neophyte went down into it to the sound of sacred music. He wore magnificent vestments, his forehead was bound with decorations and a golden crown was on his head. The covering above the pit had an opening in it, and on to the covering they led a bull, whose horns had been gilded and flanks thickly garlanded with flowers. Temple attendants would make him kneel down, whereupon a priest would inflict a large wound on him with the sacrificial knife. The blood would flow freely and the pit would fill with its warm vapour. The novice would stand with his arms outstretched and head thrown back in an effort to ensure that no drop of blood touched the ground before he had intercepted it. His ears, eyes, lips, mouth, and the whole of his body had to be steeped in it. When he reappeared, streaming with "the life-giving rain", he was regarded as a fortunate being, "regenerated for eternity",—rather than an object of horror and disgust.

The priests of such cults were no longer men who undertook to pray for the republic in the temple, and when out of the temple became citizens and magistrates again, as the priests of Rome did. They were a real clergy, dedicated to the service of the god or goddess, who claimed to be responsible for divine affairs alone, and wore a special from of dress.

Many people had a strong yearning for the unknown and they would discuss how to approach it with anyone who claimed to know a path. All believed in magic, to begin with the government which was very afraid of it, and including also pagans, Christians and Jews. The law dealt very severely with it, condemning those who practised it to be burnt, and those who studied it to be thrown

A statue of Minerva in the temple dedicated to her. Above, a temple of Isis below, the temple of the Sibyl at Tivoli.

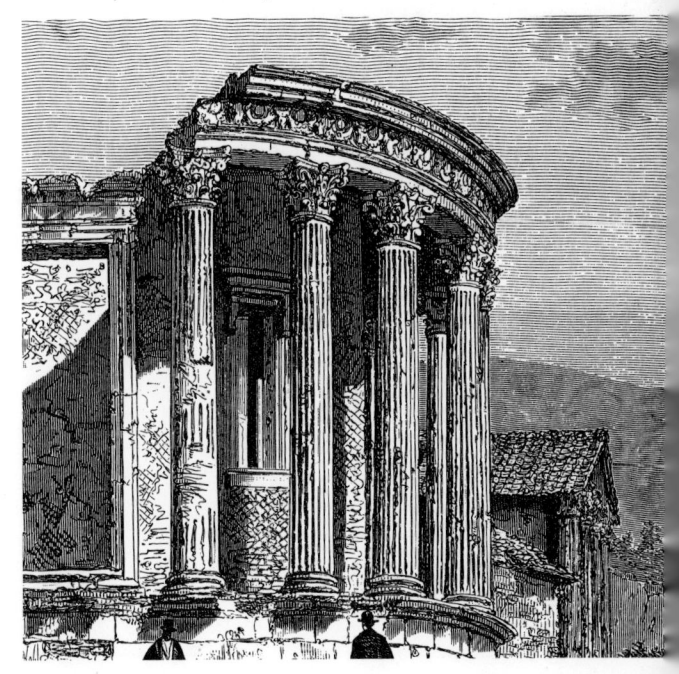

137

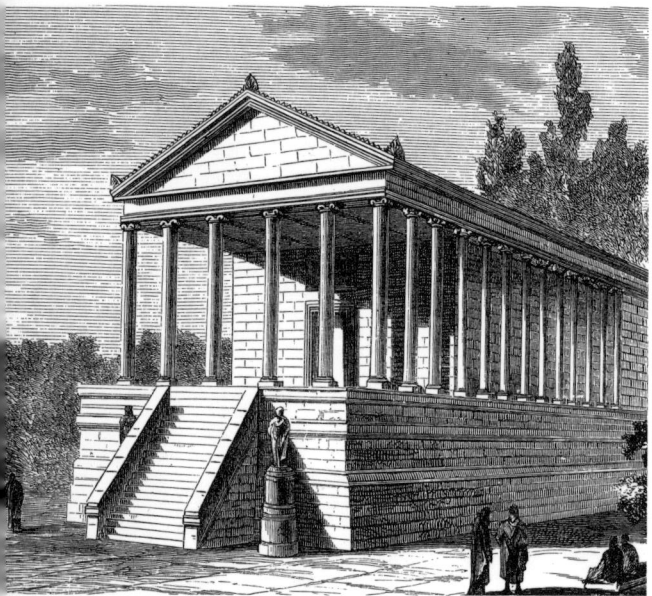

to the animals. Practice of magic only became the more common however, and its secrets added to the confusion of men's minds. The most sceptical thinkers left a trail of superstition behind them as inevitable as their own remains. Pliny the Elder, who did not believe in God although he believed in virtue, accepted omens and miracles, recounting them with imperturbable seriousness. They still practised the careful study of the entrails of sacrificed victims, and dreams were examined for revelations of the future. The Chaldeans created "nativity themes" which sometimes became sentences of death when they promised great fortune to certain contemporaries of Tiberius, Domitian, or Caracalla. Predictions made by astrologers and the sibylline prognostications supposed that destiny had decided everything in advance, whilst the oracle, on the other hand, gave one to believe that the gods intervened liberally in everything that takes place on earth.

Monotheism, vaguely conceived by primitive peoples, is the basis of Hinduism as much as of Hellenism. The Semites, surrounded by their desert of sky and land in Arabia had naturally preserved it, but in both India and Greece it was masked and hidden by the rich drapes that poets had hung around the doorways of the holy sanctuaries. Anaxagoras found this to be true of Athens and Cicero of Rome. Cicero set out to produce the most unsullied speculations on Greek thought, and arrived at the idea of divine unity and immortality of the soul, not in consequence of rigorous deductions from a philosophy based on everything being linked together, but through a noble warmth of heart. The Stoics had replaced the incomprehensible God of Plato, and the solitary God of Aristotle by a living God who penetrated the universe and filled it with his own life.

Philo, whose influence had been so great on the school of Alexandria, and even on some Fathers of the Church, had developed the theory of the triple God in one, post Augustus and Tiberius. Such a Trinity had

Left, restoration of the temples of Saturn and of Venus, Rome. Above, Christian hand drawings in the catacombs.

been worshipped by Egypt, Chaldea, Persia, India, Pelasgian Greece and Gaul. From the bosom of the Eternal God, who was withdrawn into the impenetrable depths of his being there sprang the very first emanation. Out of it emerged "the elder son of God, the oldest of the angels." Philo also calls him "the divine man" because man on earth had been created in his image.

The first-born of God, Creator of the universe is the "Word of God" or Divine Wisdom which governs the world. He in turn engenders the "Spoken Word" of the Holy Spirit which gives life by its grace, "The Holy Virgin who acts as a mediator between God who gives and the human soul that receives."

For many years, the Christian faith was propagated only amongst the lower levels of the population, where it offered consolation for every kind of suffering, and charity, as preached at its inception by Christ himself and Saint Paul. It condemned wealth which it considered to be "the fruits of iniquity or the inheritance of injustice". Christianity cherished poverty and suffering as a means of redemption of life on earth. Philosophers, who opened their heavens to the souls of the elite only, reproached christianity for its concern with the humble. How sweet to the ears of the disinherited were the words of equality before God, of the redemption of souls by the son of the Father, insulted, derided, beaten and condemned to death on a cross of slavery for them! Christ's passion was the story of themselves, and the Good Tidings seemed to apply especially to the children. Their heroes of ancient time had been the strong and the valiant like Hercules and Theseus. Then it was the sage, and now the new hero was to be the saint, whom all could become, and it was through sentiment, and not through knowledge, that Christianity intended to conquer the world.

The Christian cult was pure. There were no bloody sacrifices and nothing which did not aim to arouse the best sentiments in us. The services consisted of hymns, prayers, the reading of the Gospel and the supreme act of direct communion with God. If there were some already making Christianity the religion of the God of divine vengeance, who wanted to attribute sad and lugubrious characteristics to him, for most it was the religion of the Good Shepherd looking after his sheep, defending them against the ravaging wolves, and bringing back on his shoulders the sheep that was lost. This was the image of grace, kindness and love, often repeated in the catacombs of Rome, that was the favourite symbol of the Christian faith at that time. Then as now, hope was everything, and there was peace and serenity even in death. A dove represented the spirit rising to heaven.

Men of letters and Roman high society did not know Christianity in the second century, or if they did, it was an imperfect version. Examples are Tacitus, Suetonius, Juvenal, Pliny the Younger, Plutarch, Lucian, Hadrian, and Marcus Aurelius himself. Some took it for one of the philosophical sects.

However, the Church began to emerge from the shadow that had protected its beginnings. Already a number of pagan doctors had joined its ranks, and Justinian had just been courageous enough to bring it right out into the open. It was destined to spread rapidly, and after the reign of Commodus, to truly penetrate the high ranks of Roman society. The simple powerful originality of its dogma offered it an enormous power of attraction.

Left, "the good shepherd" from a Christian sarcophagus.
Above, the head of a Fury asleep.

Bust of a Roman goddess and statue of the Marine Victory at Ostia. (See page 96.)

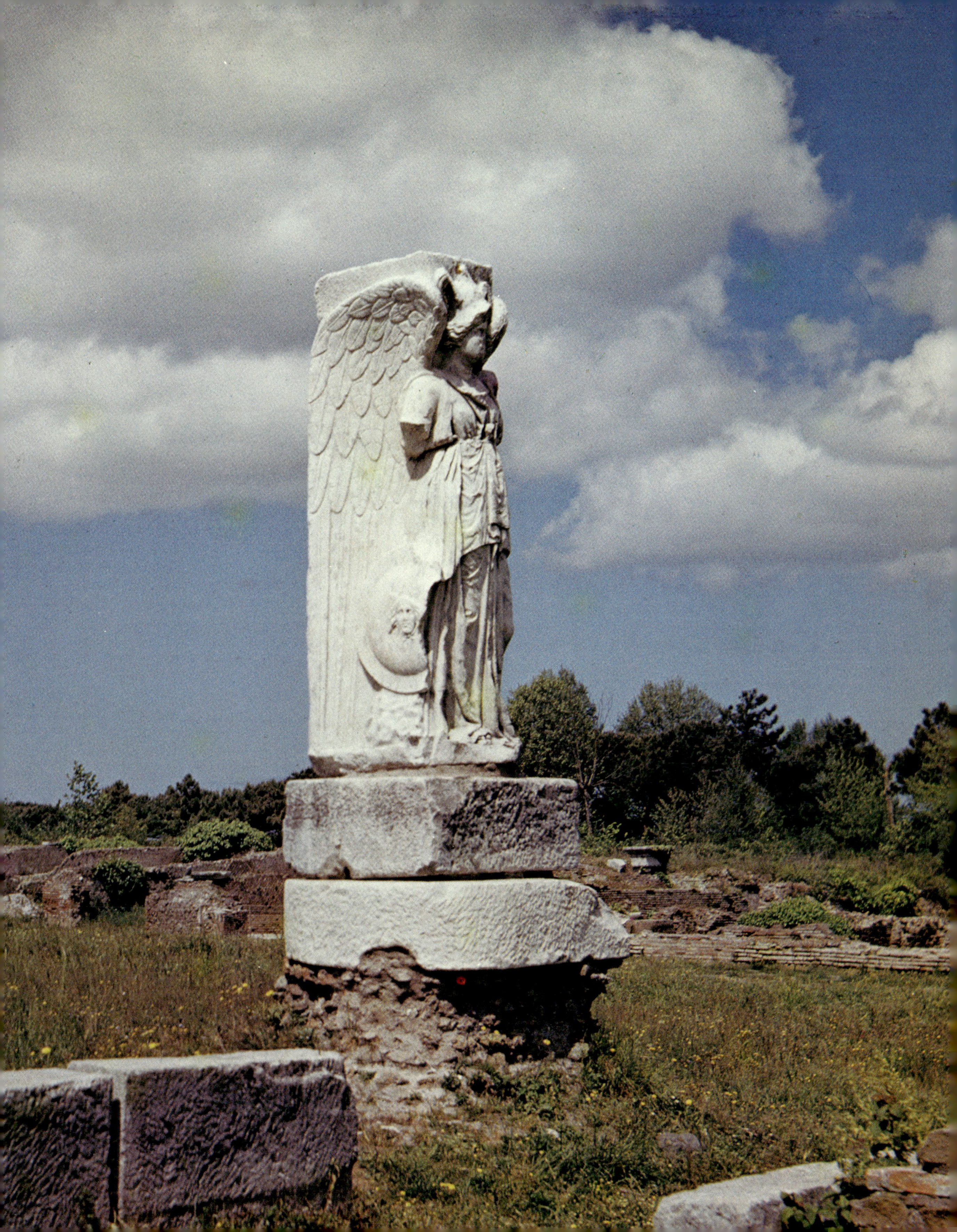

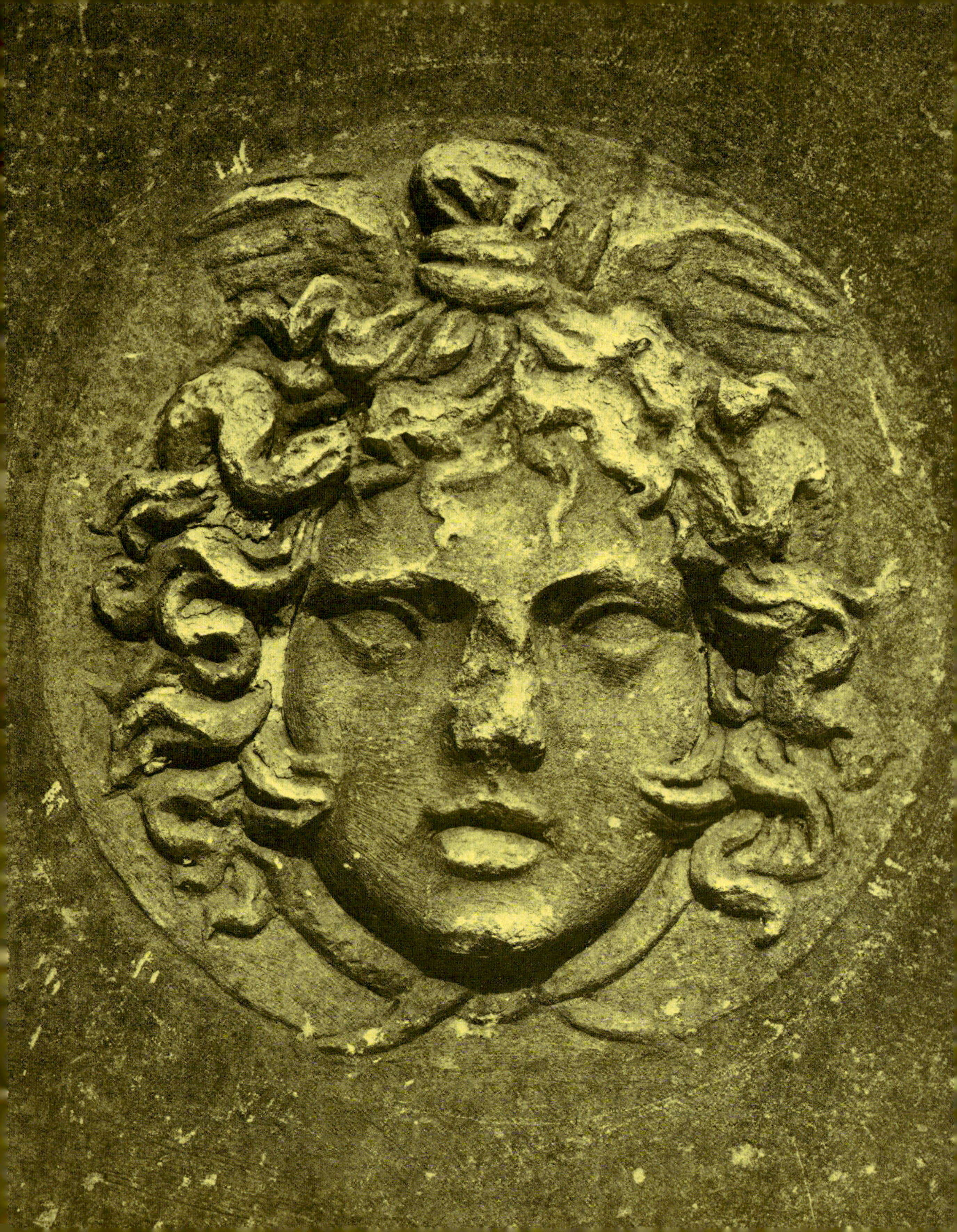

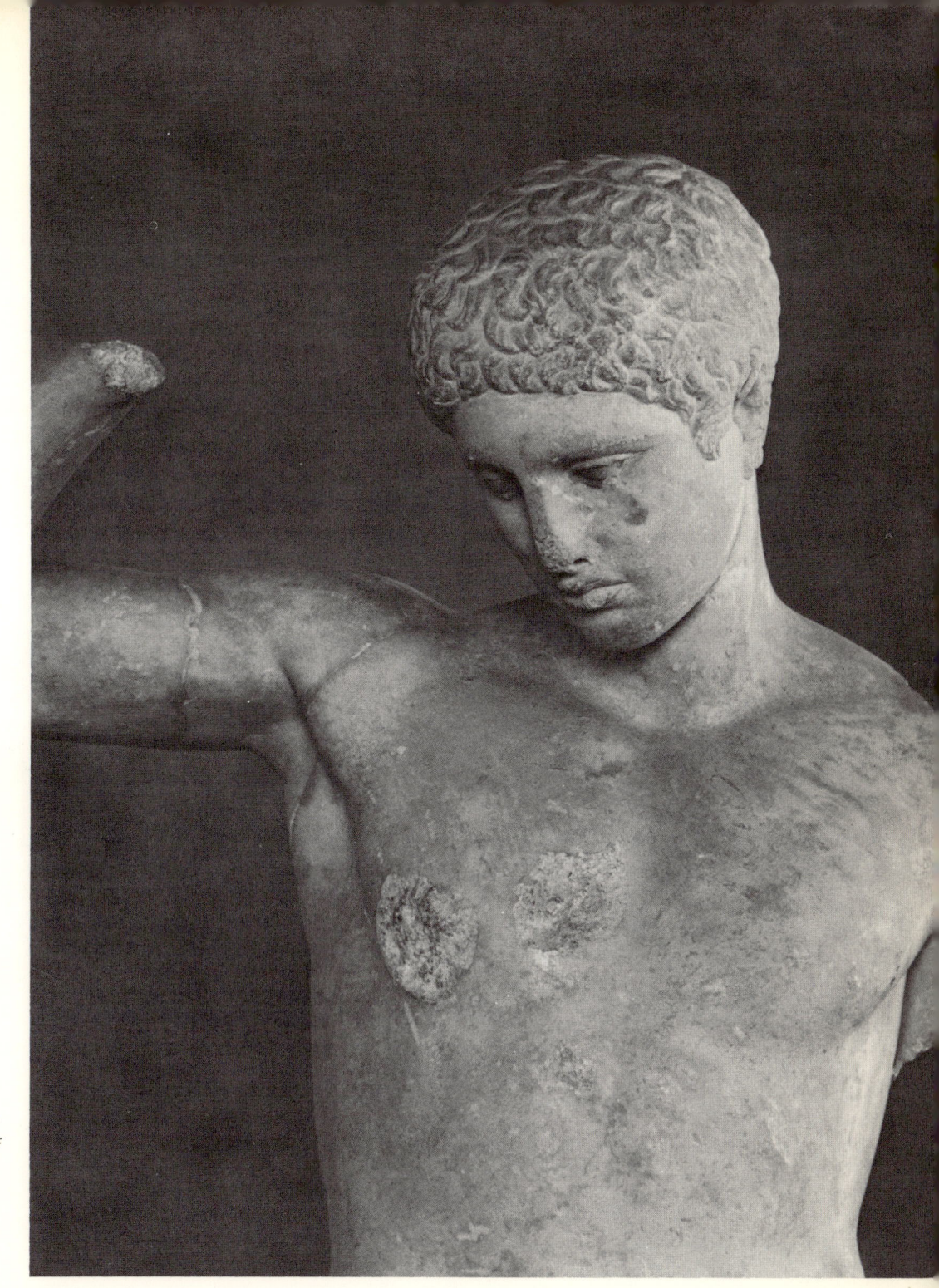

Decoration on a sarcophagus and bust of an athlete bestowing the victory crown upon himself.

145

Conclusion

Empires are like people. They hold places of honour in the minds of men only because of the greatness of the works they have achieved. Greece, the sanctuary of all art and thought, is like her poet, "youthful still in her glory and immortality."

Rome deserves less admiration, but nevertheless remains a model to the world for her politics, law, administration, and art of war.

Her legal advisers stated the true bases of justice and the moral sciences when they inscribed the following definition of law made by Celsus as a heading to their books: "Jus est ars boni et aequi", or the three precepts of Ulpius: "Honeste vivere, alterum non laedere, suum cuique tribuere".

Her system of municipal organisation has endured longer than one would think, and has handed down administrative rules that still exist. Widespread domination of Rome and the accompanying wave of Greek philosophy which was a monotheistic movement that appealed to the more enlightened intelligences, and the wretched conditions of life experienced by the vast numbers of "humiliores" all contributed to the growth of Christianity. The early groups of believers were protected by the laws which had been set up for the funeral colleges, and the Church used the imperial institutions as a model for her own hierarchy, for the empire had preserved so many pagan customs that could now draw people gently to her fold.

Rome did nothing for theoretical science, for the day of great conquests of nature had not dawned; she holds second place in respect of arts and literature, a rank she holds honourably, the arts and letters being the booty of her wars. Phidias was not born on one of the Seven Hills, and there is only one Parthenon, yet by copying Greek temples, statues and medallions, the Romans added importance to elements in art that Athens and Corinth neglected or ignored. Take the arch and the vault, for example, neither of which were used during the golden age of Hellenic art. The Romans like the Greeks had of course built quadrangular temples but they had also constructed triumphal arches for their great captains, and for the needs of their empire and the pleasures of their cities, the domed Pantheon, aqueducts, circuses and amphitheatres. In addition they made military roads which carried their legions and their will to the ends of the earth; they also built bridges over the great rivers, some of which we have not restored. They built too the Colosseum and the Baths of Caracalla, whose mountains of stone, though massive and ponderous, rise from the ground with such majesty that they could be taken as a symbol of Roman domination. Greece has no claim at all to work of this kind, at most the hands that carried it out, not the spirit that was behind it. Rome created a civil architecture and made people understand the need for large-scale public works. Mosaic is also a Roman art. If the literature of Rome was but an echo of Greece, Rome brought civilisation to the west, where Greece had done nothing. Her language which gave birth to the national tongue of the Latin nations, can if need be, become a means of communication between scholars of all countries, and her books if chosen with circumspection, will always provide the best literature for engaging the mind at the highest possible cultural level. Roman literature has truly deserved the title "litterae humaniores" the literature that creates men.

It is true that when the Romans put their hands on the treasures of Alexander's successors, the scandal of their orgies surpassed anything that had been seen in the distant Orient for a century long. Her pleasures were bloody sports or immoral shows, and Roman thought which had been temporarily fortified by Greek philosophy became lost to oriental mysticism. Finally, lover of freedom though she was, Rome accepted despotism, as if wanting to astonish the world by the magnitude of her corruption as well as by her greatness of empire. But have not other periods in history known spiritual servility, excesses in public entertainment, and an ostentatious way of life such as you find anywhere where idleness and wealth go together?

Left: Forum walls, Pompeii. Above, Roman soldiers (Rome, Constantine's Arch).

One more legacy must be attributed to Rome, and one which should be regarded as the most precious. Despite the poetic piety of Virgil and the official credulity of Titus Livy, the predominant characteristic of Latin literature is the indifference of Horace, since it is without the audacity of Lucretius. In the eyes of Cicero, Seneca, and Tacitus, and also of the legal advisers, the most imperious of all requirements was the free possession of self, and independence of philosophical thought, which all owed to the Greeks. This spirit, the true spirit of pure reason, was almost buried during the Middle Ages, but it was to reappear when the age of antiquities was discovered again.

On one of Constantine's medallions, his son is presenting him with a globe surmounted by a phoenix, symbol of immortality. This time the courtesans had been right. The sacred bird, which rises from its own ashes is the very emblem of ancient Rome which died sixteen centuries ago and still lives through her genius. "Siamo Romani".

Below and opposite: remains of the Forum, Rome.

OBREMPVBLICAM RESTITVTAM IMPERIV
INSIGNIBVS VIRTVTIBVS EORV

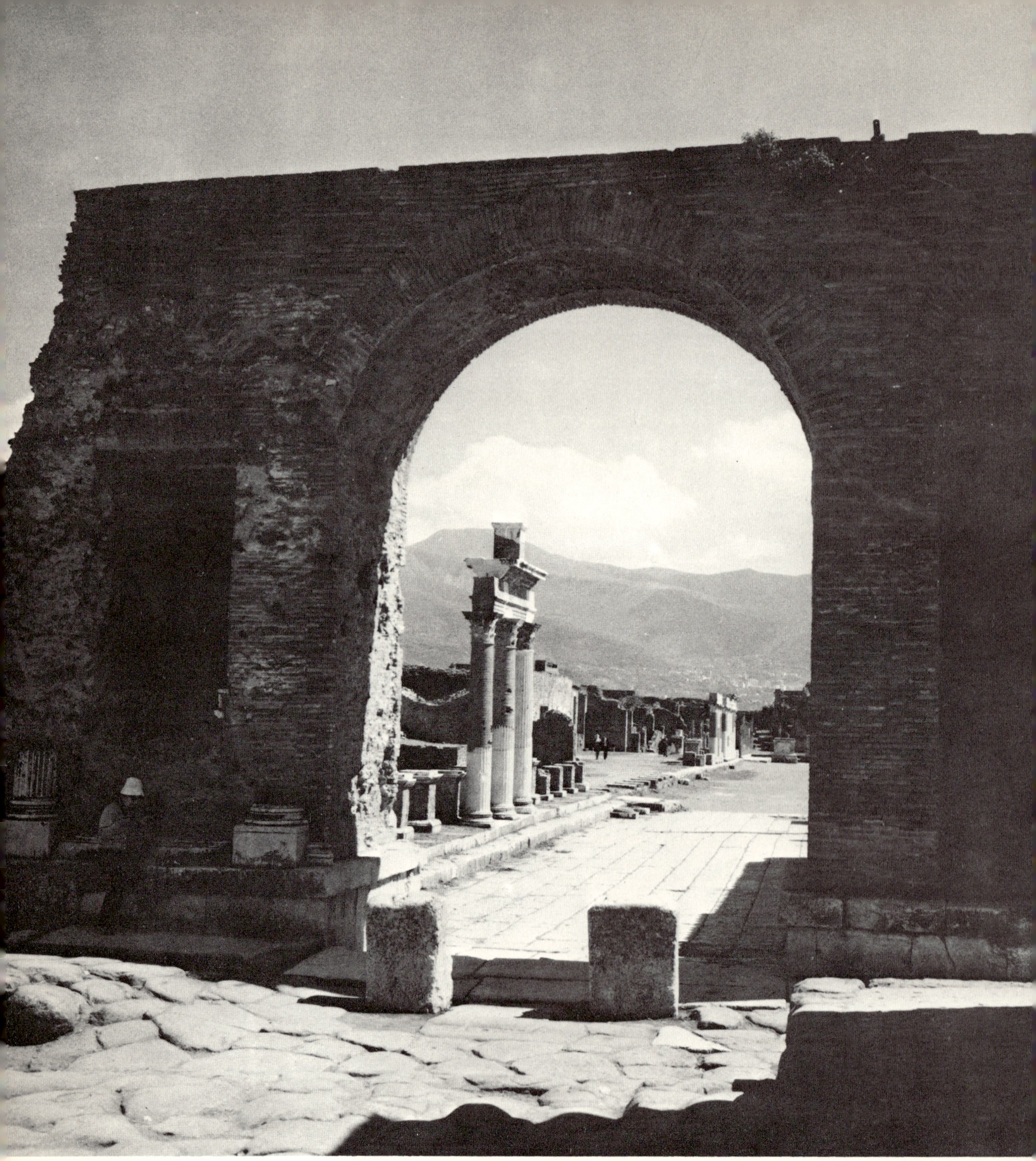

Outline of Roman History

The actions of a people are in the first place the result of their surroundings and geography. By this I mean that the sum total of the influence of soil and climate accounts for half their history. Particular virtues are even attached to particular places. "Constantinople is worthy of an empire", said Napoleon. Put Rome in Naples or Milan, and there would be no more Roman history, as there would be no more England if the two sides of the Channel were to join.

At a spot between the plains of Latium and Etruria at the foot of the Sabine hills, there arose the city which had to be the Eternal City—five leagues from the sea, stretched along the banks of the Tiber, the largest river of the Italian peninsular, and on seven easily defensible hills out of reach of malaria. Rich lands to the north and south invited plunder, whilst to the east, the mountain dwellers kept the army invicible by subjecting it to harmless but continual attacks. Near enough to the sea to know it yet not to fear it, and far enough away not to dread piracy from Greeks, Volscians or Etruscans, Rome was neither Sparta nor Athens, neither exclusively maritime nor exclusively continental. The Romans, originating from semi-mountainous country near to the plains and the coast, united all the three characteristics of the Italian races, shepherd, tiller of the soil, and sailor, without resembling any one of them. The result was that there was no conflict of custom or belief between the Romans and any one type to prevent the establishment of a large strong and united State, including the whole of the peninsula. Rome could show a familiar face and hold out a friendly hand to all her neighbours when the battle was over.

Just as Rome was the centre of Italy, Italy was the centre of the ancient world, and as such she was very vulnerable to outside attack, though impregnable if her citizens could build her into a fortress; such people were the Romans. Furthermore, the only enemies they had to fear were the Greeks and the Carthaginians. The Carthaginians had expressed their ambitions in the east and the Greeks in the west. The Gallic peoples of the Po valley, whilst offering the danger of an incursion, were no menace to any durable organisation surrounded by so many fortified towns ringed with massive ramparts; if they reached the foot of the Capitol it was in consequence of a surprise.

You have to add the influence of hereditary instincts to the influence of geography if the Romans belong to one common ethnic group, and also the traditions they bring from their various places of origin if they are a mixture of several tribes. Also to be considered are the reactions of all these elements on one another to form the national character, and finally, the circumstances of history, or in other words, external influences which determine the course of her fortune.

The way of life of the earliest Roman was strict, sparing, and industrious, whilst his religion was a cult stripped of all grandeur just as his spirit was stripped of ideals. His was the religion of the peasant bent over his plough, for he was concerned only with defending himself and staying alive. His gods were little people, his prayers self-interested demands and his sacrifices bargainings with the divinity. He made his offertory on condition that the divinity would give back in return, and was always ready to say, as one of the high pontiffs said one day to Jupiter; "If you do not, then I will not."

No one could equal him in courage and tenacity on the battle field, yet in ordinary

Tiberius' Arch, Pompeii.

life he would tremble at the flitting bird, the scurrying mouse and the unaccustomed sound. His deep sense of superstition and unrelieved piety which limited him to the recitation of incomprehensible formulae and rituals took away all poetry and gaiety. He did not know how to dream nor how to sing because he had had no youth.

But how well ordered his life was! The same discipline applied to the family as was applied to society. At home, the "pater familias" was the priest of his gods, and absolute master of his wife, sons, and slaves, just as the "patres gentium" were the heads of the republic. His civic station was that due to him through birth and possessions, and nothing was left to chance. On the days when the elections or the combats took place, each person would take up the rank that the law assigned to him, and all had a sense of duty in public life that their inexorable discipline created in them. Because the Romans preserved this very sentiment throughout the centuries, they became a great nation.

Another sentiment again plays a considerable role in their history. Their whole society was dominated by religion, which allowed for no deed of a serious nature to be performed without heaven being consulted first...

The various elements which went to make up the Romans combined to create two distinctly different peoples: patricians and plebeians. The patricians founded the towns with the ones whom they had permitted to share their laws or who had had a share of such legal rights thrust upon them. They owned the land that their clients and slaves cultivated. Their leaders would meet together in the senate to discuss the affairs of the city and all of them in the assembly would nominate the magistrates and vote for their laws. They were not a nobility nor an aristocratic sect; they were unto themselves Rome in her entirety.

The Roman people did not come up with the principal organisations for running their society until after their monarchs had been driven out and their republic set up. The revolution had been made for them by the great, and everything in their new institutions had been worked out ro prevent the return of a master. The king, sovereign for life, was replaced by two consuls elected annually. The consuls were always of patrician stock.

The two consuls being endowed with equal powers, one counterbalanced the other, for they had the power to veto each other's actions merely by declaring opposition. This was the right of "intercessio", and the short duration of the magistracies made usurpation so difficult that for more than four centuries not a trace of it was seen. As a final resource against any danger that might threaten the State or the constitution, the senate set up a sovereignty again, this time temporary, the dictatorship; its legal life span was six months, and in fact right up till Sylla's time, it was never more than a few days. Except in the case of the dictatorship, Rome never had single magistrates. All the civic responsibilities were shared by several—within the censorship consulate, priesthood, town counselling, tribuneship, and sacred offices—and they grouped themselves together into colleges so that the principle of "intercessio" could always be applied.

After the fall of Carthage and Macedonia, the Romans had an empire, and they no longer retained their customs, gods and institutions which they had founded. They had adopted the arts, literature and philosophy of the Greeks, and Greece in her dying hours had avenged her defeat by handing over the sort of corruption that had degraded her riper years. In the Orient,

Brick designs on a wall in Pompeii.

where commerce and industry had accumulated vast wealth over the years, now to be handed over to the conquerors, the proconsuls no longer showed the moderation of their fathers. When they returned to Rome with their spoils from the provinces, they set up feasts at court sittings, spread vice such as had not been known before, and scorned everything they considered beneath them. Uncouth characters such as these, who had lived for so long without solving any one major problem, and who were impressed by the glories of Greek civilisation, had set up a similar school of philosophy, which incidentally brought great destruction to their national religions.

At a later date, soldiers took the place of the people and generals the place of the tribunes. Three of the most famous, who were either taken aside by someone of importance or felt that they had been unfairly rewarded for their services, pooled their bitternesses and ambition to attack the government.

Whilst Caesar gained the reputation of being the greatest of all Roman captains beyond the Alps, Crassus, another of the Triumvirs foolishly allowed himself to be killed by the Parthians, and the third, Pompey, was wounded during the full pride of his reputation, which was still on the increase, as conqueror of the Gauls. He moved into the realms of the great.

Rome abdicated in favour of Caesar. The people and the senate handed over all power to him, and because authority was concentrated thus, the interests of the governed finally became confused with the interests of the governors. The civil war and the assassination however, left the dictator little time to carry out his proposed reforms. However, some that he managed to achieve are significant.

Caesar perished at the hand of the majestic, and the State fell into terrible disorder for fourteen years. Augustus pacified the shaken world with greater flexibility but less genius.

He took upon himself all the powers of the republic, but allowed all the positions of responsibility to continue, so that judging by all appearances, Rome had acquired but one more magistrate. "The land, wearied by civil strife, accepted Augustus as its head", wrote Tacitus, "and the provinces acclaimed the fall of an incompetent government that could not restrain greedy magistrates or insolent nobles."

The Augustan administration was sufficiently wise and paternal to assure the leader a peaceful reign of forty-four years. But where were the guarantees for the future?

Rome endured hateful tyrants like Caligula, Nero, Caracalla and Elagabal whose corruption and cruelty compare only with the bloody orgies of certain Asiatic contests. She also had fine princes who gave her new light and arrested her decline. At first, the prince governed rather than administered, and the successful municipal system prepared men whose talent and experience were needed by the empire for leadership in high office.

These inheritors of Augustus, who originated a long way from the ancient land of Saturnus, were first of all the glorious Antonines from Spain and Gaul, and then the African Septimus Severus. Having been recently drawn into the Roman way of life, their provinces had embraced it with so much ardour that they had already sent orators, poets and philosophers to the Tiber, and they had also preserved, as an ineradicable imprint of the genius of Rome, the greatest quantity and the most beautiful of all ruins to be seen outside Italy. Their reign marks the brilliant period of empire, and a happier one humanity has never known. Charity, so little known in the ancient states, even entered into public affairs. Trajan's great food institution was a noble effort at official welfare that a number of cities and individual people imitated. It is a fact that the emperors were the servants of those countries which in the fourth century were servants of the princes. They preserved discipline in the army, freedom in the towns, justice in the administration, and the Barbarians' respect for a domination which seemed unshakeable. Legal advisers styled themselves priests of the law, and the senate had been recruited from every talent revealed in the cities, public office, and the army. Tacitus was afraid at the thought of a reversal of fortune. "If the Romans were to unfortunately disappear from the face of the earth, would that the gods intervene! What would happen, if not universal war between nations?" And this in fact happened when the colossus fell. Towards the middle of the third century, unfortunate circumstances handed the imperial power to men born in countries of either very old culture or crude barbarism, to Syrians made decadent by luxury or effeminacy, and to a Goth, and also to the son of an Arab thief. They heralded the beginning of convulsions in the political field which threatened the empire with approaching dissolution, and in the religious field with the invasion of oriental cults which changed the spirit of Roman society.

Change, the mighty law of the physical world, is also the law of the moral world. Roman society, which became like a body weighed down by the ties that are all around it, acts and thinks no longer. There are no more writers and artists, and no more poets to charm and excite it with their ideals.

Yet in the midst of this world which was approaching its end, there were men who were acting and thinking on their own, but with their eyes to the heavens rather than the earth, and with preoccupations of the life beyond the grave and not of this life. The Christians were not perturbed by the slavery which had replaced the free lives of the ancient Graeco-Roman cities. At first they had wished to do no more than pursue their cult peacefully, even in obscure retreats. For them Roman society was the "great prostitute", condemned by their Holy Bible. They shrank from its honours, for they did not wish to fulfil the duties thus entailed. Their misfortunes left them indifferent, and as they did not see the Barbarians as enemies, they refused to fight them. When they no longer had to fear persecution, they spent a century in bitter dispute over their beliefs, bringing no benefit to social order. During that period, the Germans arrived. The Gospel had produced saints but had not trained citizens or statesmen. The Christians had been the undoing of the pagan empire but when they were themselves its master, they did not know how to defend it: The role of the Church in the State did not begin until the Middle Ages.

Left: fragment of mosaic from the Thermal Baths of Caracalla.

Index

A

Adonis 136
Agricola 60
Agrippa 99
Agrippina 32, 61, 78, 93
Antinoüs 59, 93
Antonines 59, 77, 155
Apicius 26
Apulia 140
Architecture 93, 104
Astrology 91
Atrium 34
Augustus 32, 33, 61, 67, 76, 82, 84, 90, 91, 92, 98, 120, 154
Aurelius 57

B

Bacchus 74, 76, 128
Brutus 59

C

Caligula 33, 41, 61, 134, 154
Capitol 75, 98, 105, 118, 123, 151
Caracalla 48, 88, 104, 138, 154
Cato 15, 20, 44, 121
Celibate 84
Celsus 91
Ceres 64, 110
Caesar 24, 32, 59, 83, 91, 153
Christians 128, 129, 130, 137
Cicero 30, 59, 90, 92, 117, 138, 148
Circus 57, 130
Claudius 50, 61, 67, 78, 90
Clients 10, 13
Colosseum, Coliseum 48, 104, 147
Commerce 22
Concubinage 82
Constantine 149
Contract 79
Convenient 57, 140
Corporation 14
Crassus 42
Cybele 123, 136

D

Diocletian 88
Dionysius Chrysostomes 7, 42, 44
Divorce 84
Doctor 92
Domitian 10, 32, 42, 61, 64, 74, 138

E

Ediles 8
Election 7
Engagement 78
Epicurus 27, 30
Esquiliae 60, 98

F

Farmer 60 (see Agricola)
Feast 20, 87
Forum 85, 104, 120
Fortune 85, 140, 120
Fraternity 11
Freed slave 90
Funeral rites 14, 84, 87, 120

G

Galen 27, 57
Games 50, 56, 57
Ganymede 59
Ghosts 111, 115, 117, 120
Gladiators 9, 57, 58
Gods 105
Gospel 140
Gracchi 58, 82
Greeks 5, 20, 91, 92, 110, 121
Guild 14

H

Hadrian 58, 59, 76, 93, 140
Hall 34 (see atrium)
Hippocrates 12, 91
Horace 59, 61, 77, 148

I

Isis 123

J

Jews 128, 129, 137
Josephus 129
Juno 68
Jupiter 13, 105, 117, 123, 134
Jurisconsult 12, 80
Juvenal 11, 31, 40, 42, 58, 61, 84, 140

L

Lares 111, 112
Legal adviser 12, 80
Libel 74
Liberalia 76
Livy 33
Lucretius 15, 123, 148
Lucullus 24, 26

M

Macrinus 57
Macrobus 26, 27, 88
Maecenas 83, 98
Magicians 121
Malaria 33
Mark Antony 27
Marcus Aurelius 134, 136, 140
Marcellus 48
Marriage 78, 79
Mars 105, 117
Marseilles 60
Martial 32, 42, 60, 68, 83, 91
Messalina 31, 62, 65
Metellus 27
Minerva 27, 105
Mosaic 93

N

Nero 10, 24, 26, 32, 33, 57, 61, 62, 129, 130, 133, 134, 154
Nerva 14
Nurse 68

O

Octavia 61

Oracle 121
Ostia 104
Ovid 40, 74

P

Painting 93
Pantheon 99
Paternity 67
Patrician 152
Paul (Saint) 42, 128, 134, 139
Penates 111, 112
Persia 68
Petronius 58
Plautus 61, 68, 77, 82
Plebeian 152
Pliny 13, 22, 23, 26, 30, 33, 41, 60, 62, 68, 84, 86, 92, 137, 140
Pluto 85
Polybius 20, 121
Pompey 34, 41, 42, 90, 93
Pontiff 118, 121
Poppaea 32, 129
Possessor 8
Praetexta (robe) 74
Propertius 74, 75
Purifications 68

R

Roads 44

S

Sacrifice 84
Sallust 120
Saturn 105, 110
Saturnalia 90
Satire 58
Scipio 121
Sculpture 93
Senator 50, 91
Seneca 23, 30, 40, 58, 74, 134, 148
Sestertius 6, 7, 26, 41, 57, 134, 140
Slave 9, 14, 74, 90
Spirits 111
Spoliarium 56
Strabo 91
Styx 84
Suetonius 33, 58, 60, 130
Surgery 92

T

Tablet 7
Tacitus 22, 24, 60, 130, 140, 148, 153, 155
Tenniores 8
Tertullian 134, 140
Theatre 50
Thermal Baths 48, 104, 147
Tiberius 22, 24, 26, 32, 57, 61, 90, 130, 138
Tiber 111
Titus Livy 20, 111, 128, 148
Toga 32, 74
Trajan 50, 59, 61, 77, 93, 155
Triclinium 34
Trimalcion 10

V

Varro 42
Vassals 10, 13 (see : clients)
Veda 138
Verus 58
Vespasian 48, 57, 82
Vesta 64, 105, 112, 118
Virgil 59, 110, 148
Viriplaca 83
Vitellius 26
Vitruvius 91
Vulcan 105

Photos: Alinari-Giraudon: 11, 75, 76, 80, 94, 99b, 132a, 140, 141 - Alinari/Viollet: 59, 67, 72, 93, 125 - Anderson/Giraudon: 16, 28, 29b, 30, 31a, 51, 63, 70, 73, 79, 81, 114, 117, 118, 121, 122, 123, 131a, 135a, 144 - Anderson/Viollet: 111 - Archives: 5, 6, 9a, b, 21, 24a, 25a, 31b, 39a, 42, 43a, 52, 56, 57, 74a, 78, 82, 100a, b, 116b, 138 - Brogi: 110 - Giraudon: 35, 50b, 64, 67, 71, 83, 85, 112, 113b, c, 119a, 133b - Harlingue/Viollet: 46, 84 - Lauros-Giraudon: 109, 142 - Marigny/Atlas: 17 - N.D.: 129 - Small/Atlases: 18 - Roger-Viollet: end papers, 2, 7, 10a, b, 13, 15, 20a, b, 22, 23, 24b, 25b, 27, 36, 37a, b, 38, 39b, 40a, b, 41a, 43b, 44, 48b, 49b, 50a, 53, 54, 55a, 69a, b, 77, 86, 87, 88, 89, 90, 95, 96, 97a, b, 99a, 101a, b, 102a, 103, 104, 106, 107, 108, 113a, 115, 116a, 120, 124, 126, 128, 132, 135b, 139, 143, 146, 147, 148, 149, 150, 151, 152 - Tomisch/Atlas: 145 - Walmann: 8, 19, 29a, 33a, b, 48a, 55b, c, d, 61, 68, 92, 98, 102b, 127, 137.

Printed in Germany.

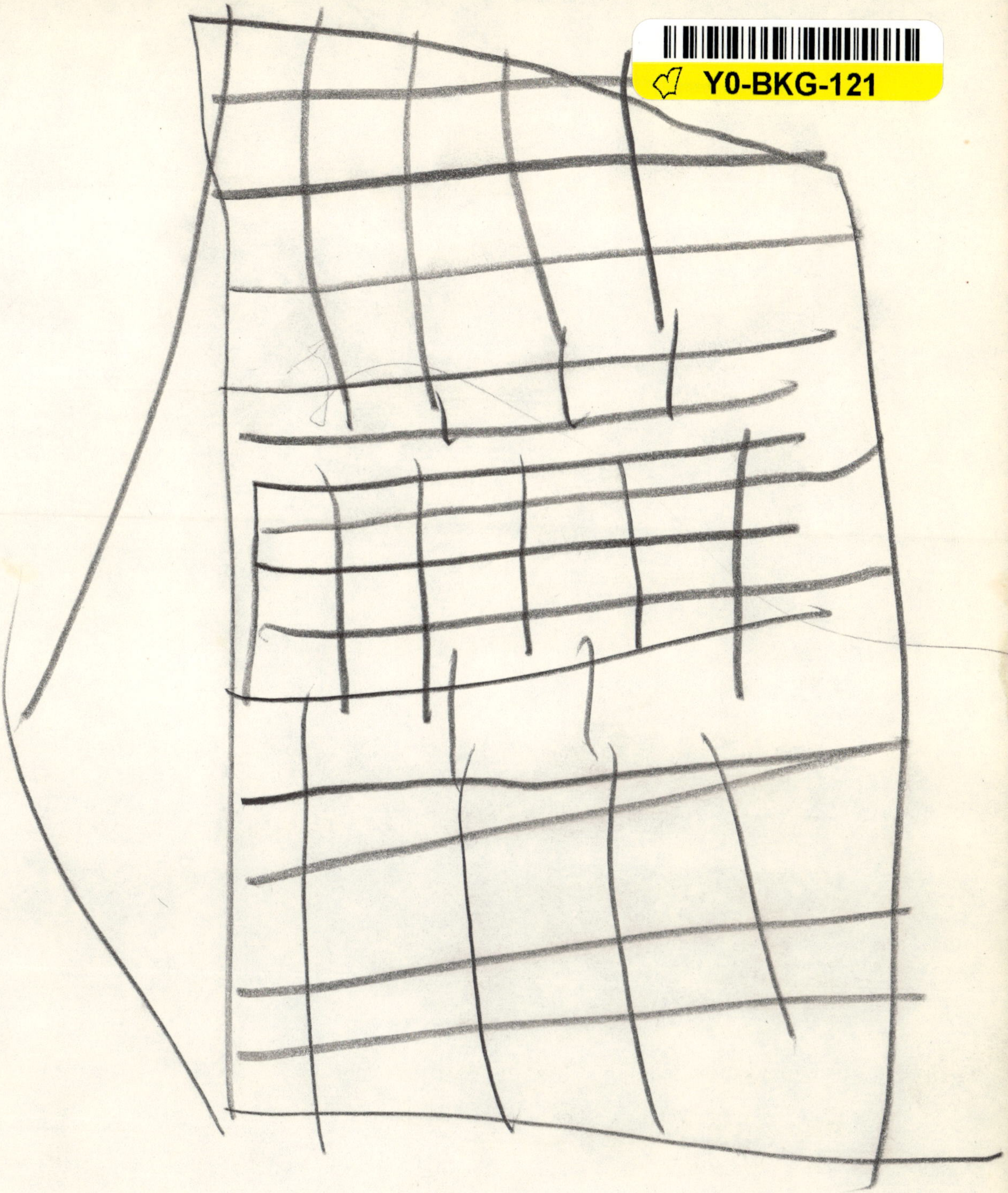

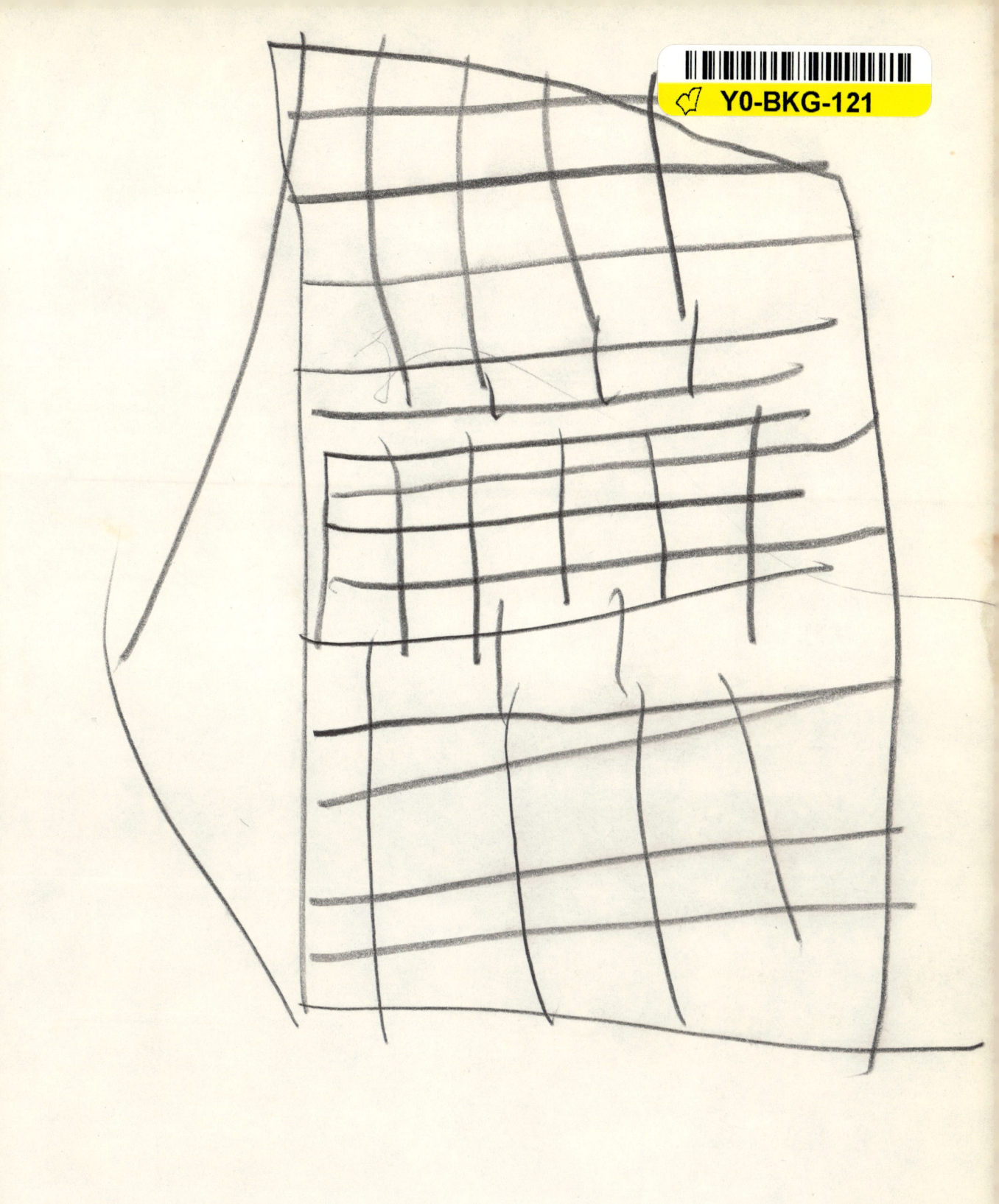

OUR NEEDS

Carol S. Prescott and Marion H. Smith

Carol S. Prescott and Marion H. Smith are writers and editors of textbooks for young people. Miss Prescott, a former teacher, is a graduate of the University of Colorado. Mrs. Smith is a graduate of Michigan State University and has also studied at the University of Michigan. Both Miss Prescott and Mrs. Smith have a deep interest in developing ways of helping children learn more about our world and its people.

COPYRIGHT 1978, THE FIDELER COMPANY

All rights reserved in the U.S.A. and foreign countries. This book or parts thereof must not be reproduced in any form without permission. Printed in the U.S.A. by offset lithography.

Earlier Edition Copyright The Fideler Company 1970
LIBRARY OF CONGRESS CATALOG CARD NUMBER: 76-17684
ISBN: 0-88296-013-X

BOOKS IN THIS SERIES

FAMILIES*
FAMILIES AROUND THE WORLD*
OUR NEEDS *
OUR EARTH *
GREAT IDEAS THAT BUILT OUR NATION *

UNITED STATES*
THE NORTHEAST
THE SOUTH
MIDWEST AND GREAT PLAINS
THE WEST

CANADA AND LATIN AMERICA
CANADA   SOUTH AMERICA
MEXICO   CARIBBEAN LANDS
AMERICAN NEIGHBORS

WORLD CULTURES*

BRITISH ISLES   GERMANY
FRANCE   SOVIET UNION
INDIA   SOUTHEAST ASIA
AFRICA   SOUTH AMERICA

(Dual editions)
EUROPE—BRITISH ISLES AND GERMANY
EUROPE—FRANCE AND SOVIET UNION
ASIA—INDIA AND SOUTHEAST ASIA
AFRICA AND SOUTH AMERICA

ASIAN CULTURES

JAPAN
CHINA
INDIA
SOUTHEAST ASIA

*Teacher's Guide is available

THE FIDELER COMPANY   Grand Rapids, Michigan / Toronto, Canada

CONTRIBUTORS

R. DALE BELLINO
Principal
Greater Plains Elementary School
Oneonta, New York

GEORGE F. CARTER
Distinguished Professor of
  Geography
Texas A & M University
College Station, Texas

ROBERT E. CONNORS
Chairman, Department of
  Elementary Education
Edinboro State College
Edinboro, Pennsylvania

DOROTHY McCLURE FRASER
Social Science Coordinator
Teacher Education Program
Hunter College
New York, New York

PAUL WALLACE GATES
John Stambaugh Professor of
  History
Cornell University
Ithaca, New York

CATHERINE E. GOODRICH
Instructional Supervisor
Oakwood School
Ramapo District No. 2
Spring Valley, New York

DON E. HAMACHEK
Professor of Educational Psychology
Michigan State University
East Lansing, Michigan

FLORENCE JACKSON
Assistant Director
Bureau of Social Studies
New York City Public Schools

HELEN McGINNIS
Consultant in Education
Sacramento County Schools

G. ETZEL PEARCY
Chairman, Department of Geography
California State College at Los Angeles
Los Angeles, California

ROBERT B. RUDDELL
Professor of Education
University of California
Berkeley, California

GEORGE D. SPINDLER
Professor of Anthropology
Stanford University
Stanford, California

ELAINE STOWE
Program Specialist, Language Arts
Sacramento City Unified School
  District
Curriculum Development Center

RAYMOND E. FIDELER
  Editor and President

D. MARIE JONES
  Manuscript Editor

ROBERT K. KINNING
  Project Supervisor

JOYCE KORTES
  Manuscript Editor

MARY MITUS
  Map and Design Editor

BEV J. ROCHE
  Design Editor

ALICE W. VAIL
  Manuscript Editor

RITA VANDER MYDE
  Picture Editor

AUDREY WITHAM
  Manuscript Editor

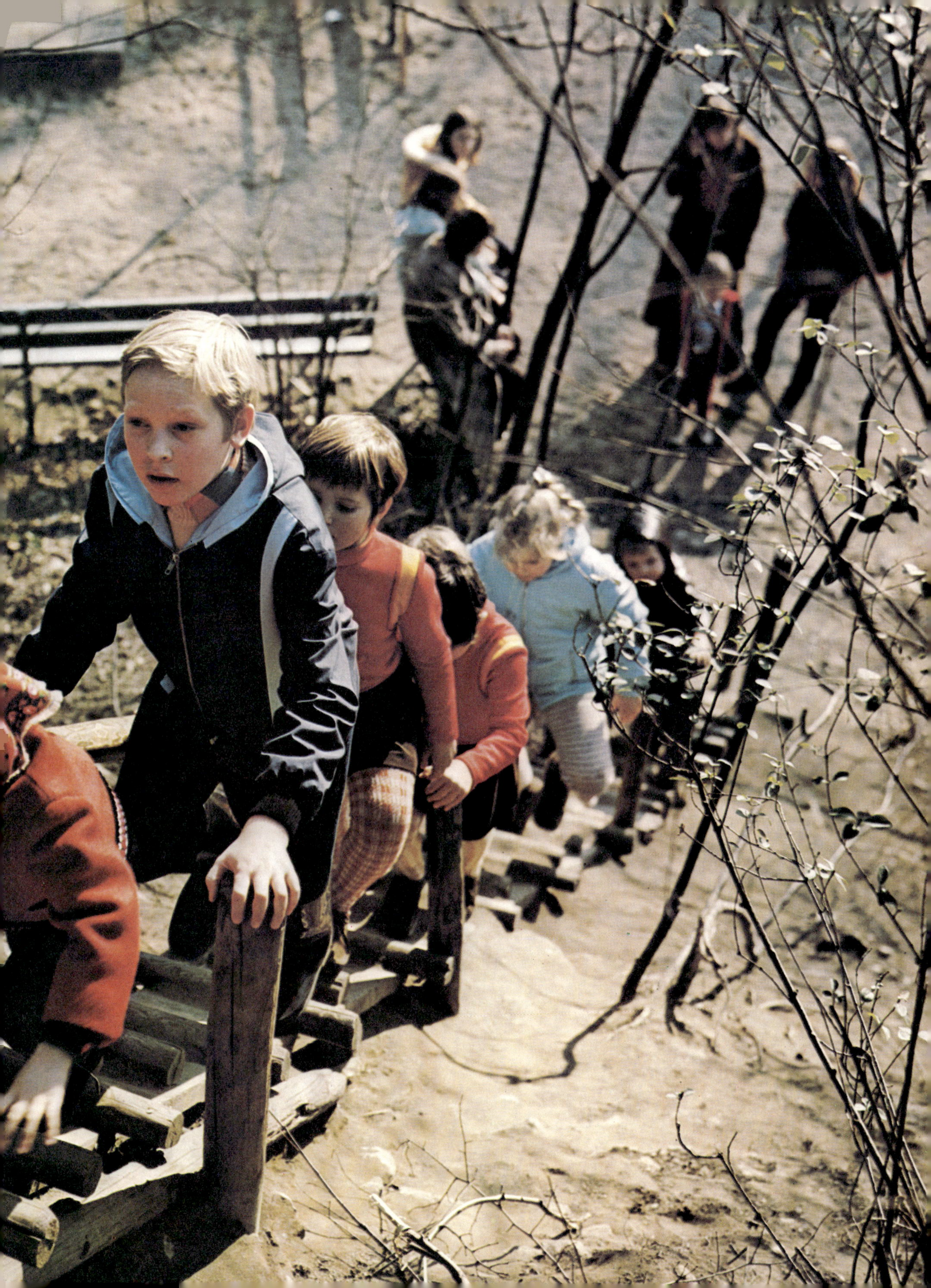

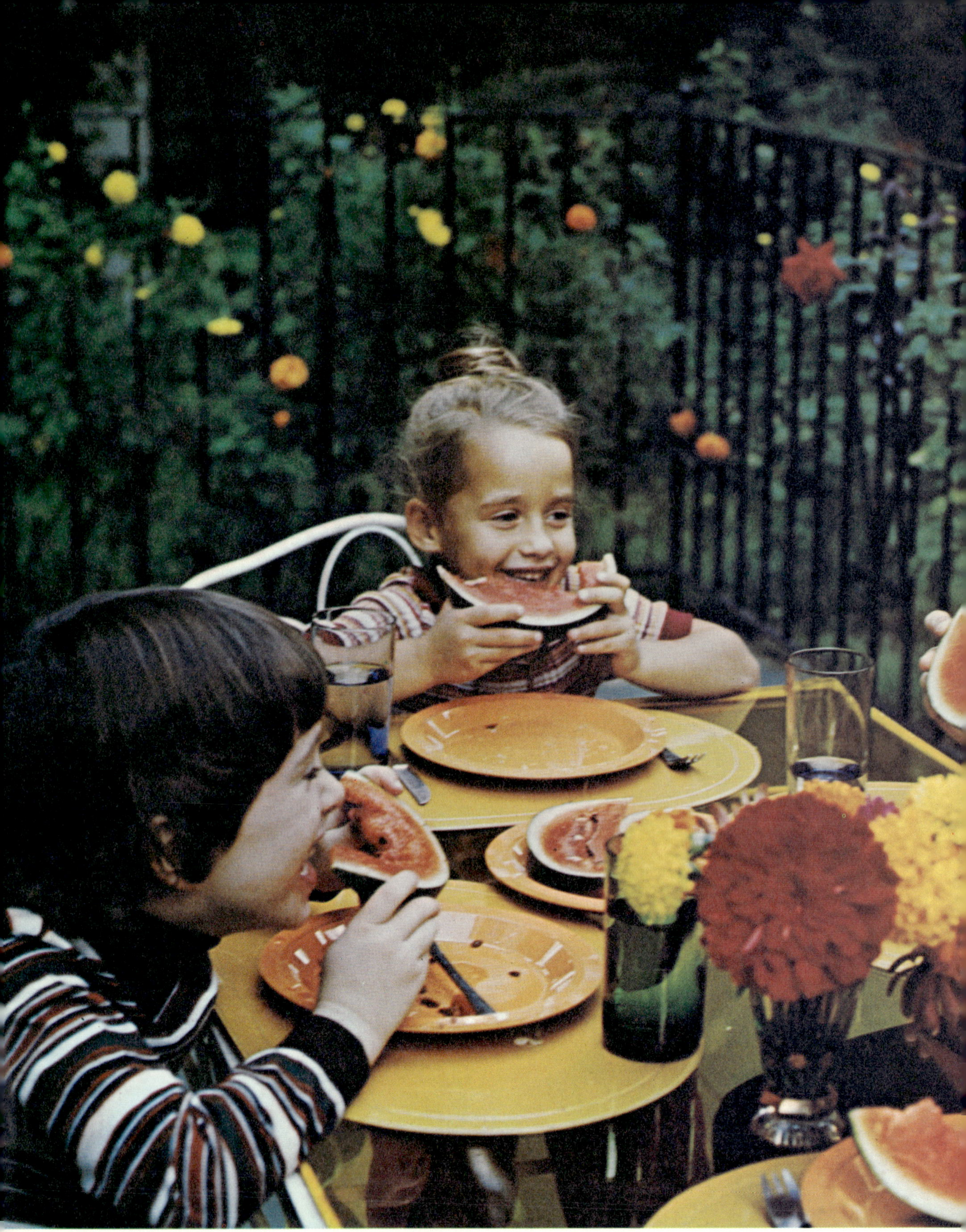

CONTENTS

What Do People Need? 6

PART 1 What Are Our Physical Needs?
    Air. 14
    Water. 18
    Food. 23
    Exercise. 28
    Sleep and Rest. 33
    Clothing 36
    Shelter. 42

PART 2 Our Social Needs
    Families. 52
    Friends 60
    Goals. 65
    A Chance To Think and Learn 70
    A Feeling of Accomplishment. 82

PART 3 Our Need for Faith
    Faith in Yourself. 90
    Faith in Other People 95
    Faith in Nature's Laws 100
    Religious Faith 104

Word List 110

What Do People Need?

7

This is the earth.

The earth is our home.

Millions of people live on the earth. One of these people is you. No one else on the earth is exactly like you. But you ARE like all other people in some ways. You have the same needs that they have.

What do you and all other people need?

How do people meet their needs?

Let's find out.

TOMATOES
UITS & VEGETABLES
EXIT
FRESH IS BEST
POTATOES
Florida
Acme

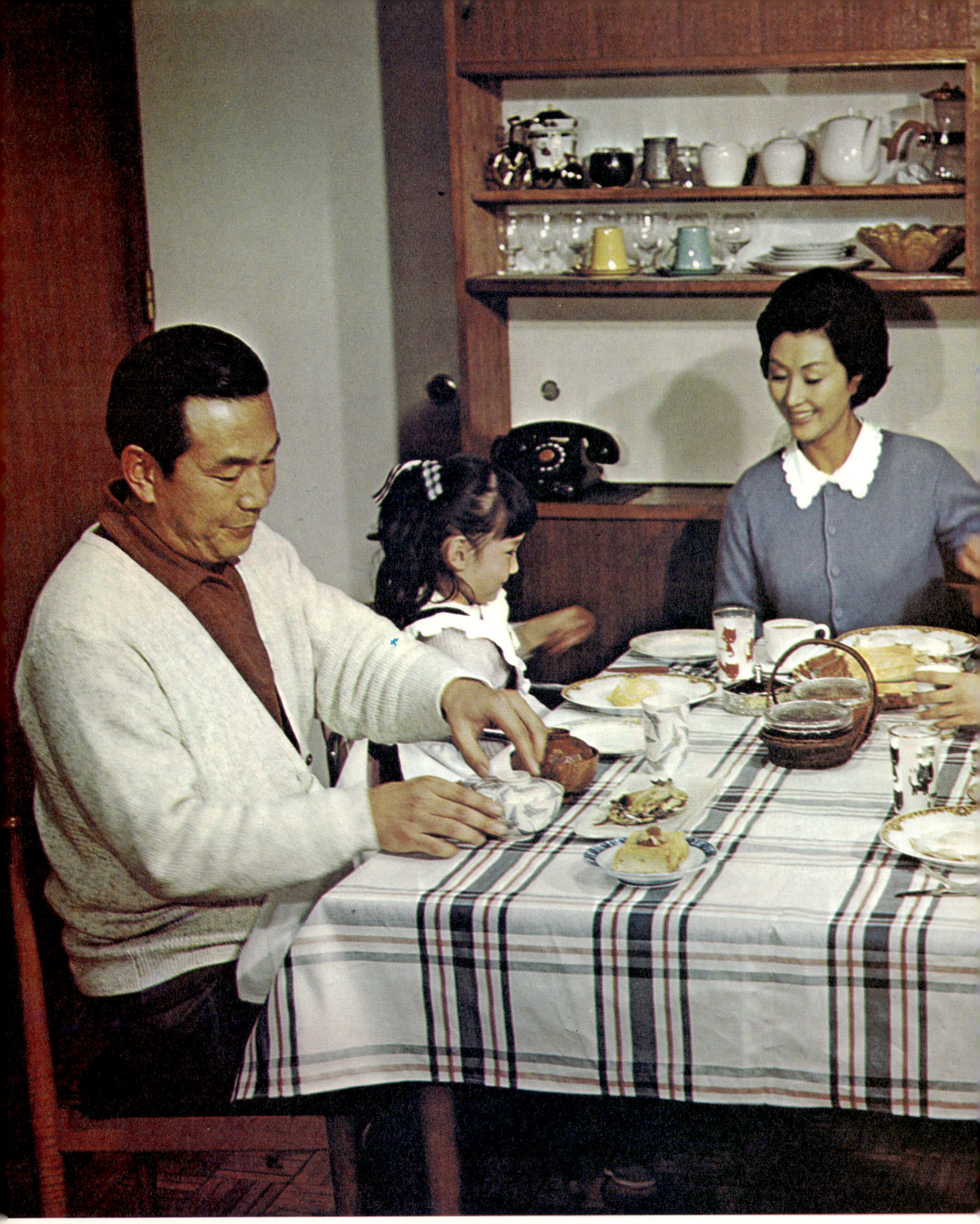

PART 1
What Are Our Physical Needs?

The Mitsui family lives in Japan, a country in Asia. Each member of this family needs certain things to stay alive. We call these needs physical needs.

What do you think these people need to stay alive? What physical needs do you think they are meeting now?

Do you think you have the same physical needs that these people have?

Air

Ann, Susan, and Patty are enjoying a day at the beach with their father. The sun overhead is bright and warm. It makes the water sparkle. The air smells fresh and clean. The girls and their father like the warm sunshine and clean, fresh air.

These people are skiing high in the mountains. They enjoy being outdoors in the bright sunshine. The air is cold, but it is fresh and clean.

People everywhere like clean air and sunshine. They must have clean air and sunshine to stay healthy. Why?

This is a large city in the United States. The sun is shining. But the people who live here can hardly see it. Today, the sun is almost hidden from sight by the fog and dirt in the air.

What do you think makes this air dirty? What would it be like to breathe this air? Would you enjoy it? What can happen to people if they do not have clean air to breathe?

What do you see in this picture? How does this picture help explain why air becomes dirty?

This city is also in the United States. The air here was once very dirty. But the people in this city decided they wanted clean air.

How can people in a city make sure that they have clean air to breathe? How can you and your family help to keep the air clean? Does your community have rules about keeping the air clean? If so, what are they?

Water

Jack has been playing tag with his friends. Now he is very hot and thirsty. Can you imagine how good this water tastes to him?

Jack needs water to drink. You need water too. Why?

These people need water to drink. They also need water for other things. In what other ways do people use water?

19

Where do people get the water they need?

In some communities, people dig wells to get water that is deep in the ground.

In other places, people get water from rivers or lakes. This picture shows a plant where river water is made ready for the people of a large city.

Where does your community get the water that its people need? How does the water reach your home?

People everywhere need water. But sometimes people do not have all the water they need.

Where this boy lives, there is almost no rain in winter. Many streams dry up and the land gets dusty. Sometimes people do not have enough water to drink.

Is there ever a shortage of water where you live? How would your life be different if your community did not have enough water for all the people?

This is a river in the United States.

Would you like to swim in this water?

Would you like to drink this water?

Once this water was clean. It was so clean that people could drink it. Now the water is dirty.

How does water get so dirty?

What can people do to keep rivers and lakes clean?

Food

The Millers are on a camping trip in the western part of the United States. Right now it is lunch time, and everyone is hungry. The food is cooking on a camp stove.

Each person in the Miller family needs food. You need food, too. Why?

These people are Chinese. In what ways is mealtime in their home like mealtime in yours? In what ways is it different?

All people in the world do not eat the same foods. Why? What foods do you think this family eats? If you do not know, how can you find out?

Many people in the world do not meet their need for food.

Some people do not have all the food they need. They are hungry most of the time.

Some people do not eat the right kinds of food. They do not eat foods that will help them to stay healthy. What kinds of food do you need? Would you stay healthy if you ate only cake and cookies? Why do you think this?

How does your family get its food?

In what other ways do people get the food they need?

How does this family get food?

Could you get your food in this way? Why do you think this?

What is this man doing? What kind of food is he trying to get?

Where does the food sold in a grocery store come from?

Exercise

Jeff and his father are shoveling the snow that fell last night. They need strong bodies to do this work. And shoveling snow helps them keep their bodies strong.

Why do you need a strong body? What work do you do that helps keep your body strong?

What are these boys and girls doing? Who do you think the man is? Why are the children looking at him?

Do you think the children need this kind of exercise? Does the man need it? Why do you think this?

Do you enjoy this kind of exercise? Why, or why not?

Look at these two pictures. Where do the people live? What are they doing? Do you think they are strong and healthy? What makes you think this?

Do you think that exercise can be fun? Why do you think this?

Do you get exercise every day? What kinds?

Do you think you need more exercise than you get? Why, or why not? If you think you need more exercise, how can you get it?

Sometimes people cannot get the exercise they need. What happens to their bodies then?

Mary was sick for a long time. She stayed in bed for many weeks. She feels better now, but her body is still weak. She cannot run and play with her friends. She cannot even walk very well.

How do you think Mary will make her body strong again?

Sleep and Rest

This is Jim. All day long he was busy. He got up early and walked to school. In school he worked hard. When school was over he played baseball with his friends. After supper he helped wash the dishes.

How do you think Jim feels?

Tamiko and Suki live in Japan. They are in bed too. In what ways is their bed different from the bed Jim sleeps in? How is their bed like his?

Do you think the girls sleep well in this bed? Why do you think this? How well do you think you would sleep in a bed like theirs?

Tamiko and Suki live far away from Jim. But they need the same thing Jim needs - a good night's sleep. Why?

34

You need more than a good night's sleep each night. You also need to have some rest during the day. Why? How do you feel when you do not get enough rest?

Do you think grown-ups need rest too? Why do you think this?

What do you do to rest your body during the day?

Clothing

Mrs. Perkins has taken her daughters shopping. She is helping Pam try on a coat.

Why do you think Pam needs a coat? Do you suppose she needs it to wear right now? Why do you think this?

Do you wear the same kind of clothing every day of the year? Why, or why not?

How do you decide what clothes to wear outdoors? Think of times when you chose the WRONG clothes to wear. How did you feel?

What clothes do you think this girl will put on before she goes outdoors?

In some lands, people never wear many clothes. In other places, people wear heavy clothing nearly all year. People in some lands need to wear different kinds of clothing at different times of the year.

Look at the people on these two pages. What does their clothing tell you about the weather in the places where they live?

What things besides weather help to explain why people in different places wear different clothing?

39

Some people wear special clothing when they work.

This doctor is taking care of a patient. What special clothing is she wearing? Why do you think she wears this clothing?

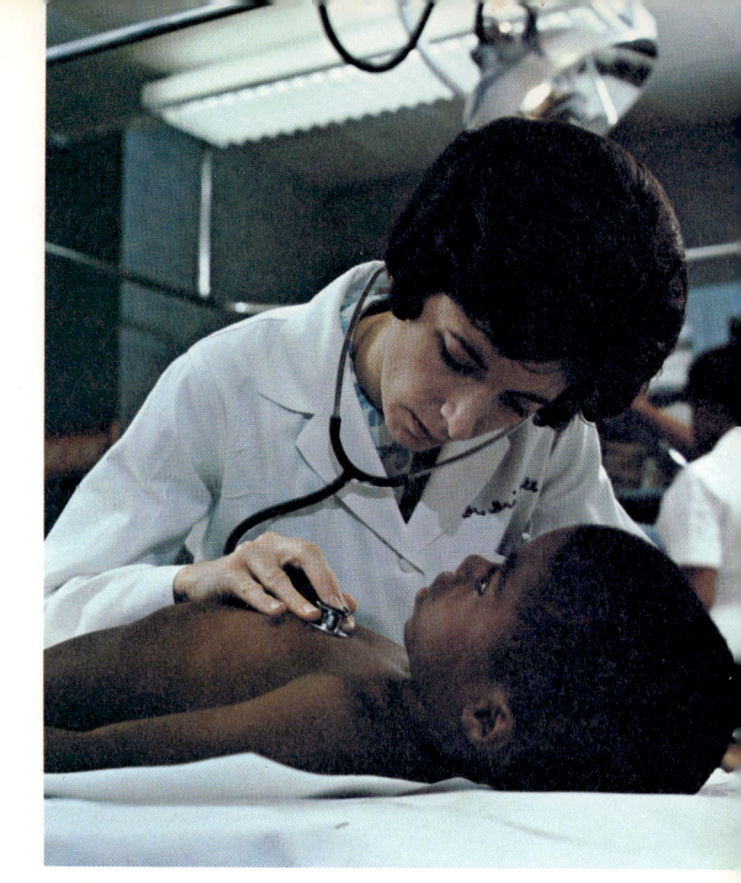

This man is a welder. What special clothing is he wearing? Why does he need this clothing?

What other people can you think of who need to wear special clothing when they work?

How do people get the clothing they need? How do people in your family get their clothing? Do all people in the world get their clothing in the same way? What makes you think this?

Do you think this mother makes all the clothing her family needs? Why do you think this?

Shelter

The picture on this page shows buildings where people live.

What does the place where you live look like?

Many people in large cities live in buildings that reach high into the sky.

What do we call these buildings?

Do you think people in small towns live in buildings like these? Why do you think this?

This picture shows another building, where people will live.

How many families do you think will live here? What makes you think this?

We call the place where people live their shelter. Why do people need shelter? What kinds of shelter have you seen?

People everywhere in the world need shelter. But all people do not need the same kind of shelter. Why?

Where these people live, a house like this is a good shelter. Why do you think this is true? Why do you suppose this house is built on poles?

Would this house be a good shelter for you and your family? Why, or why not?

44

These people live in a very dry place called a desert. Summer days here are hot, but nights can be cold. Sometimes a sandstorm blows across the land.

What would you call the kind of shelter these desert people live in? Why do you think they have this kind of shelter?

There are deserts in many parts of the world. Do you suppose all desert people live in homes like these? If you do not know, how can you find out?

How do people get the materials they need to build their shelters?

What materials were used to build the shelters you see on this page? Where do you think the people got the materials?

What materials did people use to make the shelters shown on pages 44 and 45?

46

Pablo and Maria live in Mexico. They are watching their father make adobe bricks.

First he mixed clay, straw, and water together. Where do you suppose he got these materials?

Now he is shaping this mixture into bricks. Then he will let the bricks dry in the sun for several days. Why?

Some of the bricks the father has made are already dry. Can you find them? What do you think he will do with these bricks?

What have you discovered?

What physical needs do all people have? Why do we call these needs PHYSICAL needs?

Look at the pictures on these two pages. What physical needs are these people meeting? How are they meeting these needs?

How do you meet your physical needs?

49

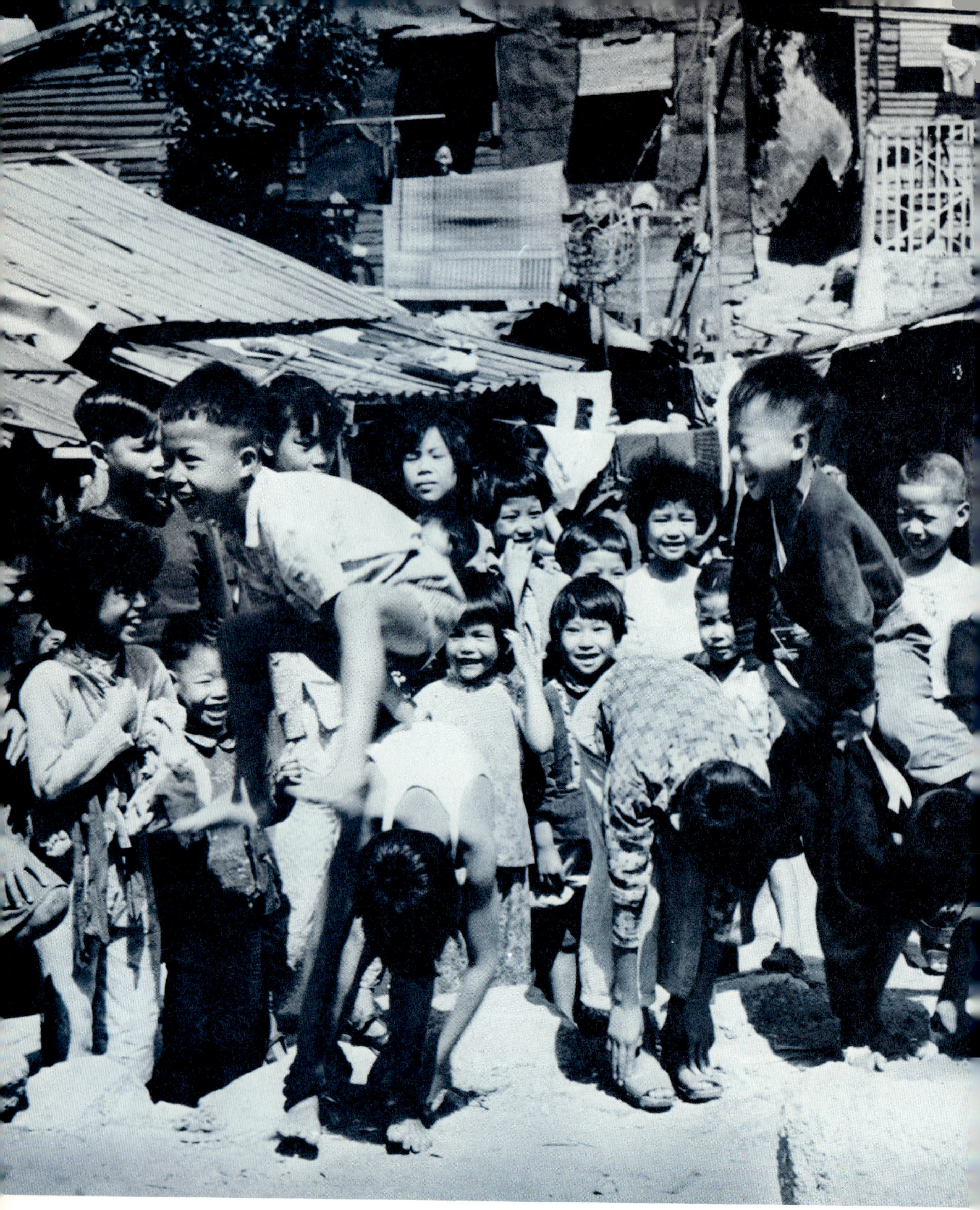

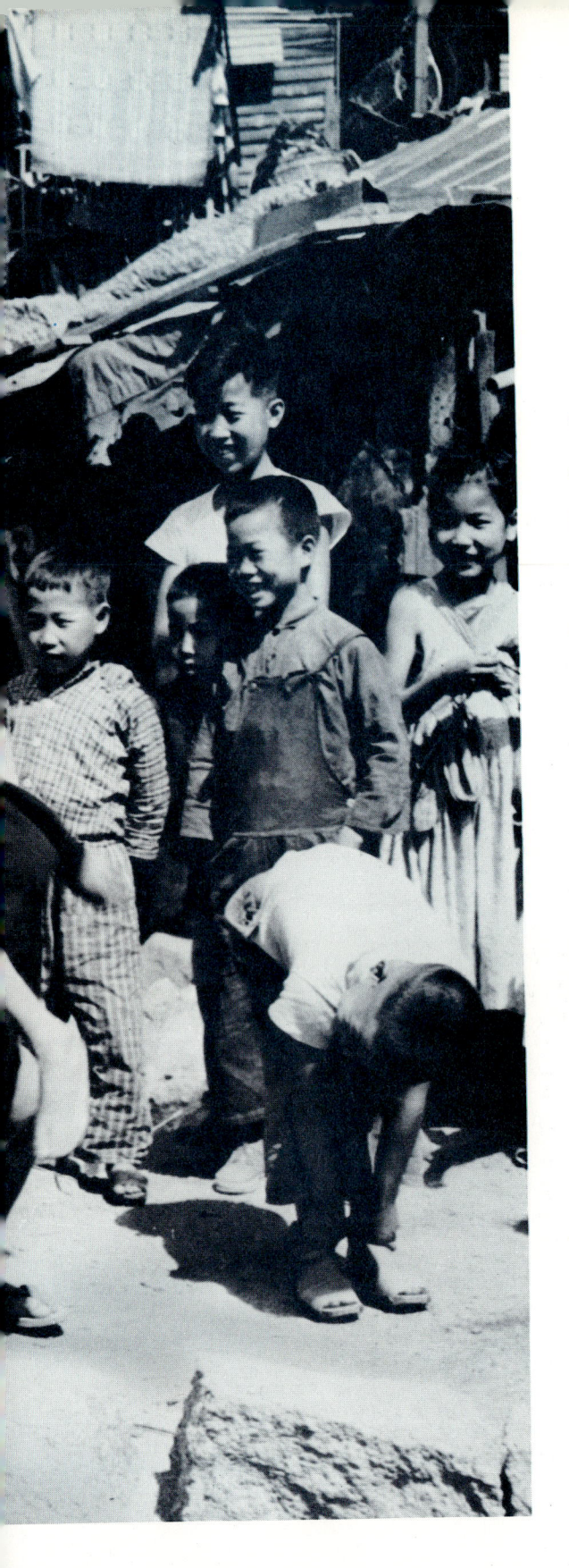

PART 2
Our Social Needs

These children live in a place called Hong Kong. What are they doing? Are they happy? Why do you think this?

These children are like all other children in the world. Each of them has physical needs, just as you do. Each of these children also has social needs. Everyone must meet these needs to be happy.

What makes you happy? Do you think the same things would make these children happy? Why do you think this?

Let's discover what some of our social needs are.

Families

Imagine that you are taking a trip around the world. Everywhere you go, you meet families. Some families are large, and some are small. Some are very much like your family, and some are very different. But they are all families.

What is a family?

Why do people need families?

This family lives in the United States. In what ways is it like your family? How is it different?

Where do these families live? In what ways are they like your family? How are they different from your family?

53

Everyone needs a family because we all need someone to love and someone who loves us.

What do you think love is?

Do these brothers love each other? What makes you think this?

How do people in your family show their love for each other?

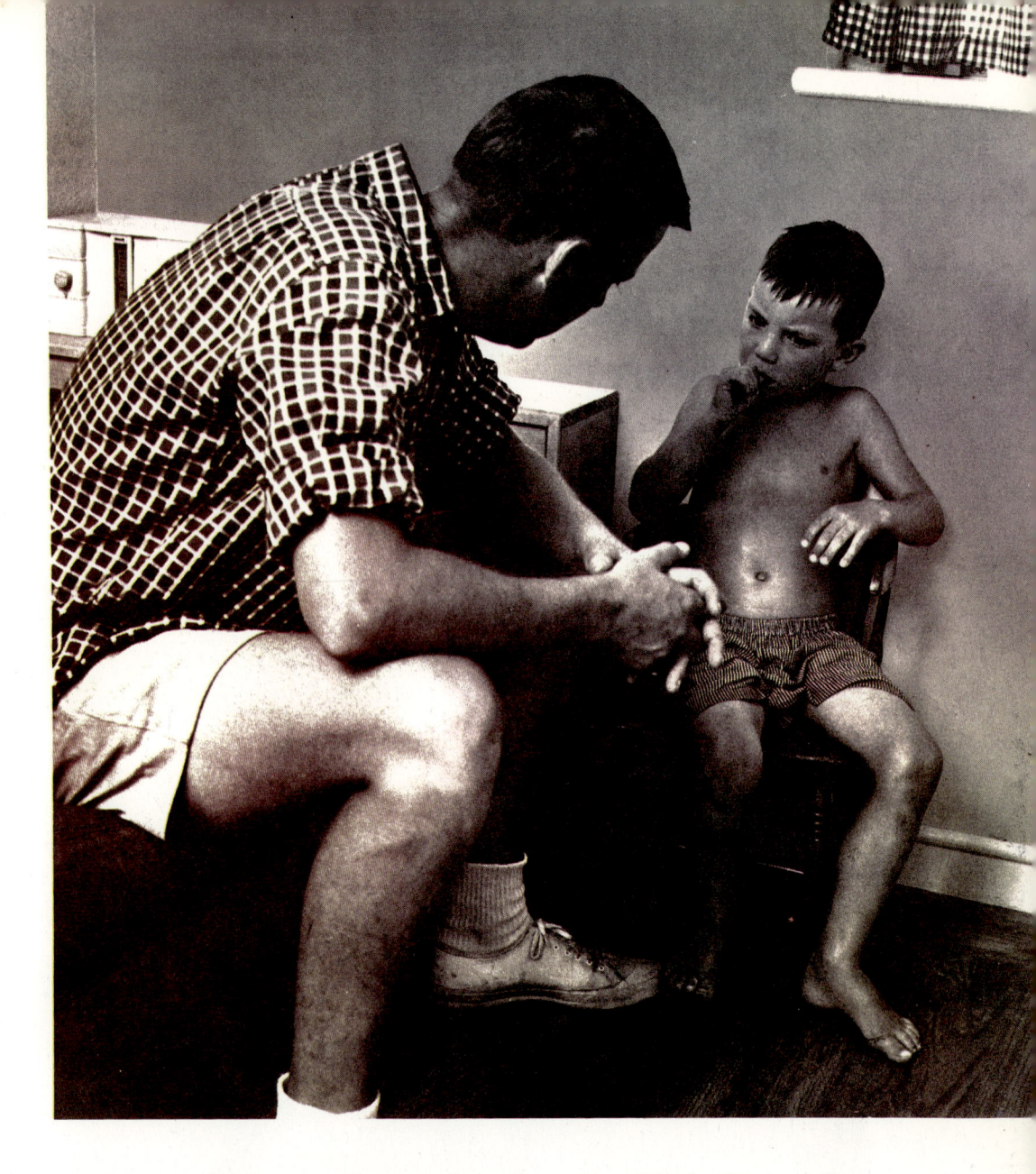

Steve did something that he shouldn't have done. What do you suppose it was?

How do you think Steve feels? How do you think his father feels? Does he love Steve? Why do you think this?

Tell about a time you were angry at someone in your family. Can you be angry at people and still love them? Why do you think this?

Look at the pictures on these two pages. In what ways are the members of these families helping each other?

What do you do to help people in your family? What do they do to help you?

56

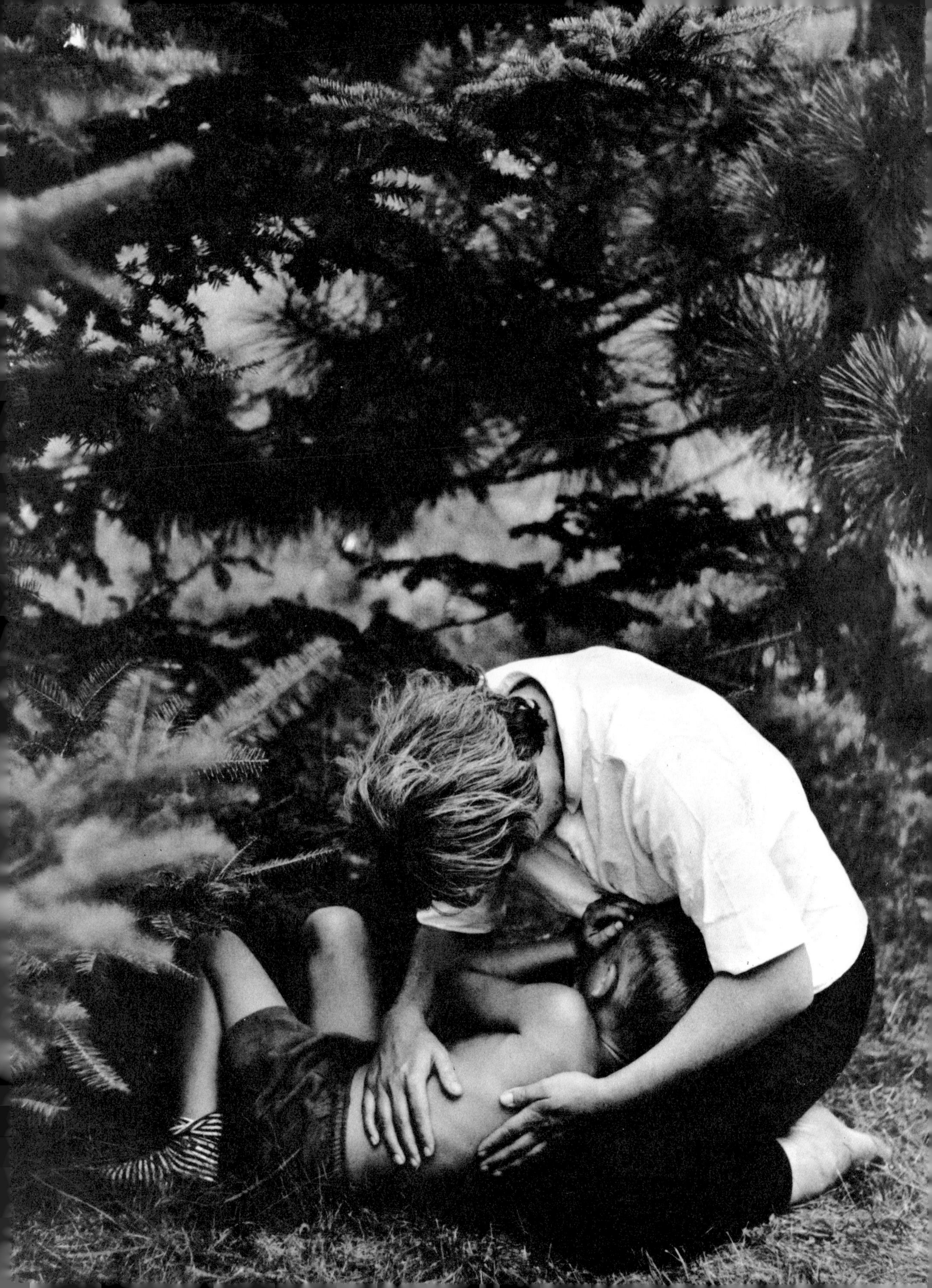

People in families like to have good times together.

What are the people in these families doing? Are they having fun? Why do you think this?

What do people in your family like to do together?

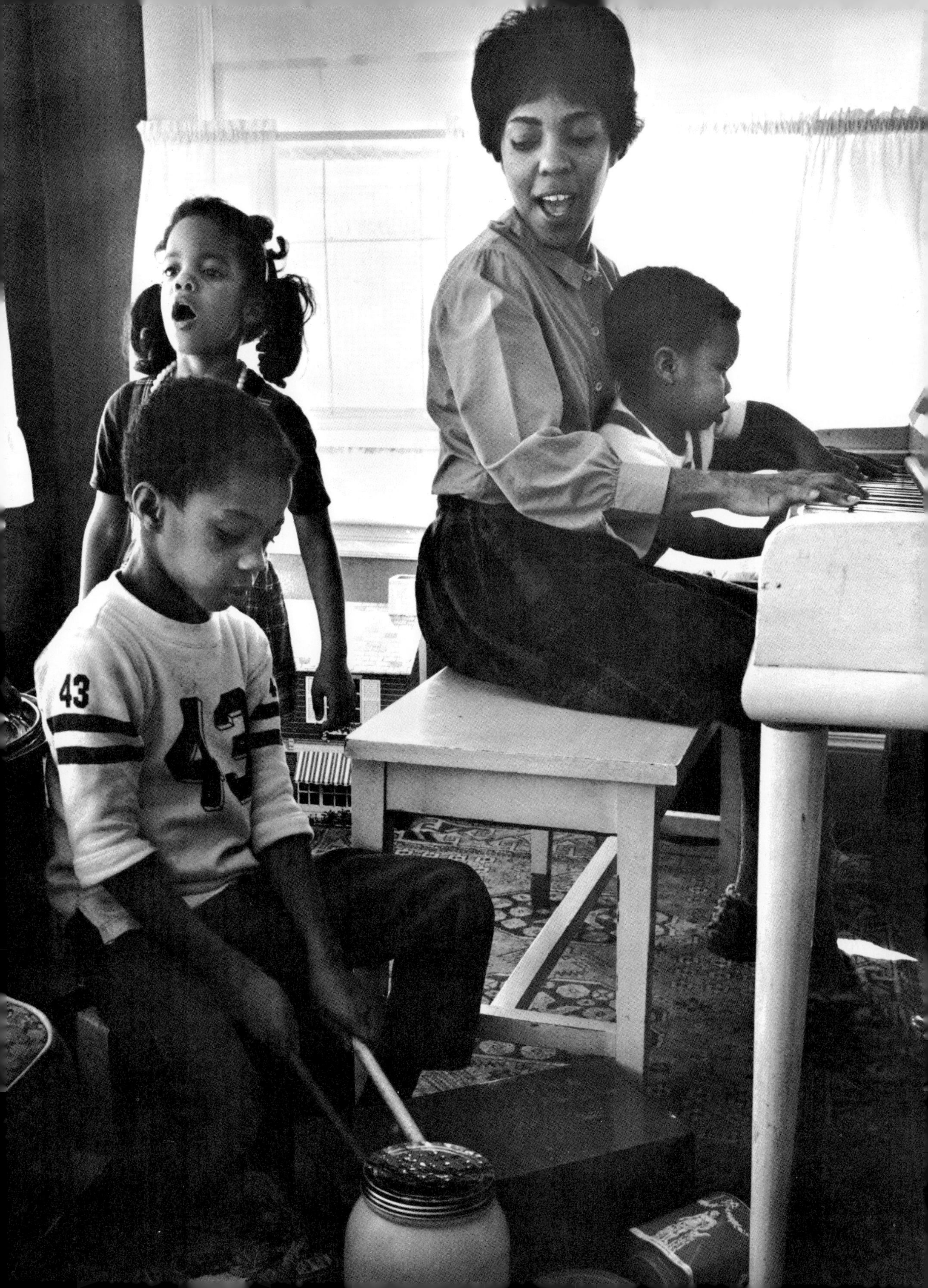
43
43

Friends

It's recess time. Judy and Susan are sitting on the swings, laughing and talking.

What do you suppose they are talking about?

Do you think Judy and Susan are friends? What makes you think this?

What is a friend? Do you think all people need friends? Why, or why not?

Molly is a new girl in school. She had many friends where she used to live.

How do you suppose Molly feels now? How could you help her?

Is it easy to make new friends? How do you make friends with someone?

People have different kinds of friends. Some friends are "best" friends. We share our biggest secrets with them. We spend more time with them than we spend with other friends. Do you have a "best" friend?

Some people are not our "best" friends. But they are still friends. We like to talk, play, and work with them. What friends do you have like this?

What are these boys doing?

What do you and your friends like to do together? Do you like to play games? Do you like to "make believe"? Do you like to laugh and talk together?

We like to share happy times with friends. Have you ever shared unhappy times with friends? What happened?

What do you see in this picture? What do you think has happened?

Tell about times when you and a friend have not agreed with each other. Do you think people can disagree and still be friends? Why do you think this?

Goals

Lu-chu and her friends live in China. They go to gym class in their school. They learn to do different kinds of exercises.

Lu-chu has a goal. She wants to become a good gymnast. What do you think Lu-chu will need to do in order to reach her goal?

What is a goal? What goals do you have? Why do people need goals?

This boy has many goals. One goal is to play the violin well. What other goals do you suppose he has?

This man has many goals too. One of his goals is to earn enough money to buy the food and clothing his family needs. What other goals might he have? What goals do your parents have?

These students in Thailand are playing an exciting game of volleyball. The winners of this game will be the new champions.

Do you think that the members of a team must plan what they are going to do before they play a game? What makes you think this?

What kinds of plans do you make? How can plans help you reach your goals?

What is this family doing? Why are they working together?

Sometimes people can reach goals all by themselves. But to reach some goals, people must work together. They must cooperate.

Tell about times when you have cooperated with other people to reach a goal.

How do people in your community work together to reach important goals?

Sometimes people change their goals before they reach them. Why?

Diane wants to be a doctor when she grows up. Do you think she might change this goal? Why do you think this?

What goals have you changed? Why did you change them?

What do you think your life would be like without goals to work for? How do goals help you to have a happy life?

A Chance To Think and Learn

I wonder why
I seem to hear the sea
when I hold a shell
to my ear.

    I wonder how
    an astronaut feels
    when he walks in space
    and looks at the earth,
    far away.

        What makes it possible
        for me to see
        pictures on TV?

            And why do children
            in other lands
            speak languages
            I can't understand?

                I wonder . . .

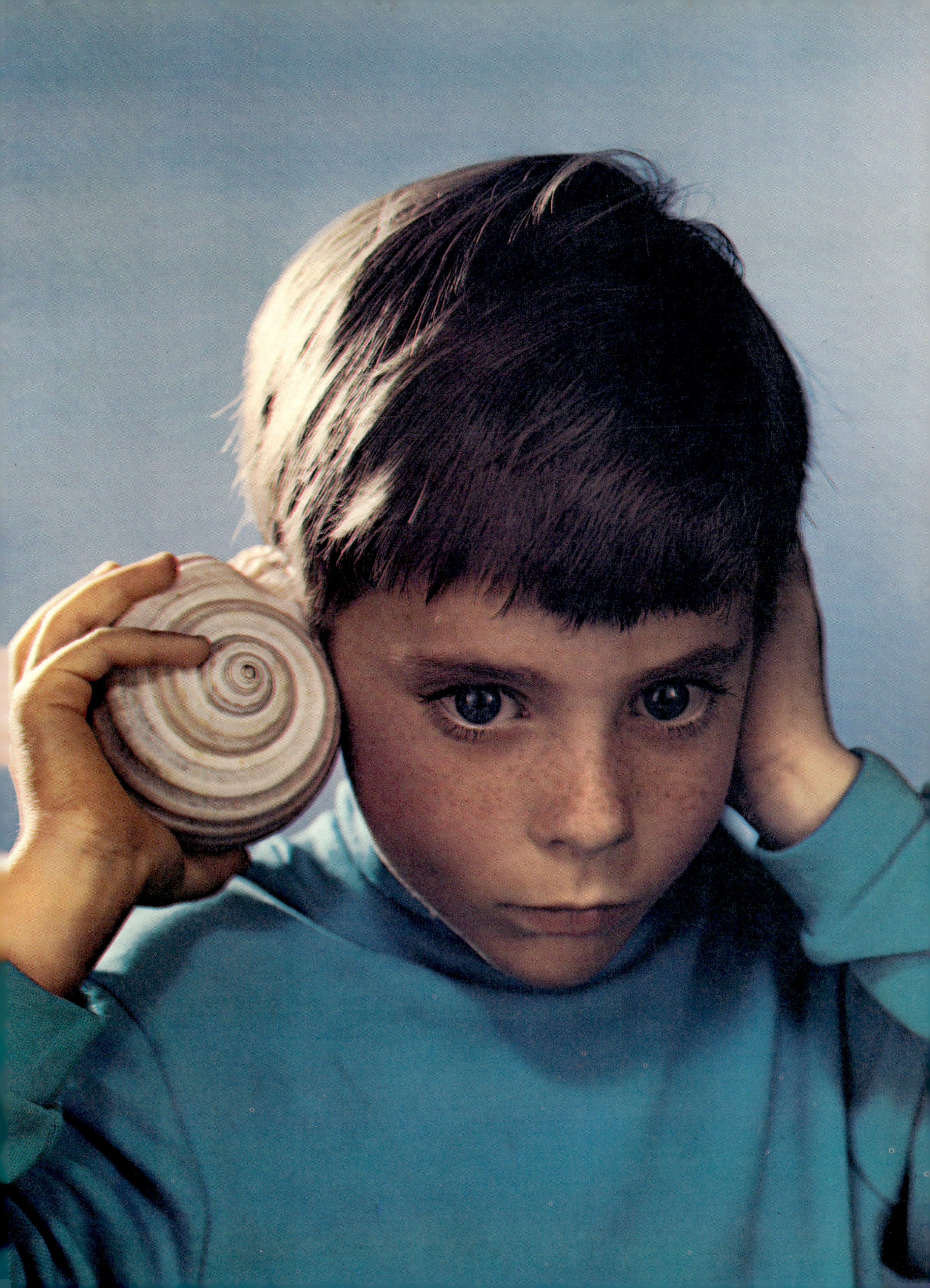

What do YOU wonder about? What questions are in your mind? Do you have a chance to find the answers to your questions? Why do you think this?

To be happy, all people need a chance to learn about things that make them curious. They need a chance to make discoveries about themselves, about other people, and about the world they live in.

People also need a chance to learn how to do something well. They need a chance to learn to . . .
> hit a baseball
> or fly a plane
> or bake a cake
> or read a book
> or play the piano.

What would you like to learn to do well? Why?

There are so many things that people can learn. Where and how do they learn?

Children everywhere learn many things at home. How are these children learning? What are they learning?

What have you learned at home? What have you learned from other people in your family? What have you learned by yourself?

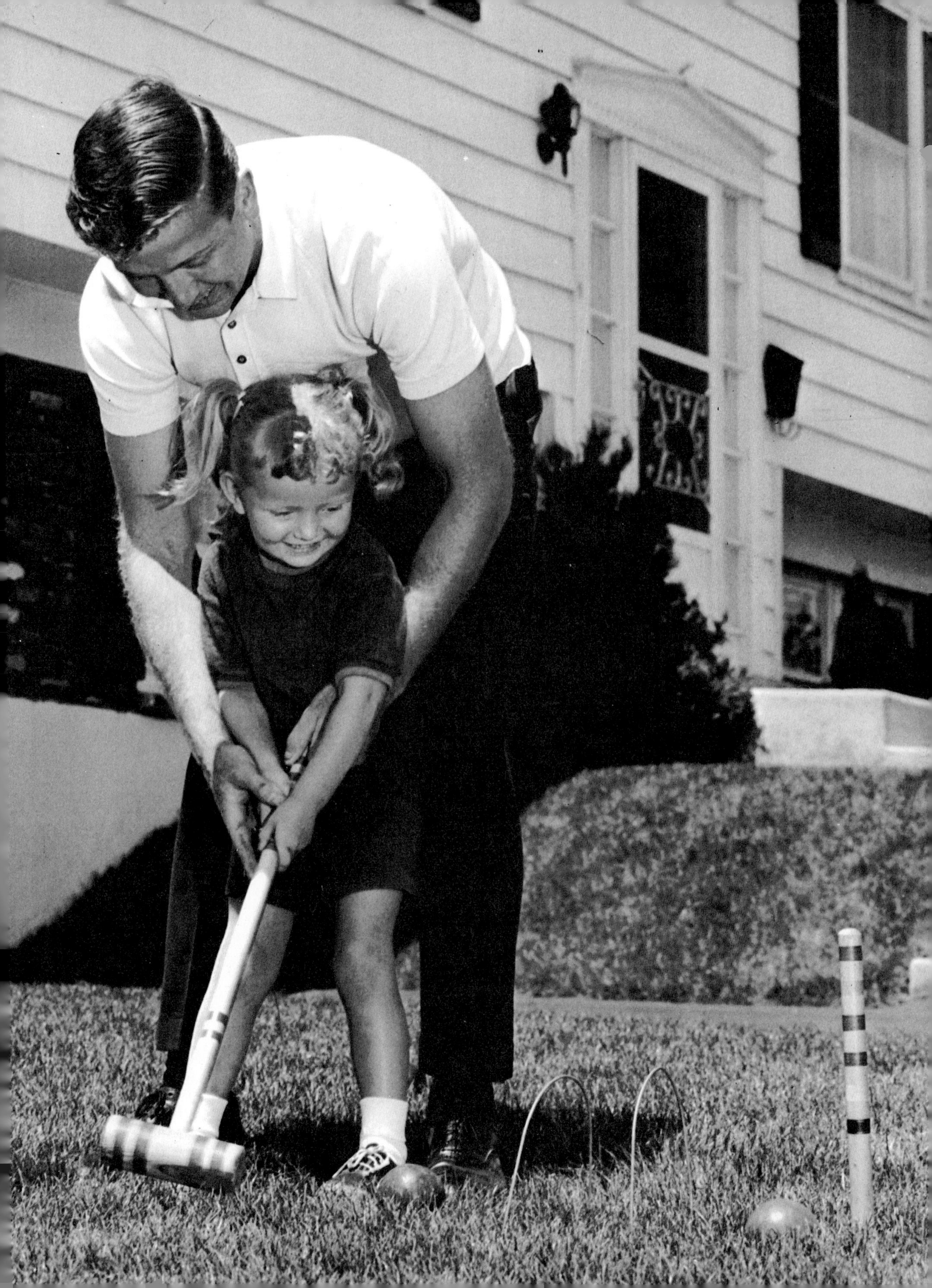

People also learn many things in school. What do you learn in school? How do you learn?

Can the things you learn in school help you to have a happy life? Why do you think this?

In our country, there are many kinds of schools. There are schools for people of all ages.

The picture below shows high school students. What kinds of things do students learn in high school? Why do young people need to go to high school?

Many people go to other schools after they finish high school. Why?

Children in all parts of the world go to school. In school, they have a chance to think and learn.

Do you think all children in the world NEED a chance to think and learn? What makes you think this?

Look at these three pictures. Where do these children live? What do you suppose they learn in school? Do you think they learn any of the things you learn? Why do you think this?

79

In some countries, all the children do not have a chance to go to school. Why do you think this is true?

The people in this picture live in South America. They did not have a chance to go to school when they were young, so they did not learn to read and write. Now they have a chance to learn these things. Will learning to read and write help them have a happy life? Why do you think this?

You can learn in many places and in many ways. Where are these children learning? How are they learning?

Do you learn in the ways these children are learning? How else can you learn? Do you always use the chances you have to think and learn? Why, or why not?

What do you think your life would be like if you didn't have chances to think and learn?

81

A Feeling of Accomplishment

This is Ricky.

How do you think he feels? Why does he feel this way? Tell about times you have felt the way Ricky feels.

Ricky has a feeling of accomplishment. He is proud and happy about what he has done.

All people need to have a feeling of accomplishment. They get this feeling when they reach a goal, or when they learn something new, or when they do their work well.

This baby has a feeling of accomplishment. Why?

What kind of work does this woman do? Do you suppose she enjoys her work? Do you think her work helps her have a feeling of accomplishment? What makes you think this?

This boy is doing a science experiment. How do you think he will feel when he makes a discovery?

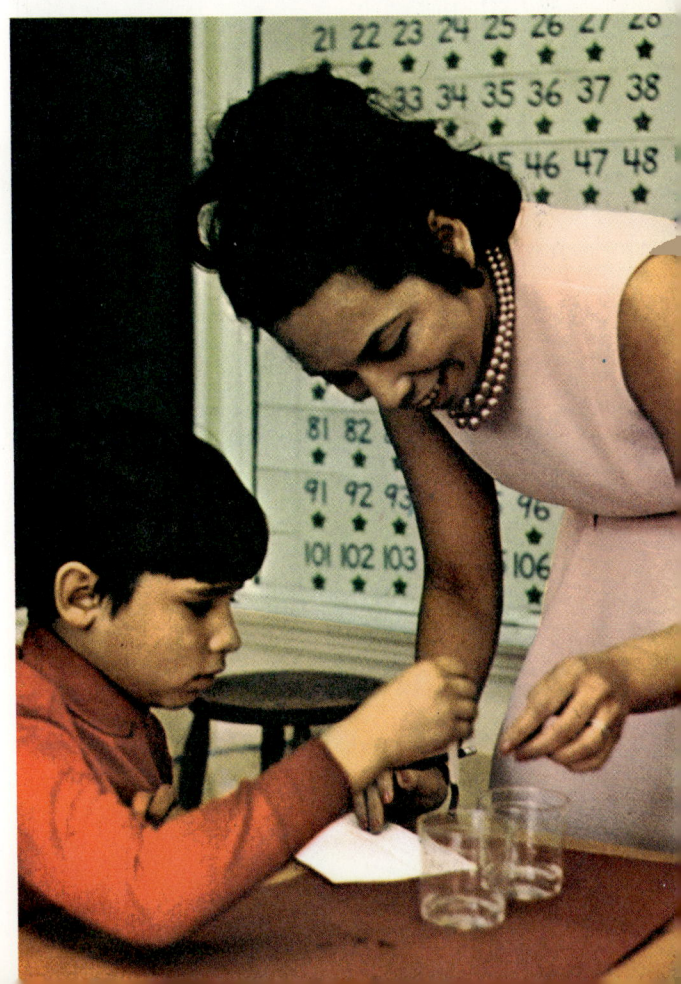

You can get a feeling of accomplishment when you do something all by yourself. But sometimes you share this feeling with other people.

Look at the picture of the boy and his father. Does each of them have a feeling of accomplishment? Why do you think this?

Who has a feeling of accomplishment at the end of a successful space flight? Are the astronauts the only people who have this feeling? Why do you think this?

These boys are playing a championship baseball game. What kinds of rewards do you think the members of the winning team will get? Will they get only a reward they can feel and touch? What makes you think this?

What kind of reward do you most like to get when you do something well? Why?

What have you discovered?

What social needs do people have?
Look at the pictures on these two pages. What social needs do you think these people are meeting? How are they meeting these needs?
How do you meet your social needs?

87

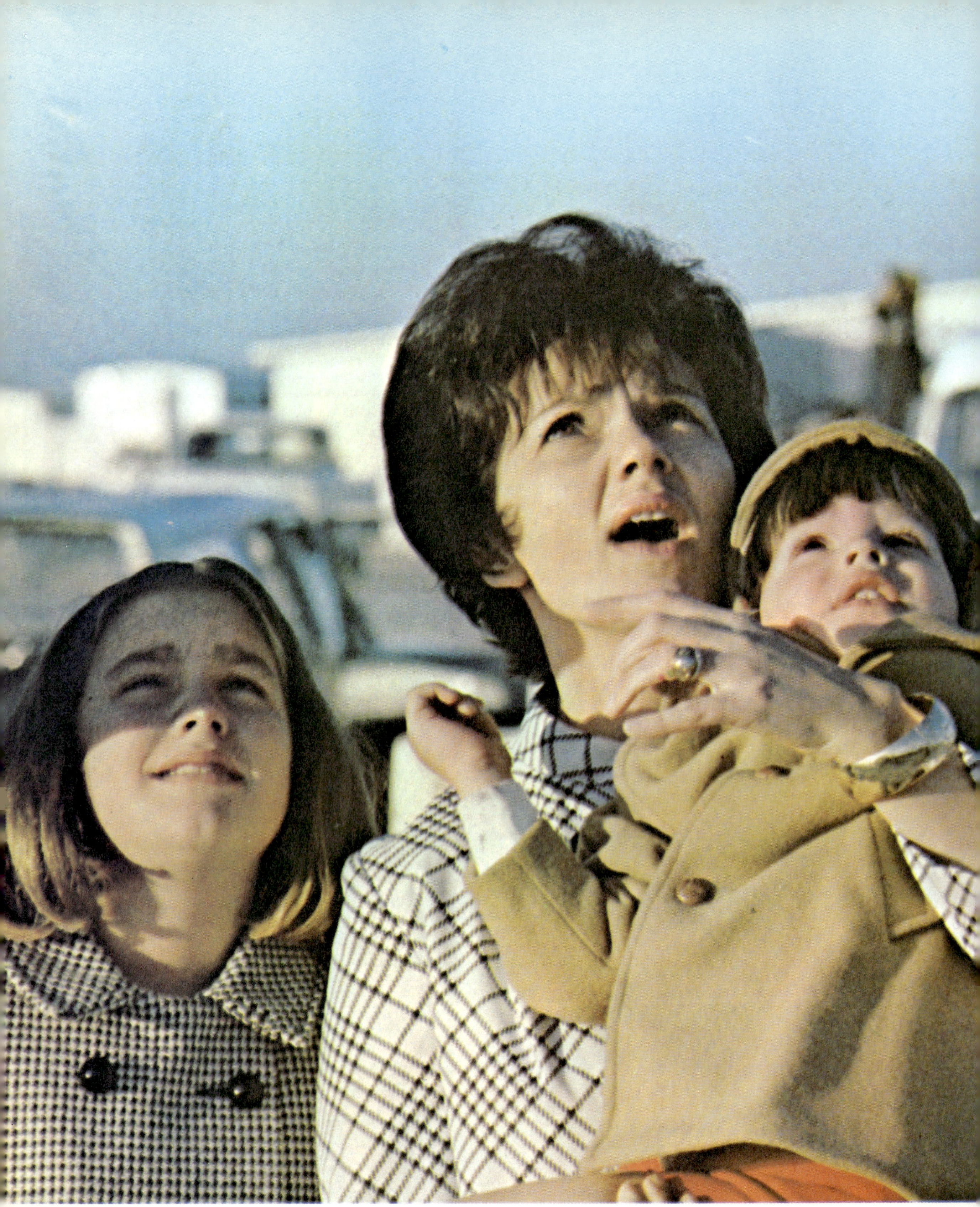

PART 3
Our Need for Faith

These children are members of the Lovell family. With their mother, they are watching a spacecraft being launched. Their father, Astronaut James Lovell, is in the spacecraft. Soon he will be thousands of miles away from the earth.

The Lovells believe that the spacecraft will return to earth safely. They have FAITH that Astronaut Lovell will be home again in a few days.

Why do the Lovells have faith?

Do they need faith?

Do you need faith?

Faith in Yourself

This is Becky.

What is she doing? How does she feel? Tell about times when you have felt the way she feels.

Becky has faith in herself. What does this mean?

Look at the picture below. What is the man doing? Do you think he has faith in himself? What makes you think this?

What things are you sure you can do? Does this mean you have faith in yourself?

Do you think all people need faith in themselves? Why, or why not?

This is Roberto. He has lived in Spain all his life.

Now Roberto and his family are moving far away. They are leaving their home in Spain and going to a new home in South America.

How do you think Roberto feels? What problems might he have? Do you think he has faith he can solve his problems? Why, or why not?

Every day we have problems to solve. Some problems are big, and others are small.

What problem do you think this boy is trying to solve? How would you solve this problem?

What problems have you had to solve lately? Do you have faith you can solve your problems? Why, or why not?

How do you feel when something goes wrong? Do you still have faith in yourself?

What do you do if you have a problem you think you can't solve by yourself?

Faith in Other People

Find the astronaut in this picture. He is ready to climb into a spacecraft. Soon a huge rocket will send him and two other astronauts far into space.

How do you suppose this astronaut feels? Do you think he has faith in himself? Does he have faith in other people? What makes you think this?

Look at the pictures on these two pages. What do you see? Which people are showing faith they have in others? How do you know they have faith?

What people do you have faith in?

Do you think you need faith in other people? Why, or why not?

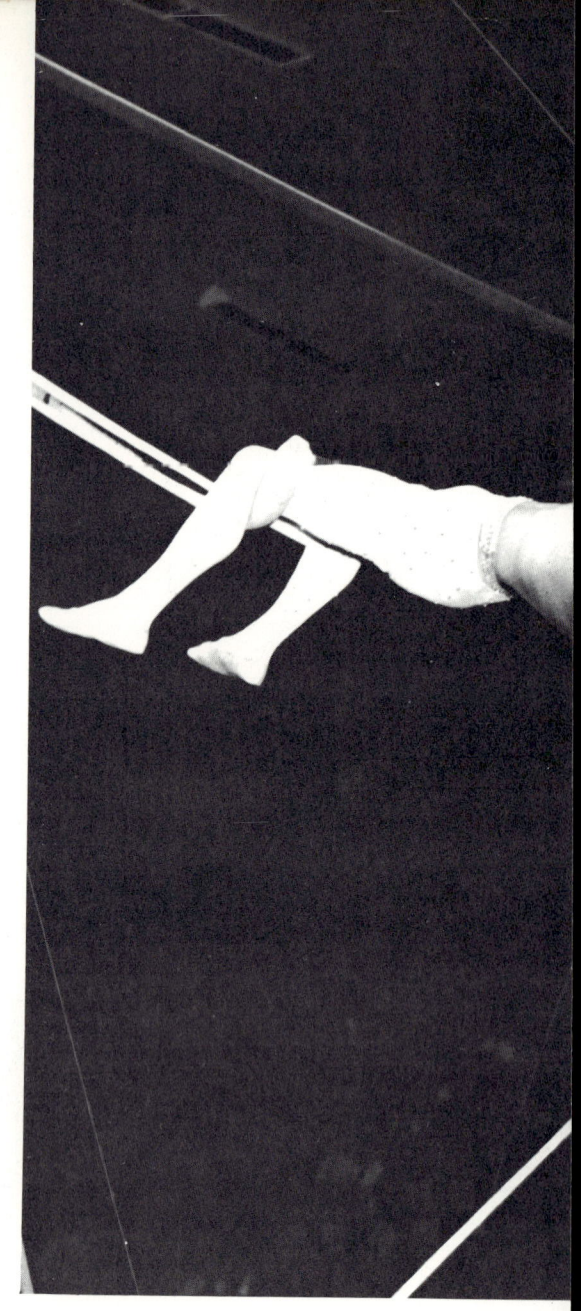

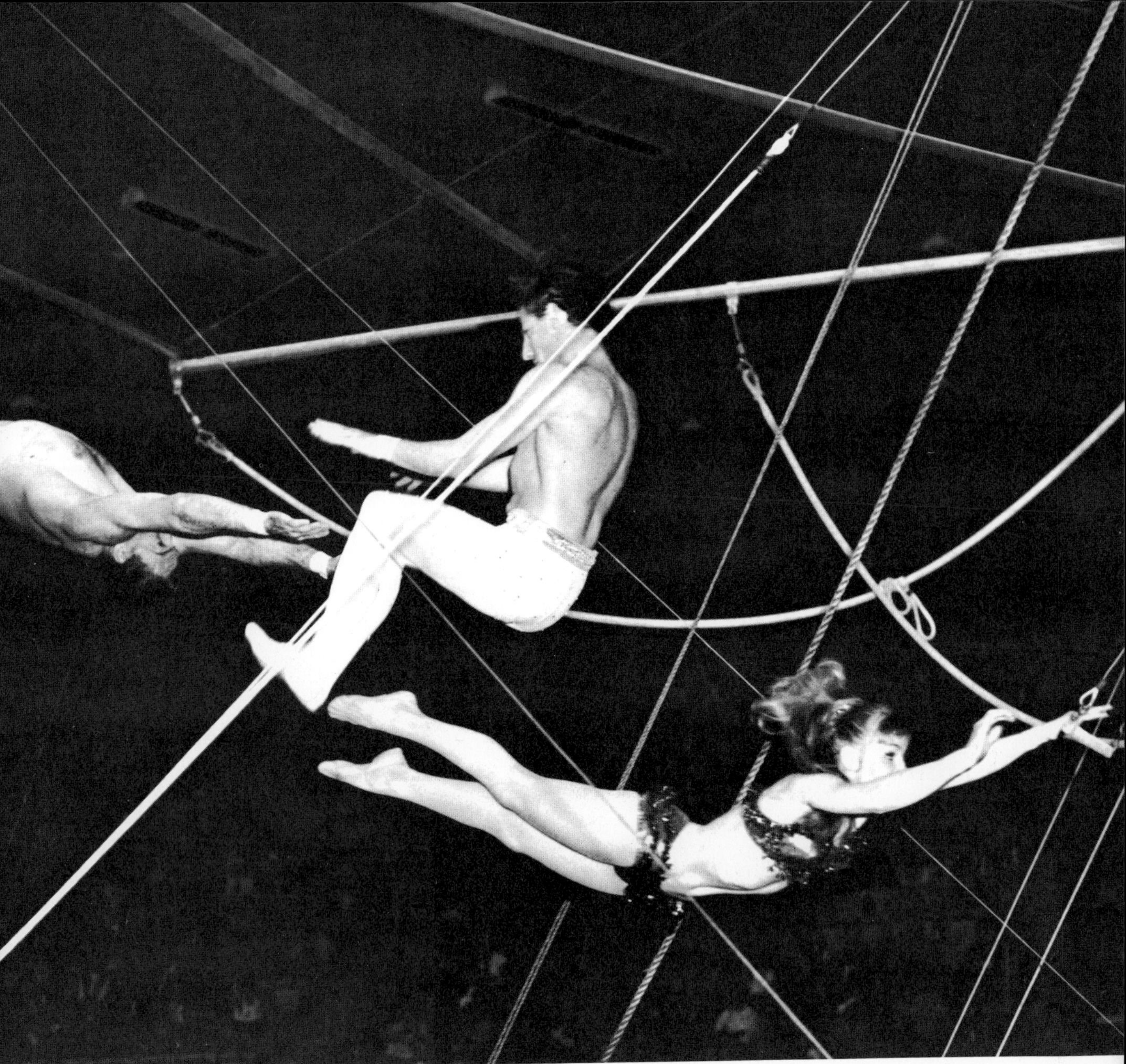

Rosa is playing jacks with her friend Nita. She has faith Nita will follow the rules. Rosa trusts Nita. But what if Nita cheated, and Rosa KNEW she cheated? How do you think Rosa would feel?

How do you feel when someone you trust lets you down? Can you still have faith in that person? Why, or why not?

Can you think of a time when another person trusted you and you let that person down? How do you think that person felt? Do you want other people to have faith in you?

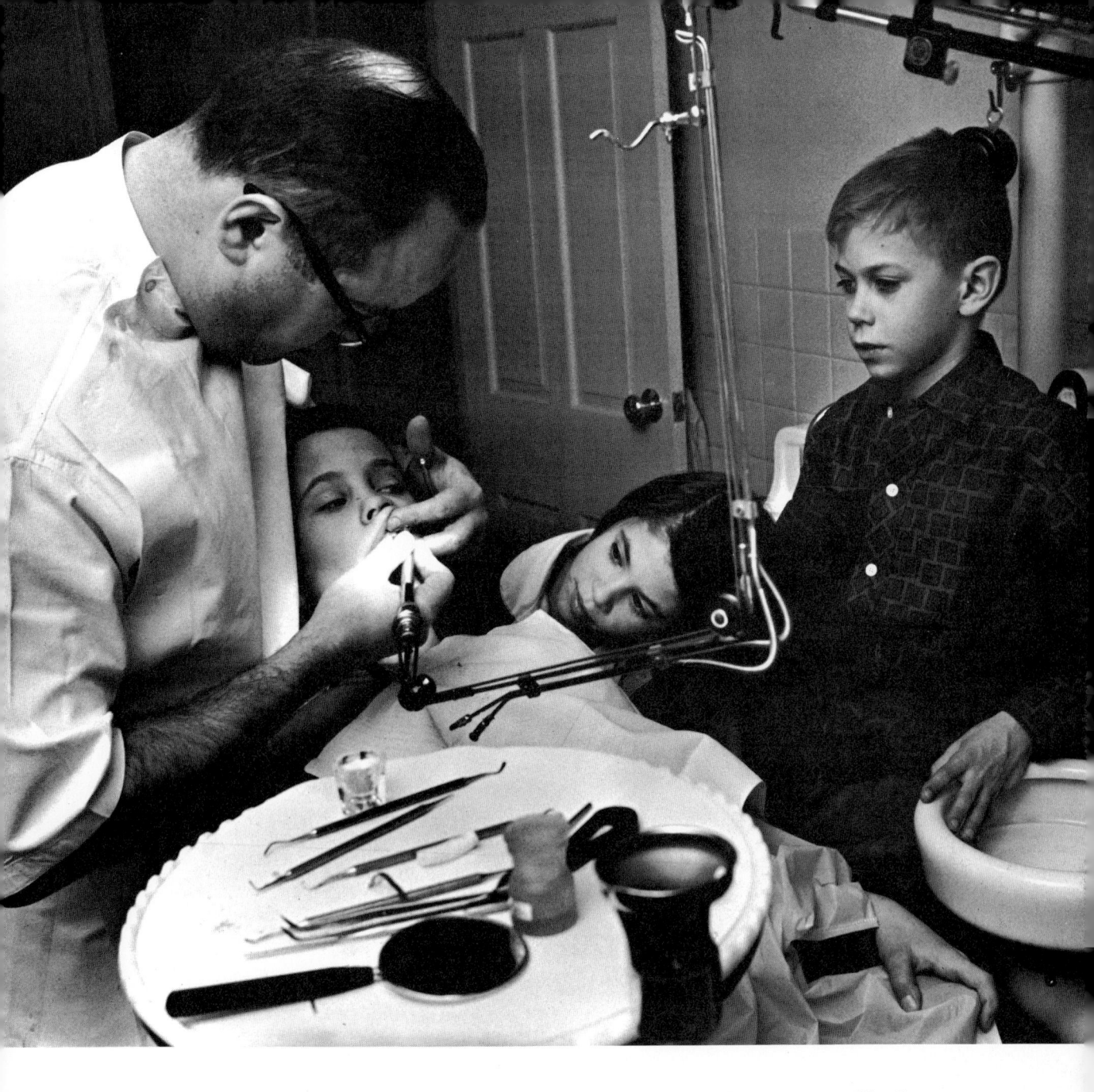

Do these children have faith the dentist will do his work well?

What do you think our world would be like if we couldn't count on other people to do their part,
or to help us when we need help,
or to play by the rules and treat us fairly?

Faith in Nature's Laws

The golden sun is setting. Soon it will disappear from the sky, and night will be here.

But in the morning the sun will appear again, and there will be light.

How do we know this? How can we be sure the sun will appear in the sky each morning?

Beth is watering some vegetable seeds that she planted. She has faith that these seeds will grow into vegetables in a few weeks. Do you think she would be surprised if the seeds grew into flowers instead of vegetables? Why do you think this?

Beth feels that she can depend on nature. She has faith that nature's laws won't change.

What is nature? What are the laws of nature you know about? Do you have faith in these laws? Why, or why not?

We do not ALWAYS know exactly what will happen in nature. But we CAN use laws of nature to make good guesses about what will happen.

The men in the picture above are predicting what the weather will be like. How do they make their predictions? How do their predictions help people?

Just imagine. What if . . .
   you couldn't depend on the sun to rise each day?
   you couldn't depend on summer to follow spring?
   you couldn't be sure that a ball someone hits in the air will come back to earth?
How would you feel? What would your life be like?

Religious Faith

These people live in Morocco. They are worshiping God in a mosque. Allah is their name for God. Their religion is called Islam.

This family lives in the United States. Their religion is called Judaism. Each week this family worships God in a synagogue. They also worship God in their home.

These people live in the United States too. They are worshiping God in a church. Their religion is Christianity.

The people in these three pictures have different religious faiths. They worship in different ways. But they all have faith in one God.

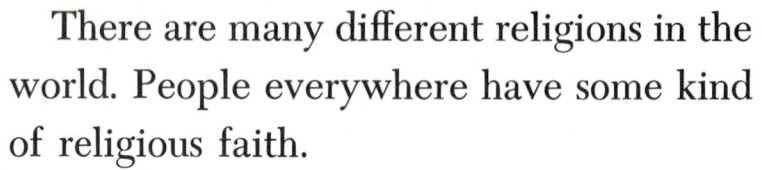

There are many different religions in the world. People everywhere have some kind of religious faith.

Not all people believe in only one God. Some people worship more than one god.

This family lives in India. Their religion is called Hinduism. They are worshiping their family god. They also worship other gods.

Why do people have religious faith? How does their religion help them?

Religion can help people understand themselves and the world they live in. It can bring them joy, and it can give them courage in times of trouble. Religion can also help people live together happily. For example, most religions teach people to be honest and to love and help their neighbors.

These people had to leave their homes because of a flood. They were given shelter in a church. Why do you think the members of this church are helping these people?

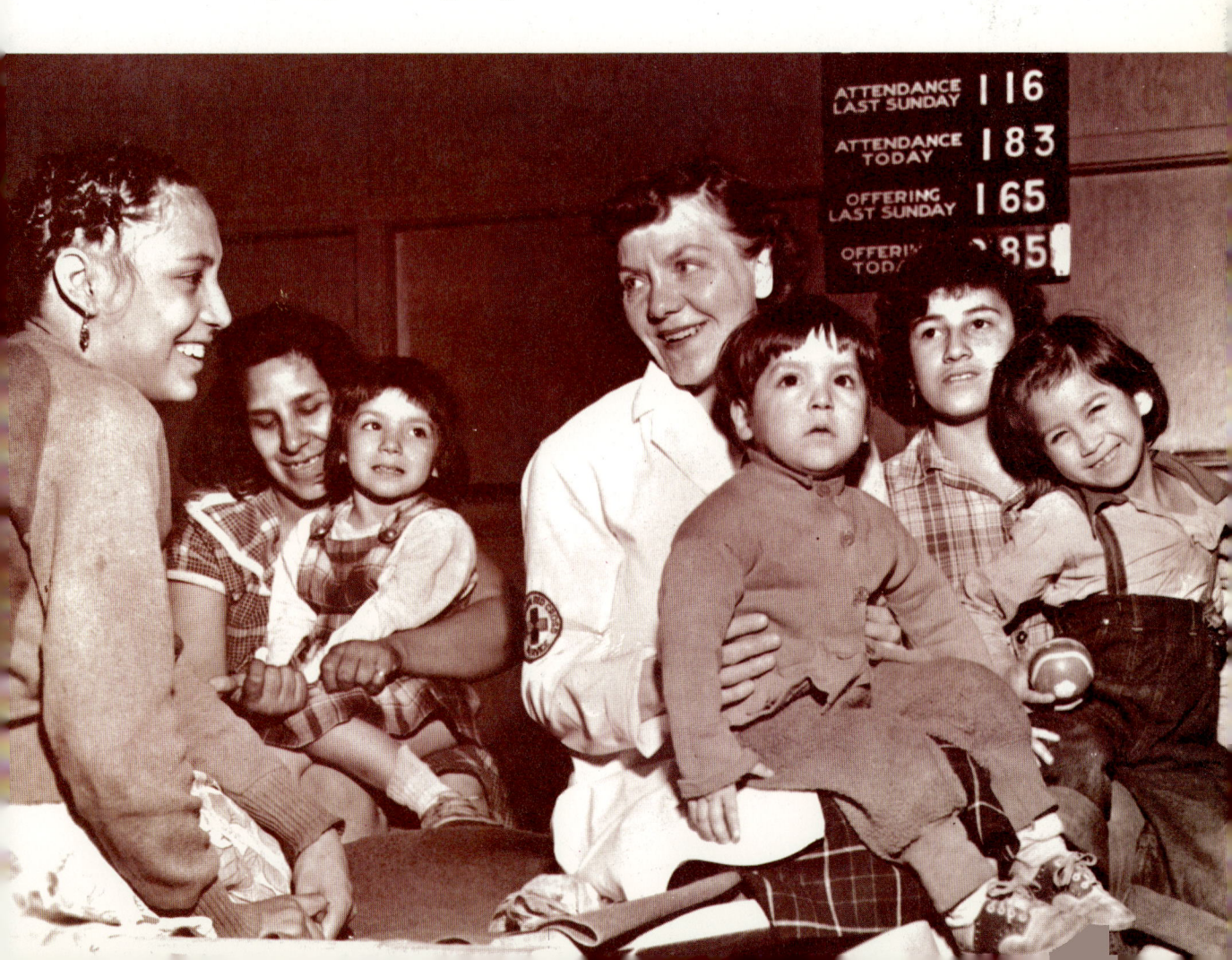

What have you discovered?

Why do all people need faith? How can people meet their need for faith?

What kinds of faith do you think the people in these pictures have? Why do you think this?

How do you meet your need for faith?

109

WORD LIST

What Do
People Need?

8 earth
10 millions
   exactly
   meet

PART 1

13 physical
   Japan
   Asia
   member
   certain
   alive
14 enjoying
   beach
   overhead
   sparkle
   fresh
   sunshine
15 skiing
   outdoors
   healthy
16 fog
   dirt
   breathe
17 explain

   becomes
   also
   decided
   community
   rules
18 thirsty
   imagine
   tastes
20 plant
   reach
21 streams
   dry
   dusty
   shortage
23 camping
   western
   everyone
   camp stove
   person
24 Chinese
   mealtime
27 sold
   grocery
28 exercise
   bodies
32 sick
   weak
33 baseball

35 during
   grown-ups
36 clothing
   daughters
37 chose
38 pages
   weather
40 special
   doctor
   patient
   welder
42 shelter
44 built
   poles
45 desert
   sandstorm
46 materials
47 Mexico
   adobe
   bricks
   mixed
   clay
   straw
   shaping
   mixture
   several
   already
48 discovered

PART 2

51 social
   Hong Kong
60 recess
62 share
   spend
64 agreed
   disagree
65 goals
   China
   gym
   gymnast
66 violin
   parents
67 students
   Thailand
   exciting
   volleyball
   champions
   team
   plan
   plans
68 themselves
   cooperate
70 chance
   learn
   shell
   astronaut
   possible
   languages
   understand
72 mind
   curious
   discoveries
73 plane
   piano
77 ages
   below
   high school
80 South America
82 accomplishment
83 science
   experiment
84 successful
   flight
85 championship
   rewards
   touch

PART 3

89 faith
   spacecraft
   launched
   thousands
   miles
   safely
92 Spain
   problems
   solve
95 huge
   rocket
98 jacks
   trusts
   cheated
99 dentist
   treat
100 nature
    laws
    golden
    setting
    disappear
    appear
101 vegetable
    instead
    depend
102 predicting
    predictions
103 rise
104 religious
    Morocco
    worshiping
    God
    mosque
    Allah
    religion
    Islam
105 Judaism
    synagogue
    church
    Christianity
106 India
    Hinduism
107 joy
    courage
    example
    honest
    flood

ACKNOWLEDGMENTS

2-3—H. Armstrong Roberts
4-5—H. Armstrong Roberts
6-7—Shostal Associates, Inc. by Charles Bear
8—NASA
9—Shostal Associates, Inc.
10—Shostal Associates, Inc.
11—Publix Pictorial Service by David W. Carson (upper); Alpha Photo Associates, Inc. by Fred M. Dole (lower)
12-13—Japan Information Service
14—Shostal Associates, Inc.
15—DeWys, Inc.
16—Ken Heyman
17—Laurence R. Lowry (upper); Shostal Associates, Inc. (lower)
18—William Froelich
19—Gianni Tortoli (upper); Bavaria—Verlag by Schmidlin (lower)
20—Ernst A. Jahn
21—C. S. Wong, Bangkok, Thailand
22—U. S. Department of the Interior
23—Texas Highway Department
24—Stockpile
25—Bob & Ira Spring
26—Photo Researchers by Hermann Schlenker (lower)
27—Maryknoll Fathers (upper); Japan Information Service (lower)
28—H. Armstrong Roberts
29—Alpha Photo Associates, Inc.
30—Photo Researchers by Andy Bernhaut
31—Japan Information Service
32—Publix Pictorial Service
33—Shostal Associates, Inc. by Jim Pond
34—East-West Photo Agency by Horace Bristol
35—DeWys, Inc.
36—Freelance Photographers Guild
37—Shostal Associates, Inc. by John Mechling
38—George Hunter
39—Carl E. Östman by P. O. Stackman (upper); Rapho Guillumette by Allyn Baum (lower)
40—Black Star (upper); Shostal Associates, Inc. (lower)
41—DeWys, Inc.
42—Chicago Department of Development & Planning
43—H. Armstrong Roberts
44—Paul Almasy
45—Shostal Associates, Inc.
46—Shostal Associates, Inc. (upper); Photo Researchers by Carl Frank (lower)
47—Philip Gendreau
48—William Froelich
49—Harrison Forman (upper); A. Devaney, Inc. (lower)
50-51—A. Devaney, Inc.
52—Shostal Associates, Inc.
53—Bavaria—Verlag by K. H. Hock (upper); Photo Researchers (lower)
54—Ken Heyman
55—Esther Bubley
56—William Froelich (upper); Alpha Photo Associates, Inc. (lower)

57—Ken Heyman
58—Photographic Library of Australia (upper); H. Armstrong Roberts (lower)
59—Magnum
60—Ken Heyman
61—Shostal Associates, Inc. by R. Dorman
62—Shostal Associates, Inc. by John Mechling
63—H. Armstrong Roberts
64—Design Photographers International
65—United Press International
66—UNESCO (upper); Authenticated News International (lower)
67—Shostal Associates, Inc.
68—DeWys, Inc.
69—Shostal Associates, Inc.
71—Shostal Associates, Inc. by John Mechling
72—Shostal Associates, Inc. by Ozzie Sweet
73—Shostal Associates, Inc. (upper); Rapho Guillumette by Hella Hammid (lower)
74—Publix Pictorial Service by C. A. Peterson
75—H. Armstrong Roberts
76—Alpha Photo Associates, Inc.
77—Shostal Associates, Inc.
78—Shostal Associates, Inc.
79—Shostal Associates, Inc. (upper); George Hunter (lower)
80—Ken Heyman
81—Freelance Photographers Guild (upper); Shostal Associates, Inc. (lower)
82—Shostal Associates, Inc. by John Mechling
83—Harold M. Lambert (upper); Shostal Associates, Inc. (lower)
84—Shostal Associates, Inc. by John Mechling (upper); NASA (lower)
85—Shostal Associates, Inc.
86—Photo Researchers by Andy Bernhaut
87—Shostal Associates, Inc. (both)
88-89—NASA
90—DeWys, Inc.
91—Shostal Associates, Inc.
92—Authenticated News International
93—Ken Heyman
94—Eastman Kodak Company
95—NASA
96—Shostal Associates, Inc.
96-97—Ringling Bros. & Barnum & Bailey
98—Alpha Photo Associates, Inc. by Postner
99—Ken Heyman
100—Gianni Tortoli
101—Alan Cliburn
102—Shostal Associates, Inc.
103—Design Photographers International by Dunn
104—Photo Researchers by Thomas Hollyman
105—Magnum (upper); Shostal Associates, Inc. (lower)
106—Dugan
107—Religious News Service
108—Shostal Associates, Inc.
109—Bavaria—Verlag by T. Heibeler (upper); Carl E. Östman (lower)

Grateful acknowledgment is made to © Rand McNally & Company for permission to use all of the globes in this book.